Strategic Alliances as Social Facts

Business, Biotechnology and Intellectual History

How can we explain a proliferation of alliances when the probability of failure is higher than success? And why have we emphasized their order, manageability, and predictability whilst acknowledging that they tend to be experienced as messy, politically charged, and unpredictable? Mark de Rond, in this provocative book, sets out to address such paradoxes. Based on in-depth case studies of three major biotechnology alliances, he suggests that we need theories to explain idiosyncrasy as well as social order. He argues that such theories must allow for social conduct to be active and self-directed but simultaneously inert and constrained, thus permitting voluntarism, determinism, and serendipity alike to explain causation in alliance life. The book offers a highly original combination of insights from social theory and intellectual history with more mainstream strategic management and organizations literature. It is a refreshing and thought-provoking analysis that will appeal to the reflective practitioner and academic researcher alike.

MARK DE ROND is University Lecturer in Strategy at the Judge Institute of Management Studies, University of Cambridge.

Strategic Alliances as Social Facts

Business, Biotechnology, and Intellectual History

Mark de Rond

CAMBRIDGE
UNIVERSITY PRESS

PUBLISHED BY THE PRESS SYNDICATE OF THE UNIVERSITY OF CAMBRIDGE
The Pitt Building, Trumpington Street, Cambridge CB2 1RP, United Kingdom

CAMBRIDGE UNIVERSITY PRESS
The Edinburgh Building, Cambridge, CB2 2RU, UK
40 West 20th Street, New York, NY 10011–4211, USA
477 Williamstown Road, Port Melbourne, VIC 3207, Australia
Ruiz de Alarcón 13, 28014 Madrid, Spain
Dock House, The Waterfront, Cape Town 8001, South Africa

http://www.cambridge.org

© Mark de Rond 2003

First published 2003

Printed in the United Kingdom at the University Press, Cambridge

Typeface Plantin 10/12 pt.   *System* LaTeX 2_ε [TB]

A catalogue record for this book is available from the British Library

ISBN 0 521 81110 4 hardback

To Ed and Greetje de Rond

Strange is our situation here upon earth. However, there is one
thing that we do know – man is here for the sake of other men –
above all, for those upon whose smile and well-being our own
happiness depends, but also for the countless unknown souls
with whose fate we are connected by a bond of sympathy.

Albert Einstein

Contents

Figures

Foreword

The contributions of this book are threefold. First, the three empirical studies of strategic alliances in biotechnology research add to an already considerable literature on the pharmaceutical industry and its evolving structure. Second, the approach to understanding these increasingly pervasive strategies exemplifies the utility of moving away from theoretic 'silos' towards multi-theoretic analysis. This approach can be usefully juxtaposed with contrasting arguments about how management research might achieve more depth and maturity, as outlined in more detail below. The third contribution of the book is to relate a pluralist perspective to the work of Isaiah Berlin. This section of the book not only provides a stronger ontological foundation for Mark's effort, but introduces a philosophical depth that has been missing from most discussions of management theory around the world. All in all, this is a fresh, ambitious and welcome agenda. Though complex, the book is brief enough to be accessible to many readers; I encourage you to be one.

The empirical study begins with the puzzle of why alliances continue to flourish despite widely agreed statistics showing that at least half of previous efforts have failed, often miserably. Those interested in alliances, especially their strong role in the pharmaceutical industry, will be interested in the (disguised) descriptions of three specific connections. None of these collective efforts fulfilled its initially stated purpose; the most apparently successful was terminated the most quickly. De Rond's analysis is compatible with Czarniawska's (1997) argument that managers are in, and help create, never-ending dramas, in which purpose cannot be expected to match the firm expectations of textbooks and a-priori rhetoric. De Rond's story of how and why initial objectives were modified is plausible, and brings into partial question, at least, attributions of alliance failure. It also supports a stronger interpretive strand in future work on alliances.

Alliances constitute an important strategy in an internationalizing and globalizing world, and the empirical aspect of the book is therefore useful in and of itself. The contribution that moves beyond empirical observation is de Rond's approach to theory building. Here, the work on alliances becomes the springboard for observations that are relevant to a much wider audience.

De Rond claims that useful theory building *must* be pluralist. This is a contribution to an increasingly sophisticated discussion of the purposes of management theorizing and research. In the last fifty years, almost all business schools have increased their social science capabilities. Spurred on by ranking schemes that heavily influence acceptance by journals, there has been remarkable progress recently in relating theories from economics, psychology, sociology, anthropology, geography, and other fields to the contexts of business and other organizations. De Rond's position, however, is that analysis from a single theoretical basis, the thing that is most easily rewarded by highly regarded journals, is at best a useful intermediary. Single science perspectives cannot shed significant light on the contexts we claim to be trying to understand; in fact, they tend to obscure it.

The assertion that a pluralist perspective must now be developed can be contrasted with two other points of departure. The first of these argues that management must become more of a 'design science'; the second escalates a critical, or at least a non-managerialist, stand.

The design perspective, recently explored in a conference inaugurating the new Weatherhead School of Management building designed by Frank Gerry (http://design.cwru.edu), is just beginning to coalesce. My summary of this point of departure is that management must take its standing as a profession more seriously. Following colleagues in architecture, medicine and engineering, proponents for this agenda claim scholars of management should put more effort into creating a coherent language of practice and offering specific, empirically verified, templates for application. Design proponents feel we are less relevant than other professional schools; we are behind colleagues helping to fight disease or reach the stars.

A critical perspective, rooted in but now rather independent of Marxist thought, finds this highly problematic. Henry Mintzberg and others repeatedly point out that too many management theorists, especially in America, tacitly assume their job is to support managerial action, thereby ignoring larger conditions and consequences. Zald (2002) introduces a special issue of *Organization* (August 2002) with an essay suggesting that it may be time to move these concerns to a more central position if the management field is to develop. Recent events, easily signified by Enron and Andersen's debacles, have further escalated this worthy agenda. If a critical perspective were closer to centre stage, theorizing would be more firmly rooted in the humanities and in history, and place organizational activity into a more contestable frame.

De Rond's book establishes a third position. The key to his argument is that the shortcomings of management theory are more closely tied to our efforts of the past. The key issue is not that we have been standing too close (as critical theorists argue) or too far away (as most design theorists would argue), but that we have been too narrow in understanding our current ground. What our field needs, de Rond suggests, is not more theoretical variety but theories *of* variety. We need theoretical approaches that accept heterogeneity as a starting point in drawing observations from the empirical world of organizations. This is an interesting third perspective on the purpose of management theory. It is particularly attractive because it most clearly leverages our current skills as scholars, and most clearly links a management theory agenda to university and public pressures for strong science from business schools.

After establishing the logic, De Rond goes on to provide a philosophical basis for this third alternative in the works of Isaiah Berlin (1909–97), an Oxford-educated philosopher who became one of the most versatile intellectual historians of the twentieth century. Throughout his long life, Berlin remained sceptical of anything all-embracing and rational, as it denied too much of what we know to be true of social life. This depiction of Western intellectual tradition is highly relevant to the study of organizations. Management theory tends to share with much work from the social sciences, the humanities, and the sciences an unquestioned belief that to every problem there is a solution; that solutions can be found by applying reason; and that solutions found must form a coherent, all-embracing body of theory. De Rond believes that our thinking about alliances has been dominated and stunted by this tradition. Berlin's thinking supports a compelling alternative lens, a perspective that is not unknown in the field, but again one that supporters could easily claim has not been adequately explored. I believe this is an important third path to greater maturity of our field. We need a deeper and more developed pluralist tradition, even while recognizing a responsibility for design and the importance of critical distance.

As a potential reader, you may feel overwhelmed by the breadth of de Rond's agenda, and the larger debates it engages. Yet the brevity of this book is its strength. It should be read as a guidebook, rather than a definitive text. Consistent with Berlin's vision, we each must make our own extensions. Let us begin.

ANNE SIGISMUND HUFF
Director
AIM – The Advanced Institute for Management
London Business School

Acknowledgements

It remains for me to thank those who were helpful (albeit often unbeknownst to them) in shaping the ideas behind the manuscript, though the responsibility for them remains mine alone: Donizete Antunes, Patrick Baert, David Barron, Sarvapreet Bedi, Steve Casper, Chris David, Christian de Cock, Sue Dobson, David Faulkner, Elizabeth Garnsey Mary Ann Glynn, June Grindley, Henry Hardy, Roger Hausheer, John Kay, Thomas Kern, Valerie Leroux, Sonja Marjanovic, Deirdre McCloskey, Alan Miller, Edwin Moses, John Roberts, Emmanuel Raufflet, Raymond-Alain Thietart, Richard Whittington, several anonymous reviewers, and many of my students. I appreciated the readiness of Hamid Bouchikhi, John Child, Ranjay Gulati, Duane Ireland, Ray Loveridge, and Andy van de Ven to read a first set of proofs and comment on them. I have benefited from each. I thank John Child and Raymond Loveridge in particular for suggesting I write this book in the first place. I have greatly appreciated the patience and guidance of Chris Harrison at Cambridge University Press. He is everything one expects from an editor as well as being thoroughly humane. He is a useful source also on contemporary British fiction. Kate Gentles, my copyeditor, patiently toiled away at what must have seemed, to her, a rather cluttered and confused text. She did much to improve the book. I am grateful to Ian MacMillan, Rosalie (Roz) Cohen, and the Sol. C. Snider Center for Entrepreneurship at Wharton for their generosity in providing a stimulating research environment during the spring and summer of 2001. I thank PricewaterhouseCoopers for their financial support of part of this study. I am deeply indebted also to the case study participants and interviewees. Although the names used in the cases are fictitious, the cases are anything but. ESSEC (*Ecole Supérieure des Sciences Economiques et Commerciales*) has been my intellectual home for the past three years. Its faculty were kind and patient as I stumbled, as an Anglo-Saxon, into its professional corps. Elizabeth Demars provided excellent last-minute assistance. I am especially appreciative of my colleague Hamid Bouchikhi. In Hamid I have found a compatriot in

contemplating the epistemology of organizational life. Our many conversations at *La Musarde* (a tiny but typical French crèperie), becoming
increasingly more daring as the Bordeaux took its toll, have found their
place in this book.

I owe much to Charles J. Stokes. His extraordinary intellect, curiosity,
and spirited treatment of whatever subject happened to interest him at
that time, were sources of inspiration and ambition for ten intimate years
of friendship. His was a splendid capacity for finding specks of beauty in
the dreary, excitement in the dull and unexciting, prospect in disappointment. I often found solace in our monthly exchange of letters. Sadly, he
is no longer here to appreciate the book, parts of which he patiently read
and commented on.

I am grateful also to Anne Huff for providing a Foreword to this book.
I was flattered by her agreement to do this, as one would be, and have
deeply appreciated her support for this effort. Her keen intellect, integrity,
candidness, and dedication continue to inspire.

Last, but certainly not least, I thank my family. My wife Roxana
and Shelby, my two-and-a-half-year-old, became pleasant diversions
during the writing process. Repeatedly, having left my computer
to pour another cup of coffee, I would return to find my screen
plastered with 'tyyulopo vvvvvvvvjjjjjjjjjjjjjjjjjjjjhjnmhhjnuuu,..........
vvhgt8u8nnnrrewwsaaa', or worse, disappeared altogether. Fortunately
computers have memories, and these distractions became sources of com-
fort – subtle reminders of the normality of life and the relative insignifi-
cance of one's aspirations.

I owe everything else to my parents. It is to them that I dedicate this
book.

Introduction

I cannot quite think of myself as on the side of authority, judgment...
and I hear myself chatter and the only excuse for it is that one is full
of unsifted ideas and too chock-a-bloc to have time to think and too
warm-blooded to reckon the consequences...

Isaiah Berlin[1]

Isaiah Berlin's startling admission befits the mood of this book. It is
written not from the wisdom of old age but the folly of youth. It is a book
about alliances and yet alliances are quite unimportant to it. They illustrate my argument, but this argument itself potentially has much wider
implications as well as applications. Our theorizing about alliances, so
I argue, may benefit from relaxing any a-priori assumptions we may have
traditionally taken to them: expectations of finding constancy, homogeny,
teleology, progress or pattern. This is especially important when considering that we may have relatively little empirical evidence that these are
ordinarily their properties. What if this is no more than a metaphysical attitude? True to our intellectual origins, we may have persisted in
three, relatively unexamined, beliefs, namely that to every genuine question there is but one answer; that these answers can be discovered by
applying reason; and that, together, such answers must be compatible in
amounting to a coherent, stable, and universal body of theory (cf. Berlin,
1999a). As in simple arithmetic, the parts add up reliably to the same
sum total. A comprehensive theory of alliances has, in other words, remained distinctly possible. Even if we have not found it yet, one day we
will – for the ideal exists, at least in principle. In this respect, Einstein's
aside may not be entirely irrelevant: 'so far as the laws of mathematics
refer to reality, they are not certain. And so far as they are certain, they
do not refer to reality.'[2] In this book, I examine the implications of this
monist epistemology and propose pluralism as a compelling but largely
untried substitute. In pluralism, we may find the means to legitimize the
relative messiness of strategic alliances whilst finding in them also a sense

---

[1] As cited in Ignatieff (1998: 208).   [2] As cited in Kosko (1993: 3).

1

of social order. Their messiness, in other words, is an inherent, and not dysfunctional property. That, in a nutshell, is the gist of my argument. To paraphrase Bertrand Russell, I cannot prove that my view of alliances is correct. I can only state my view and hope that as many as possible will agree – or, if not agree, at least find it intellectually useful.[3]

The three-tier characterization of monism, as an intellectual tradition, was Isaiah Berlin's first great discovery. It simplifies monism but does so deliberately to illuminate a deep-rooted philosophical issue. Drawing on the works of Machiavelli, the eighteenth-century Romantics Vico, Herder, Herzen and Hamann, and the Russian novelist Tolstoy, Berlin fought to crack its moral fibre and became one of the most celebrated intellectual historians of the twentieth century. A keen observer of social and political life, Berlin concluded that there is no one best way for human beings to live. More importantly, any such recipe can never be derived from human nature, as suggested by Rousseau, and arrived at by applying reason. Instead, conflicting ideals coexist; and as men are bound to disagree about ultimate ends, conflict is often inevitable. Some of the worst crimes of the twentieth century, Naziism and fascism included, were carried out in the firm and unrelenting belief in a final, terrifyingly rational, solution to the organization of society. This being one of the most powerful and dangerous arguments in the history of human thought, Berlin summarized thus:

Objective good can be discovered only by the use of reason; to impose it on others is only to activate the dormant reason within them; to liberate people is to do just that for them which, were they rational, they would do for themselves, no matter what they in fact say they want.[4]

To what extent are business organizations exposed to the same human divisiveness, the ubiquity of potentially incompatible interests, personalities, histories, and loyalties? Organizations, to be sure, may be more discriminating than societies in being mostly able to choose their membership. They may also exhibit more coherence when in the presence of a distinct corporate culture and shared strategic intentions. After all, organizations are seen as purposeful, boundary-observing, socially constructed systems of human activity (Aldrich, 1979; 1999: 2). Actors will, to some degree, be constrained by the institutional frameworks of their corporations. And in large measure, these institutions are the residual deposits of their own activities. Be that as it may, despite such centripetal institutional forces affording a higher probability of homogeneity than

---

[3] Paraphrased from Russell (1957: 48).

[4] As cited in Ignatieff (1998: 202), and taken by him from an unpublished manuscript entitled 'Freedom and its Betrayal' written by Isaiah Berlin.

found in some other types of organization, there may yet exist a fair amount of heterogeneity – possibly more than our current research techniques allow us to reveal (Aldrich, 1999; Starbuck, 1993). Business organizations after all remain distinctly social phenomena – political, moral, social, and personal life continues inside them. Indeed, is this heterogeneity not likely to increase exponentially when combining organizations through mergers, acquisitions or various forms of alliances? And are we who write about them not likely to exemplify this same divisiveness?

This book is an effort to try and redress this felt imbalance by humanizing the literature on strategic alliances. But it also seeks to make three specific contributions: (a) to respond to a lack of empirical research and theory-development on alliance dynamics and evolution in a governance- and performance-dominated alliance literature; (b) to help remedy a felt imbalance in this literature towards alliances as strategic, financial or economic events, at the expense of their social, contextual, and historical characteristics; and (c) to relax any monist assumptions we may traditionally have made about them. Not least among these is the expectation of discovering some stable principles in alliance life, or what Zeitz (1980: 72) two decades ago wryly described as that 'positivist idea of science . . . [which] stresses the importance of locating stable patterns of behaviour and of formulating general theories that apply *regardless* of particular circumstances'.[5] The residue in part of the Foundation Studies[6] of the mid to late 1950s (Gordon and Howell, 1959; Pierson et al., 1959; Porter and McKibbin, 1988; Porter, 2000), we still straddle the divide between the narrative world of organizations and the natural sciences, using the context of organizations but methods of the natural sciences for reasons of transparency, legitimacy, and respectability (Bailey and Ford, 1996; Pfeffer and Fong, 2002). Poole and van de Ven's contention is relevant in this respect:

Like most social scientists, organization and management theorists are *socialized* to develop internally consistent theories. The presence of contrary or contradictory assumptions, explanations, or conclusions is often viewed as an indicator of poor theory building (1989: 562; italics added).

Quoting Ralph Waldo Emerson's 'A foolish consistency is the hobgoblin of little minds', they emphasized the growing recognition that any important advances in management and organization theory will have to

---

[5] Italics added.
[6] The Foundation Studies comprise two separate studies conducted in the mid-1950s (and published in 1959) and commissioned by the Ford Foundation and the Carnegie Foundation (hence their name). The studies are still considered as landmark publications and their implications for the design of business school research have been profound.

find ways to address paradoxes inherent in human beings and their social organizations (Poole and van de Ven, 1989: 562). Like Timothy Smart, a fictional student of van de Ven's making, we 'know experientially' that organizational life is far less consistent, causally linear, and unitary than implied in any single theory available to us. Yet this very knowledge is anathema to most of our theories, which tend to rely on consensus and alignment of all members to a single vision (van de Ven, 1997: 7). There is a 'garbage can' element (Cohen, March and Olsen, 1972) to alliance life: a lack of clarity of preferences, which includes vagueness and change-ability on the definition and measurement of success and failure (Levitt and Nass, 1989: 193); ambiguous technologies and serendipity; and a relatively fluid participation, with participants entering and leaving the scene, sometimes unpredictably. These three traits alone may not convey the entire story, but the story cannot properly be told without them.

What we need, the book concludes, are theories to explain the particular *as well as* the general; theories that allow one to find the particular *in* the general, the general *in* the particular, and the general as only ever experienced *through* the particular. Such theories must allow for social conduct, including learning processes, to be active and self-directed but simultaneously inert and constrained, permitting voluntarism, determinism, and serendipity alike to explain causation in alliance life. For alliance life is likely to be the sum total of choice plus chance plus inevitability.

This book makes no promises as to *producing* that theory. It does make an attempt at it in proposing the reconciliation of Berlin's objective value pluralism (to account for the particular) with Giddens's structuration theory (to account for the general). For despite the idiosyncrasy of alliances, there *is* order. It exists in the extent to which human actors rely on deep-seated social institutions to inform and legitimize their strategic conduct, thus producing order and generality but without necessarily affording prediction as a consequence. This reconciliation is a proposition I invite readers to oppose or develop. I endeavoured to write a readable text, one that may tempt the reader to engage with it, to ruthlessly put pen to the margins of this book, to improve on the ideas inside it. My style is thus deliberately informal, often adopting a first person perspective. It was, I believe, Aristotle who suggested that in the absence of being able to know the good and the true, ultimately all questions boil down to questions of beauty. Unfortunately, to borrow from Don Quixote, I could not contravene that law of nature according to which like begets like.

The title of the book, 'Strategic Alliances as Social Facts', is perhaps somewhat misleading. The sociologist Emile Durkheim appears to have been the first to develop the notion of 'social facts' to describe institutional-type constraints on the activities of human agents over which they may have little or no influence. His *Rules of Sociological Method* (Durkheim, 1982) appears to be dedicated primarily to this proposition. In Durkheim's view, social facts are 'real', in an ontological sense; they can and do constrain the actions of individuals; they exist independently of individuals; are external to them; and cannot be reduced to a mere set of psychological facts or statements about habits or routines (Hund, 1982: 270). The treatment of strategic alliances proposed here is true to Durkheim in drawing attention to the degree to which individual actors are informed by deeper-seated social structures, some industry-specific, others specific to the alliance or a single organization, or even a function of national culture. Whilst it certainly appears true that such structure can and does curb individual action, this is not inevitable. There may exist a fair degree of voluntarism (cf. Child, 1972, 1997), and even serendipity, where structure may serve as an enabling device for human conduct and a precondition also for chance. And this, in a nutshell, is where the book departs from a Durkheimian view. It wishes to relax Durkheim's emphasis on structure as principally constraining the scope of action whilst providing a forum also for voluntarism and chance. Purists may object to my appropriation of his term 'social facts', though I hope they will be sufficiently curious to see the argument unfold. Besides, as is often the case, intellectual concepts, once released, take on a life of their own. Isaiah Berlin, for instance, brings the term into play to describe, more loosely, the internal relationships and activities and experiences of societies. And my treatment is perhaps closer to Berlin's. A more descriptive title might have been 'Strategic Alliances as Social Facts and Artefacts', the tail-end highlighting the presence of voluntarism and chance in alliance life, but it somehow sounded too cumbersome. This would have been a more accurate summing-up of the book's central argument, however.

1   Paradoxes of alliance life

Why have alliances proliferated when the probability of failure is higher than that of success? How do we explain a growing recourse to them whilst also assuming rational strategic management? Are we not learning from experience? And why have we persisted in approaching alliances with expectations of finding homogeneity whilst being well aware that they often unfold in very diverse and changing circumstances? Why are some apparently successful alliances prematurely dismantled? Why are others deemed successful whilst not having attained their primary goal, or in the absence of any obvious tangible attainments? Why do some survive despite being problematic? Why do others appear to get by despite poor managerial decisions? These questions may entail some of the paradoxes of alliance life. They can be resolved but principally at the level of epistemology. For we, in our thinking about them, may have sought constancy, homogeny, teleology, progress or principle in the absence of compelling empirical evidence that these are their usual properties. To that extent it may be helpful to relax any such a-priori assumptions and approach alliances plainly as facts – as things that simply are. The adjective 'social' in the book title is, however, intentional. Some facts cannot be abstracted from circumstance without risking disfiguration. Yet this is not to suggest that we approach them completely void of theory, for quite the reverse is true. The inevitability of interpretation has been subject to a longstanding debate in academic circles and one need not look far for support. To this extent Voltaire's quip, 'History is only a pack of tricks we play on the dead,' is quite possibly the most poignant and most famous.[1] The inevitability of having to rely on judgment, reason, and imagination in historical reconstruction (properties that belong to us rather than to the things we observe) seems reasonably well recognized in each of our three main scholarly traditions: the humanities and the social and natural

---

[1] As cited in Becker (1960: 88).

sciences. The Cambridge historian E. H. Carr, deliberating his own field, concluded this:

> It used to be said that facts speak for themselves. This is, of course, untrue. The facts speak only when the historian calls on them: it is he who decides to which facts to give the floor, and in what order or context. (1961: 9)

Catherine Morland, also a historian, wryly wondered why her field had to be so dull for she thought a great deal of it to be invention. Carl Becker called it 'that nefarious medieval enterprise of reconciling the facts of human experience with truths already, in some fashion, revealed to them' (1960: 102). Isaiah Berlin, likewise, deemed any depersonalized history but 'a figment of abstract theory, a violently exaggerated reaction to the cant and vanity of earlier generations' (2002: 140–1). And similar voices, sentient of the constructivist nature of their practices, can be heard in history (e.g. Carr, 1961; Elton, 1967; Evans, 1997), economics (e.g. McCloskey, 1998; Schumacher, 1995), the philosophy of science (e.g. Feyerabend, 1999; Kuhn, 1970), epistemology (e.g. Berkeley, 1713; Hume, 1740; Kant, 1781; Russell, 1980), physics (e.g. Feynman, 1998), chemistry (e.g. Mullis, 2000), and the organization sciences (e.g. van Maanen, 1975, 1979; Weick, 1988, 1993, 1995). A short paragraph in Michael Crighton's entertaining *Travels* summarizes it rather well:

> It's hard to observe without imposing a theory to explain what we're seeing, but the trouble with theories, as Einstein said, is that they explain not what is observed, but what *can* be observed. We start to build expectations based on our theories. And often those expectations get in the way. (1988: 351)

So it is these theories we must be careful about. Perhaps unable to rid ourselves of the tools we use to construct a workable image of the social world, we may at least seek to vary our assumptions and see where that gets us. To relax these assumptions is largely the aim of this book. But it also seeks to make two further contributions. First, it responds to repeated calls for more process-oriented research and theory development on alliances in a governance- and performance-dominated literature (Arino and de la Torre, 1998; Deeds and Hill, 1998; Doz, 1996; Koza and Lewin, 1998; Parkhe, 1993a; Ring and van de Ven, 1994; Salk and Shenkar, 2001; Shenkar and Yan, 2002). Second, it seeks to socialize and contextualize this literature (Gulati, 1998; Gulati, Nohria, and Zaheer, 2000), by emphasizing the presence and role of human agency in alliances, the ability of human actors to build and destroy, even single-handedly, and the extent to which their conduct today is informed by the memories and institutions of times past.

Paradoxes

The remarkable proliferation in cooperative strategy as a legitimate and presumably effective means towards achieving business success has not escaped the attention of academics. This subfield has been of scholarly interest since at least the mid-1960s (e.g. Evan, 1966; Guetzkow, 1966). And the growth in corporate partnering in recent years has been truly unprecedented (Badaracco, 1991; Barley et al., 1992; Beamish, 1988; Beamish and Delios, 1997; Hagedoorn, 1995; Hagedoorn and Schakenraad, 1993, 1994; Harbison and Pekar, 1998; Hergert and Morris, 1988; Inkpen 1996; Ireland, Hitt, and Vaidyanath, 2002; Mowery, 1988; Osborn and Hagedoorn, 1997; Pekar and Allio, 1994; Powell et al., 1996). Strategic alliances appear to have become the single most commonly adopted strategy (Dyer et al., 2001; Gulati, 1998), with in excess of 10,000 newly created partnerships each year (Schifrin, 2001). In biotechnology alone, the number and value of investments in alliances is reported to have increased fivefold during the last decade of the twentieth century, 50 per cent of which were targeted at upstream, drug-discovery-based projects (van Brunt, 1999; Sapienza and Stork, 2001). PricewaterhouseCoopers estimate alliances to account for 50 per cent of the pharmaceutical industry's total R&D budget, or an investment to the tune of $22 billion in 2001 alone (*The Economist*, 13 July 2002: 51). The reasons usually given for this proliferation include the need for financial resources, legitimacy, and commercial expertise provided by pharmaceutical companies, windows on new technologies, knowledge or research approaches afforded by new biotechnology firms (Leblebici et al., 1991; Leonard-Barton, 1995); resource complementarities (Harrison et al., in press); the sharing of risk and expenses, and obtaining access to new markets or information with minimum costs of redundancy, conflict and complexity (Baum and Calabrese, 2000; Ireland, Hitt, and Vaidyanath, 2002; Walker, Kogut and Shan, 1997; Powell et al., 1996). In contrast to such *exploration* opportunities, Rothaermel (2001) found that the pooling of complementary skills could provide pharmaceuticals with even better 'relational' rents through a strategy of *exploitation* (cf. Dyer and Singh, 1998; March, 1991).

On the other hand, the reported failure rates of alliances, particularly (but not exclusively) of technology-oriented collaborations, have remained surprisingly high. Alliance failure rates were estimated at 33 to 50 per cent by McKinsey's Bleeke and Ernst (1991), at 61 per cent by Accenture in 1999, and at 59 per cent by PricewaterhouseCoopers in 2000. In fact, the latter thinks failure rates for discovery research alliances (the most relevant empirical sample for our purposes) are as high as

64 per cent, while consortia disappoint in 90 per cent of cases. *The Economist* (22 July 1995), citing Boston Consulting Group studies, put the alliance failures rate at 60 per cent for regional alliances and 70 per cent for international alliances. Michael Skapinger writing in the *Financial Times* in 2001 affirmed this 70 per cent estimate. These figures suggest that alliances are anything but simple. By comparison, estimates provided by the academic community do not differ greatly. Harrigan (1985) for instance, suggested a mortality rate of 50 per cent. Beamish (1985) raised this to 61 per cent. Auster (1987) estimated that two out of three alliances failed. Kogut (1988a) found that, in the specific case of R&D alliances focused on new product development (the most relevant benchmark for comparison), 57.1 per cent were likely to disappoint. Park and Russo (1996), based on a study of joint ventures, placed their failure rate significantly lower at 27.5 per cent. Inkpen and Beamish (1997) thought this to be closer to 50 per cent.[2] Young-Ybarra and Wiersema (1999) and Spekman et al. (1998) endorsed this 50 per cent estimate.

These data, however, may be problematic on at least three counts. First, the literature lacks a precise and consistent definition of collaborative success and failure (Yan and Gray, 1995). Park and Russo (1996) suggested this is problematic even within the joint ventures literature. For instance, alliance mortality may merely be natural, even desirable, if partner firms either have achieved their core objective(s) or exit the relationship in 'better shape' competitively than when they entered it (Gomes-Casseres, 1989; Hamel, Doz, and Prahalad, 1989). In some cases, this may be true only for one partner. But longevity in and of itself is probably not the most accurate measure of success. Besides, it is only realistic to expect alliances to fail in some respects (e.g. attaining the original purpose) but succeed in others (e.g. generating spin-off projects). Or, in the specific case of pharmaceuticals that pursue real options strategies for biotechnology investments, high failure rates are to be expected. They merely reflect the serendipity of drug discovery, and even if only one in every, say, five alliances succeeds in generating a drug candidate (a failure rate of 80 per cent), the total investment is usually well worth it.

A second problem with these failure rates is their lack of specification. As Zajac (1998) suggests, the term 'alliance' has become host to a gamut of different interorganizational arrangements including, among others, licensing agreements, joint marketing agreements, buyer–supplier relationships, outsourcing arrangements, non-equity research collaborations, equity joint ventures, consortia, and even mergers and acquisitions.

---

[2] Inkpen and Beamish explain later in their paper that instability often results in the termination of alliances. Hence their estimate seems relevant.

Certain arrangements may be more likely to disappoint than others but, given imprecise definitions, this is somewhat difficult to tell. Beamish (1985), Park and Russo (1996) and Inkpen and Beamish (1997) are specific in identifying joint ventures and arriving at restricted failure or instability estimates, as is Kogut (1988a) in characterizing product development alliances, but they are among the relatively few that do. Finally, these failure rates must be considered alongside the rates of failure of the next best alternatives: internal venturing or acquisition. Unfortunately the data on each of these are somewhat sparse. Park and Ungson (1997) provided an estimate of internal venturing failure of 44 per cent, which appears lower than the average alliance failure rate. Porter's (1987) oft-cited study of corporate acquisitions put their rate of failure at 50.3 per cent, which is not markedly different. Studies that compared alliances with formal organizations suggested that the former are generally less successful and also less stable (Bleeke and Ernst, 1991; Das and Teng, 2000; Gomes-Casseres, 1987; Hennert et al., 1998; Kent, 1991; Li, 1995; Pennings et al., 1994; Yamawaki, 1997).

But perhaps the continued pursuit of an alliance strategy, even in the face of failure, should not prove too surprising. Biotechnology startups usually have little choice in the matter as they rely on alliances with pharmaceuticals for funding, legitimacy, and commercial expertise. Pharmaceuticals may conclude that the potential economic payoff of investing in alliances is worth the risk. Multiplying the expected returns by the probability that these returns will occur may render a sufficiently interesting payoff structure. Unless one finds that this payoff structure is significantly improved for in-house research, it makes perfect economic sense to collaborate. The sparse empirical evidence to date, however, is not encouraging, and perhaps we may allow the paradox to remain – at least for the time being.

Explaining cooperative strategy

In response to alliance failure and instability, Das and Teng (2000) conclude that despite the development and application of various theoretical perspectives (not originally developed to speak specifically to alliances), each remains either too incomplete or too weak in providing explanations. Their conclusions are broadly consistent with those of Child and Faulkner (1998), Faulkner and de Rond (2000),Gulati (1998), and Shenkar and Yan (2002), and call for more contextual, social, and process-friendly approaches. Whilst not intending to reproduce the various reviews here, a summary of the premises and limitations of existing theories is fitting. Broadly, theoretical explanations for cooperative strategy can be assigned to two camps. Economics has served as a foundation discipline for the development of six such perspectives: market power theory, transaction cost theory, the resource-based view, agency theory, game theory, and real options theory. The field of organization theory and its intellectual parent sociology have bred at least another four: resource dependence theory, relational contract theory, organizational learning theory, and social network theory. We will briefly look at each in turn. For those readers already familiar with this literature, feel free to skip this section.

Market power theory

Sometimes referred to as the 'positioning school' or 'strategic management theory', market power theory is often associated with the works of Michael Porter, who made the contributions of Edward Mason (1939) and Joe Bain (1951), and the structure–conduct–performance school of industrial organization,[3] accessible to practitioners by refocusing it on rent-creation. In his influential *Competitive Strategy* (1980) and *Competitive Advantage* (1985), Porter suggested that the profit potential of firms is determined by industry structure. This structure, in turn, consists of five basic forces: the threat of newcomers entering the industry (this being contingent on barriers to entry), the bargaining power of suppliers, the bargaining power of buyers, the threat of substitution (acting as a price ceiling), and the degree of rivalry between competing firms (including the ability of established rivals to retaliate). A company's strategy should be to position itself to take advantage of these forces (or to be sheltered from their ability to erode any profit potential). Consequently, a strategy of cooperation may enable alliance partners to achieve a stronger positioning together than they would have in isolation. Market power can potentially be gained through allying, in providing risk reduction, access to technologies and markets, and so forth. Porter's emphasis on industry structure and his disregard for the roles of politics and human agency betray his training in industrial organization.

Despite its obvious merits, market power theory is of limited use in informing evolutionary theories of alliances. Also, because it assumes that the industry environment dictates the pursuit of one of three generic strategies – cost leadership, differentiation, and focus – it leaves little room for genuine strategic choice (cf. Child, 1972). To quote Child and Faulkner:

---

[3] The S–C–P school argued that industry *structure* determined firm *conduct* (or strategy) which, in turn, determined its *performance*.

It is . . . a fairly deterministic perspective, which does not readily accommodate the way in which evolving relationships between firms can alter the rationalities and strategic visions held by their policy makers . . . [and] therefore has some difficulty in dealing with the processes through which cooperative strategies evolve over time. (1998: 19)

Moreover, it is relatively positivistic in assuming that the environment is 'out there', thus negating any notion of the *enacted* world, including cognitive processes, a-priori assumptions, and prejudices that may well inform decision-making processes (Smircich and Stubbart, 1985).

Transaction cost theory

Transaction cost theory (also referred to as transaction cost economics, or TCE) posits that a strategy of cooperation can be a cost-reducing method of organizing business transactions. Such costs may include those incurred in arranging, negotiating, managing, and monitoring transactions, and arise primarily from the bounded rationality and inherent opportunism of human agency. These two assumptions form the basis of Coase's (1937) and Williamson's (1975, 1985) central argument, namely that perfect contracts cannot be written, given cognitive and informational limits to the exercise of rationality, and that firms or individuals are likely to take advantage of any ensuing 'loopholes' given their self-interested orientation. Given the choice of only a limited number of partners to transact with, uncertain or complex market conditions, and limited information, the more vulnerable partner is likely to gain from internalizing the transaction by bringing it within managerial control. Hence, the attributes of a transaction, especially the degree of asset specificity, should play a key role in choosing appropriate governance structures.

Transaction cost theory has been widely used to inform alliance research (Deeds and Hill, 1998). Examples include modes of entry into foreign markets (Anderson and Gatignon, 1986), the selection and structuring of alliance forms (Hennert, 1988; 1991; Parkhe, 1993a), R&D alliances (Brockhoff, 1992; Pisano, 1990), the semiconductor industry (Gates, 1989), and the formation of new ventures (Oviatt and McDougall, 1994). Whereas market power theory stresses the relative bargaining power and profit potential gained through collaborating, transaction cost theory emphasizes instead the efficiency and cost-minimizing motives for cooperating. It has been criticized for neglecting the role of power in choosing between market and hierarchy (Francis, Turk, and Willman, 1983) and also for its inability to explain how the relational aspects of cooperation evolve over time and how these, in turn, structure the nature of transactions (Parkhe, 1993b). It is thus thought also to ignore the effects of trust, interpersonal bonding, implicit modes of governance, and reputation as a means of reducing the risk of opportunism and, conceivably, also curbing the boundedness of rationality through a growing willingness to share information (Faulkner and de Rond, 2000). Finally, transaction cost theory appears positive, rather than normative, in orientation (Seth and Thomas, 1994), and risks promoting a rather negative view on management, as managers are deemed opportunistic and untrustworthy (Donaldson, 1995). Like market power theory, it may be relatively deterministic and static in orientation in being concerned primarily with issues of efficiency and control.

Resource-based theory

In contrast to market power theory, the resource-based view does not accept the inevitability of forces driving a market towards equilibrium, nor of the necessary competing away of monopolistic rents. Instead it suggests that firms can earn Ricardian rents by configuring their resources in a way that is difficult to imitate by existing or future rivals, or by having access to capabilities that are durable and not easily appropriable, transferable or replicable (Ricardo, 1891; Barney, 1991; Grant, 1991; Peteraf, 1993; Rumelt, 1984, 1991; Wernerfelt, 1984). The resultant perspective on a firm's competitive position is as that of a collection of rare and unique resources and relationships. The task for managers is consequently that of adjusting and renewing these resources and relationships as time, competition, and change erode their value (Rumelt, 1984: 557–8).

To realize a sustainable competitive advantage by trading in imperfectly imitable and imperfectly mobile firm resources through a strategy of cooperation is possible, but only under some circumstances. An alliance can legitimately and efficiently afford access to unique capabilities, specific assets or processes, without necessitating a merger or acquisition. Things become vastly more difficult when these capabilities are tacitly held (e.g. a distinct corporate culture or social complexity within organizations). Absorbing such competencies requires that a firm develop high receptivity and a strong learning intent. It also requires that the partner has some degree of transparency in knowledge communication, and that the nature of this knowledge is itself sufficiently transferable. Indeed, to transfer the analytical skills of Stephen Hawking to a mathematically-impaired student may prove wearisome. Moreover, trading in strategic resources can be subject to high transaction costs, particularly those of adverse selection, moral hazard, cheating, and hold-up (Chi, 1994).

Agency theory

Agency theory is concerned with the ability of 'principals' to monitor and control 'agents'. Accepting the assumption of self-interest, an integral part also of transaction cost theory, agents may seek to exploit their relative positions (e.g. access to resources) and must be presided over by principals (Fama and Jensen, 1983; Jensen and Meckling, 1976). Principals can be of various kinds, including shareholders or owners, as can agents, including managers and employees. Governance systems thus become the focal point in organizational design. Traditionally, applications of agency theory have focused on the specific relationship between owners and managers of large public corporations (Berle and Means, 1932), though more recent works have extended this to include relationships between employers and employees, clients and lawyers, and buyers and suppliers (Child and Faulkner, 1998). Firms, for instance, are viewed as a mere nexus of contracts between owners of the factors of production and customers (Ramanathan and Thomas, 1997). The assumptions underlying agency theory are not dissimilar from those supporting transaction cost theory, or even the classical economics of Adam Smith. Human beings remain viewed as self-interested, opportunistic, subject to bounded rationality, and risk averse. Thus, a strategy of cooperation (especially through the formation of joint ventures) can be advantageous in accruing the benefits of teamwork, but also costly in terms of legislating for, and monitoring, the self-serving behaviour of agents. Like transaction cost theory, agency theory has significant implications for the choice of governance structure. As Das and Teng point out, 'managers are often motivated to fold the alliances into their own firms to control their own compensation or employment risk. A consequence is that many alliances are terminated rather quickly, often being sold to one of the partners' (2000: 83). And this perhaps suggests a limitation of agency theory, for whilst it seems to provide a rationale for the acquisition of alliance partners it does not explain why some firms successfully acquire partners whilst these partners themselves should be pursuing that very same objective (Das and Teng, 2000). Also, the theory may again be relatively deterministic and static in its orientation.

Game theory

Game theory is commonly credited to the work of three Princeton colleagues, the mathematician John von Neumann, the economist Oskar Morgenstern, and the much younger John Nash. Their institutional environment – the mathematics department at Princeton University and the prestigious Institute for Advanced Studies – proved a magnet for the likes of Albert Einstein, Kurt Gödel, Hermann Weyl and Robert Oppenheimer. Von Neumann's recognition that social behaviour could be analysed as a game was introduced in his 1928 article on parlour games, and extended in his collaboration with Morgenstern on his better-known *Theory of Games and Economic Behavior*, published in 1944. Trivial games, like poker or bridge, might hold the key to more complex social interactions, they reasoned, by highlighting the rational calculations that inform such interactions. This is a function primarily of the interconnected and highly interdependent interests of participating individuals (Zagare, 1984). Although von Neuman and Morgenstern's single-round Prisoner's Dilemma[4] has since evolved into more complex varieties (e.g. non-zero-sum games over multiple rounds of interaction), one principle remains unchanged: strategies of cooperation may materialize provided there exists a possibility for the parties involved to meet again in the future (Axelrod, 1984). As applied by Parkhe to the specific context of formal alliances:

In strategic alliances cooperation is maintained as each firm compares the immediate gain from cheating with the possible sacrifice of future gains that may result from violating an agreement... The assumption here seems intuitively reasonable: broken promises in the present will decrease the likelihood of cooperation in the future. By the same token, cooperation in the current move can be matched by cooperation in the next move, and a defection can be met with a retaliatory defection. Thus, iteration improves the prospects for cooperation by encouraging strategies of reciprocity. (1993a: 799)

Although game theory retains the assumption of individual self-interest, it does not also assume that competitive behaviour will follow, as is implied in Adam Smith's 'invisible hand' theory. Even von Neumann's (1928) simple, two-player, one-round Prisoner's Dilemma game shows instead that the optimum outcome is gained through a strategy of cooperation, not competition. This discovery, by John Nash published

---

[4] Assume, argued Von Neumann and Morgenstern in the original Prisoner's Dilemma, that two culprits have been arrested. The police have some circumstantial evidence to convict them, but too little to be able to persuade the presiding judge to administer long sentences. So they make each prisoner a devious offer: if you implicate your partner in the crime, we will drop all charges against you and you will get to go home. Your partner, on the other hand, will receive a prison sentence of ten years. If you refuse to cooperate with us (but cooperate with your partner, in game theoretic terms), we will still have sufficient evidence to ensure a prison sentence of one year, that is, provided your partner refuses to cooperate with us also. However, if your partner implicates you in the crime, all charges against her will be dropped and you get to go away for ten years behind bars. If both of you talk and implicate each other in the crime, you will receive sentences of seven years each. Apparently this 'trick' almost always works, particularly as prisoners are not allowed to communicate with each other. One can easily see why.

when he was a 21-year-old PhD student (Nash, 1950a, 1950b), ultimately secured him the Nobel Prize in economics in 1994 (Nasar, 2001:
15). Drawing on an early article in game theory by the mathematician
John von Neumann (1928), Nash introduced 'non-cooperative games'.
These particular games are void of enforceable contracts among players
(as is often the case in real life) but where these involve players acting on
their best individual rationalizations of other players playing their own
best strategies. Clearly, collaboration can maximize joint interest whilst
avoiding the worst possible individual payoffs. In other words, competition does not inevitably generate the best possible outcome for all. One
thus takes issue with Adam Smith, for when each player pursues their
private interests they do not also necessarily promote the best interests of
the collective.

Dixit and Nalebuff (1991) and Brandenburger and Nalebuff (1996)
have done much to popularize game-theoretic thinking. Their work out-
lines the circumstances under which strategies of cooperation may be
rewarding, and those conditions under which they may be undermined.
Axelrod's (1984) simulations contribute to these the importance of simplicity, predictability, and forgiveness, each of which is facilitated by a
'tit-for-tat' approach to alliances. What limits the usefulness of game theory at present is the almost inevitable simplification of real-life scenarios.
It is thus less helpful in accounting for the personalities of players, their
social ties, verbal communication, uncertainty about what the other
player actually did previously in the game, and the social conventions
and institutions in which these players are embedded and by which their
conduct is at least likely to be partially informed. Game theory also re-
duces firms to single actors and is less able to account for the potential
variety of perception and interest within them.

Real options theory

A fugitive from the field of finance, real options theory provides a particular explanation of firms entering alliances, namely to spread risk and
maintain a presence in rapidly developing technological fields. Within the
context of a real options strategy, alliancing helps generate a portfolio of
comparatively low-risk options, enabling small and incremental 'wagers'
to be made that can simultaneously achieve new learning and open up
further options for the future (Amram and Kulatilaka, 1999; Copeland
and Keenan, 1998; Faulkner and de Rond, 2000; Kogut and Kulatilaka,
2001). Such strategies are particularly relevant to the pharmaceutical industry, where large firms may commit to significant annual investments

in, say, twenty or twenty-five biotech startups with the expectation that only four or five will generate a realistic drug candidate. Even so, this will usually render the expenditure worthwhile.

Despite its particular relevance to high-tech industries, real options theory is comparatively limited to supplying explanations for the process of cooperating. Also, the theory affords an inherently more predatory perspective on cooperative behaviour than do most other theories, is static and fairly deterministic, and provides a much less explicit treatment of those characteristics often associated with successful cooperation, including commitment and trust.

Resource dependence theory

Resource dependence theory, developed most elaborately by Pfeffer and Salancik (1978), suggests that firms are dependent on resources that reside outside themselves. It thus focuses squarely on the contexts in which such firms operate and upon which they rely for resources. As Pfeffer subsequently explained:

Because organizations are not internally self-sufficient, they require resources from the environment and, thus, become interdependent with those elements of the environment with which they transact . . . Thus, resource dependence theory suggests that organizational behaviour becomes externally influenced because the focal organization must attend to the demands of those in its environment that provide resources necessary and important for its continued survival. (1982: 192–3)

A strategy of cooperation is thus explained by seeking to control this source of uncertainty. It can provide firms with access to unique capabilities (which is consistent with the resource-based view), financial resources, exclusive suppliers, raw materials, skills, processes, or markets. In other words, firms may seek to reduce their dependency on their environment by cooperating with key parts of it (Faulkner, 1995), although this may simply replace one source of risk with others, including freeriding, opportunism, and the unintended transfer of proprietary skills (Faulkner and de Rond, 2000).

The theory seeks to develop a more explicit awareness of organizational context and is fairly normative in focusing on rational choice and deliberate efforts to align the firm to its environment (Pfeffer, 1982). Its relative emphasis on economic and socio-political forces, and the implication of this for relationships with stakeholders, has been criticized by some (e.g. Donaldson, 1995) but welcomed by others. Finally, resource dependence theory is not entirely process-friendly, and may be unrealistic in assuming the relatively unproblematic transfer of resources, particularly when these are minimally mobile and imitable (Das and Teng, 2000).

Relational contract theory

Dissatisfied with classical and neoclassical contract theory, particularly with their narrow definition of business exchanges as discrete, Macneil (1974, 1980) developed his 'relational contract' theory. As opposed to transactions being discrete events, Macneil, and Macaulay (1963) before him, realized that most exchange relationships need ongoing interactions. Formal legal contracts, however important, seldom provide an adequate mechanism for assisting day-to-day interactions. Instead, most relationships rely on particular historical and social contexts, including trust. As put by Heide:

Relational exchange . . . accounts explicitly for the historical and social context in which transactions take place and views enforcement of obligations as following from the mutuality of interest that exists between a set of parties. (1994: 74)

Trust, in fact, is thought to be critical for ensuring smooth exchanges – a strategic alliance being considered one such relationship. But despite its helpful emphasis on trust, relational contract theory may be limited in not having generated sufficient empirical research to warrant its applicability (Kern and Willcocks, 2000). Also, the concept of trust appears somewhat ill-defined – is it calculative, predictive or affective trust (Child and Faulkner, 1998)? Does it refer to trust between partnering organizations or between individuals involved in the daily exchange relationship? Finally, as Das and Teng (2000) pointed out, a lack of trust may not explain most alliance failures as partners with no obvious historical record of partnering also succeed.

Organizational learning theory

As suggested earlier, alliances may provide opportunities for partners to learn about technologies, disease targets, processes, customers, competitors or foreign markets. Organizational learning theory focuses on the capability of organizations to acquire, disseminate, and retain new knowledge so as to improve future performance (Child and Faulkner, 1998). Partner differences are potentially important as they can provide learning opportunities and a powerful motive for entering into alliances. The paradox is, of course, that although alliances are usually intended to enhance organizational learning, the fact that the strategic and cultural fit may be less than perfect can seriously impede this learning process

(Child and Faulkner, 1998; Inkpen, 1998). Related to this is a second paradox, sometimes dubbed the 'Meno' paradox (Polanyi, 1966). It holds that partner organizations either already know what they are looking for, and hence need not search for it, or do not know what exactly they are after and thus cannot find anything. Polanyi's solution to this paradox, as Shenkar and Li (1999: 135) point out, lies in building specific capabilities that stimulate the search for new knowledge – or an 'absorptive' capability. An important concept introduced by Cohen and Levinthal (1990: 128), absorptive capability refers to the ability of firms to recognize the value of, and utilize, new information. Clearly, this faculty is rooted in prior related knowledge. An existing knowledge base, in other words, determines the degree to which partner firms search for, evaluate, and seek to effectively apply new knowledge – what can be learned is a function of that which is already known (Powell et al., 1996). Exactly what degree of relatedness is required for existing knowledge to lead to new knowledge is still open to debate (Shenkar and Li, 1999).

Not only is experience a precondition for learning, but so is a sense of community. When an alliance arises from a pre-existing membership in a common technological community, collaborating is thought to be routinized and to occur more readily, requiring less effort (Hakansson, 1990; Powell, Koput, and Smith Doerr, 1996; von Hippel, 1988).

Firms opt for sustaining the ability to learn, via interdependence, over independence by means of vertical integration. This, in turn, promotes a sense of community-level mutualism . . . Competition is no longer seen as a game with a zero-sum outcome, but as a positive-sum relationship in which new mechanisms for providing resources develop in tandem with advances in knowledge. (Powell, Koput, and Smith Doerr, 1996: 143)

Powell, Koput, and Smith Doerr (1996) provide empirical support that experience and network centrality are positively correlated with performance, though they are equally careful in suggesting network centrality as a guarantor of success.

Despite having surfaced in the literature as early as the 1970s, it has only recently been applied specifically to the study of alliances (e.g. Child and Rodrigues, 1996; Ciborra, 1991; Dodgson, 1993; Doz, 1996; Hamel, 1991; Inkpen, 1995; Inkpen and Crossan, 1995). Hamel (1991), in particular, distinguished between two types of learning in strategic alliances. Collaborative learning affords access to, and transfer of, proprietary skills and knowledge, as well as more general experiences as to the nature of partnering. Competitive learning, on the other hand, takes place when one partner exploits the knowledge and expertise provided by another. The latter type is inherently predatory, although the distinction may merely be one of intent, for partners can only reasonably be expected to put their alliance-related learning into practice in different situations. Some have suggested that the process of collaborating, particularly as it affords learning opportunities, is potentially more important than governance structure (e.g. Doz, 1996; Hamel, 1991). What is clear, however, is that the actual learning process can be fraught with difficulties (Inkpen, 2000; Inkpen and Crossan, 1995). Reflecting on his own research, Inkpen says this:

> Despite the logical notion that alliances create learning opportunities, and although organizations often talk in glowing terms about their alliances' learning potential, my research suggests that learning through alliances is a difficult, frustrating, and often misunderstood process. More significantly, I would argue that creating a successful alliance learning environment is the exception rather than the rule. (1998: 70)

In contrast to the various theoretical perspectives discussed thus far, organizational learning theory may provide a more process-friendly approach to the empirical study of alliances. What the literature still lacks are examples of such empirical studies, principally studies that move beyond in-depth case studies towards large cross-sectional samples (Simonin, 1999). The reason for this may be a common one: the variables that are most interesting theoretically are usually also those that are most difficult to identify and measure (Spender and Grant, 1996).

Social network theory

Social network theory appears to have rapidly become a fashionable intellectual lens for the study of alliance formation and evolution at a population level. Defined broadly as select, persistent, and structured sets of autonomous players who cooperate on the basis of implicit and open-ended contracts, both to adapt to environmental contingencies and to coordinate and safeguard exchanges (cf. Jones, Hesterly, and Borgatti, 1997), social networks are a macro-level phenomenon. Nevertheless, they emerge, evolve, and dissolve as a direct consequence of the actions of individual players. The contracts on which exchanges are based are mostly socially, rather than legally, binding. As Nohria (1992) explains, (a) essentially all organizations comprise social networks; (b) the actions and behaviour of individuals and organizations can be explained, at least partly, in the context of their position in this network; and (c) this network is constantly being socially constructed and adjusted or modified through the actions of individuals or organizations. This reproductive feature of networks, as social structures, is not inconsistent with Giddens's (1984) tradition in sociology, though one might contend that network analysis, by definition, emphasizes structure at the expense of action (Sydow and Windeler, 1998). It thus risks rendering a one-sided account of alliance process (Faulkner and de Rond, 2000). Social network analysis does contribute significantly to our understanding of alliance formation, dynamics, evolution, performance, and the consequences of performance, by studying the larger networks in which they are embedded (Gulati, 1998). This is an area ignored by many traditional scholars, who have focused almost exclusively on dyadic relationships. It is also process-friendly and able to produce a more socialized account of alliance life, albeit mostly at the population level.

In sum then, various theories exist to render explanations of alliance formation and optimal governance but explain to a much lesser extent their dynamics and evolution. We have briefly discussed ten of them. Zeitz (1980) contributes four additional perspectives: exchange theory (Cook, 1977; Levine and White, 1961), ecological theory (cf. Aldrich and Pfeffer, 1976; Guetzkow, 1966), systems theory (Turk, 1973), and sociometry (Anderson, 1967), though he admits that none (at the time of his writing) found widespread acceptance. Relatively little may have changed since. Despite very significant contributions, none of those reviewed has met with unequivocal adoption. Nor does any theory, considered on its own, seem able to provide that sought-after comprehensive theoretical lens. Many appear relatively deterministic, acontextual, and aprocessual, potentially lacking in balance and comprehensiveness (Child and Faulkner, 1998; Faulkner and de Rond, 2000; Parkhe, 1993a; Salk and Shenkar, 2001; Shenkar and Yan, 2002; Simonin, 1999; Wood and Gray, 1991; Zeitz, 1980). As put forcefully by Sydow and Windeler:

Although we believe that economic and organization and network theories contribute to a better understanding of creating and organizing interfirm networks, none of these focuses on structure as well as on process, takes the production of structure via action as much into account as the flow of action from structure, and deals simultaneously with power, cognition, and legitimacy issues as interrelated aspects of the process through which economic effectiveness is constituted. (1998: 270)

Lastly, existing theory appears somewhat inadequate in rendering explanations of alliance instability and failure. In the words of Das and Teng:

Although all these approaches have identified certain characteristics of strategic alliances that may lead to their undesirable dissolution, the extent of our understanding of this subject appears to be fragmented and incomplete... There is as yet no general framework that explains *why* strategic alliances are inordinately *unstable*. (2000: 84; italics added)

A promising new theory candidate is the political perspective, introduced by Shenkar and Yan (2002) as an alternative explanation for the dynamics of cooperative ventures. Drawing on the works of Cyert and March (1963), Perrow (1986), and Pfeffer and Salancik (1978), they suggest that alliances are best seen as consisting of coalitions of individuals that compete for resources and managerial attention and entertain potentially conflicting views on organizational objectives. Given the inability of a single coalition to determine these objectives, alliance life is subject to ongoing processes of negotiation. Their application of this political lens to a failed Chinese cooperative venture is insightful and bodes well. It fragments rather than unifies, making allowances for diversity, messiness, and inconsistency.

The implausibility of a one-best-way

But perhaps one cannot expect simple theoretical recipes. Maybe alliances simply reflect the heterogeneity of the larger contexts in which they exist. In pharmacology and biotechnology, as in other industries, mergers, acquisitions, joint ventures, and various other coalitions seem to have added organizational complexity. Pfizer became the largest drugmaker in the world upon its acquisition of Warner Lambert with sales approaching $25 billion per year. It is now pursuing the integration of Pharmacia. GlaxoWellcome joined forces with SmithKline Beecham. Novartis is the product of a merger of Ciba-Geigy and Sandoz, and recently took a significant equity stake in the pharmaceutical Roche. Organizations exploit opportunities by creating, acquiring, or cooperating with those that possess the relevant skills or resources. But while thus seeking to forge more competitive businesses out of potentially incompatible entities, those in charge risk rendering control increasingly illusive. Moreover, corporate success can be difficult to foretell, particularly in technology-intensive businesses. The recent volatility of the NASDAQ (a technology-dominated equity market) serves as a poignant reminder. This relative lack of constancy and predictability might well be exacerbated in drug discovery by virtue of its inherent serendipity. To take just two examples, the fortunes of British Biotech, once the wunderkind of Britain's science community, took a nosedive when its anti-cancer candidate Zacutex was forced back into expensive clinical trials. Its second drug candidate, Marimastat, fared similarly soon after. Its stock plummeted, losing over 90 per cent of its value within weeks. Pfizer's blockbuster drug Viagra, on the other hand, made over a billion dollars in its first year. A male impotency drug, Viagra was originally intended to combat angina but seemed doomed to failure upon disappointingly low rates of effectiveness in combating the disease. However, as luck would have it, side effects reported by healthy male volunteers indicated a promising alternative disease target. Pfizer wisely re-entered the drug into clinical trials but using impotent men instead and generated one of the best-selling drugs of recent history.

Inside organizations, but at the level of the individual, one may meet the potentially inconsistent and multifaceted nature of human agency. Individuals act neither in a vacuum nor in a wholly determined fashion. Rather their conduct is likely to be partially voluntaristic and partially fashioned by the raw materials of culture, tradition, prejudice, loyalty, ambition, personality, and experience. Moreover, human agency may be heir to inconsistent value systems, contriving to stick to a belief in both the morality of motive and that of consequence (de Rond, 2002). We may, for instance, marvel at the achievements of Jack Welch, in the early 1980s, and those of Al 'Chainsaw' Dunlop (in the pre-Sunbeam era) in trimming down their organizations to achieve efficiency and focus, despite incurring significant social costs on the way. Yet, at the same time, we may admire those too who, irrespective of their achievements, are moved by motives regardless of consequence. The eighteenth-century industrialist Robert Owen (social architect of the New Lanark wool mills and, in later life, the founder of the 'New Harmony' community in Indiana, USA) and, in recent times, Anita Roddick (founder of The Body Shop) may be good examples. Like characters in a Bertolt Brecht play, we epitomize the antitheses of being human: the kind and cruel, the just and merciful, the idealist and realist – these being potential divisions within the same person. Brecht, the controversial German playwright (1898–1956), drew on just such divisiveness (or the tendency thereto which exists in all) in his subversive social critiques (e.g. *The Good Woman of Setzuan*, 1948). And one finds this same sense of the multifaceted and at times inconsistent and irrational in the complex novels of the Russians Fyodor Dostoevsky and Leo Tolstoy.

What thus emerges is a dynamic and socially complex arena, anathema to traditional business principles, in which management is to take charge and which it must explain. Due to the speed at which markets and industries have been changing, the alliance route has emerged as a popular strategic route, particularly as it is often less irreversible, less complex, and usually less costly than either organic growth or acquisition while preserving some flexibility and autonomy. Their proliferation has been estimated at 25 to 30 per cent per year for industrialized nations (Anderson, 1990; Bleeke and Ernst, 1991, 1995).

This brings us to a second paradox: whilst we may have come to recognize the social complexity of alliances we may have yet to depart from the epistemological tradition that informs our thinking about them. When reviewing the process literature on strategic alliances, it seems that we may have sought constancy, homogeny, teleology or progress possibly in an effort to produce useful miniature universes, but in the absence of verification that these are, in fact, their true properties.

Life cycle approaches

The earliest of these alliance process models are generally linear in orientation. By and large, these conceptualized alliance evolution as a generic sequence of predictable life cycle stages. One is thought to progress naturally from one stage to the next (see Figure 1.1). Particularly good examples of this are: Achrol, Sheer, and Stern (1990), d'Aunno and Zuckerman (1987), Forrest and Martin (1992), Kanter (1994), and Murray and Mahon (1993). Each viewed alliance life as commencing with a period of courtship, followed by formalization of the alliance and moving towards a critical decision: to either elaborate the collaborative domain or to pack up and go home. Change is immanent in that alliances 'grow up' through a generic sequence of life cycle stages. As Aldrich (1999: 197) explains,

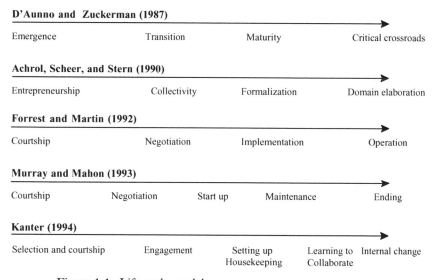

Figure 1.1: Life cycle models

life cycle models typically hypothesize that organizations (including interorganizational forms of organization) confront generic problems as they age, to which managers and members respond with generic solutions. Consequently, evolution is driven primarily by internal processes, particularly at the level of senior management.

Despite their apparent diversity, life cycle process models appear typically informed by an atomistic treatment of what is inevitably a complex phenomenon (Mathews, White, and Long, 1999). This is particularly well reflected in a shared conception of alliance life as consisting of a predetermined and orderly sequence of stages, each of which calls for a specific managerial task (i.e. courting, negotiating, formalizing, learning to collaborate, ending). These stages are mediated by 'the immanent logic, rules, or programmes that govern the entity's development' (van de Ven and Poole, 1995: 515). These assumptions may be at variance with the felt experiences of those involved in the daily life of alliances. Empirically, there is evidence from the small business sector that forces such as competition can be a far more important cause for reaction and change than the progression through life cycle stages (Dodge, Fullerton, and Robbins, 1994). Joint research programmes in biotechnology, for instance, seem to evolve in relatively uncertain and rapidly changing technological contexts, forged by serendipity in lead compound discovery and rapid industry consolidation, and there often appears no orderly and predictable sequence of stages. The history of the biotech startup Vertex, narrated in impressive detail by Werth (1994), and the case narratives to follow provide various illustrations of these properties. Similarly, Aldrich (1999: 197) cites Levie and Hay's (1998) review of sixty-three identifiable stage models of organizational growth between 1960 and 1996 to conclude with these authors that such models had made no progress towards prediction of developmental patterns. The persistence of such models, particularly in the absence of any empirical confirmatory support, is somewhat surprising.

Although some may consider biotechnology the exception rather than the norm, it is an area in which collaborations have become increasingly commonplace. Many biotech startups lack the financial resources to sustain long periods of research, the expertise to see a drug through the various clinical trials and FDA or EMEA approval, and the marketing skills and sales force to commercialize drugs. Given a relatively slow growth in venture capital investment (Gove, 1998), few if any commercial drugs to provide regular cash inflows, and the desire of large pharmaceuticals to maintain a window on novel technologies and flexible processes, strategies of cooperation have prevailed.

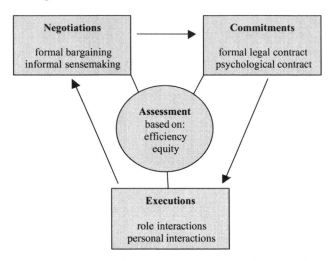

Figure 1.2: Teleological approaches: Ring and van de Ven (1994)

Teleological approaches

To overcome the limitations of life cycle frameworks, other scholars have contributed more open-ended, iterative process models. Probably the best known examples are Ring and van de Ven (1994) and Doz (1996) (see Figure 1.2), although this iterative property is present already in earlier contributions by Shortell and Zajac (1988) and Zajac and Olsen (1993). Ring and van de Ven examine process in collaborations and assume that these can be neither fully specified nor controlled by partners prior to their execution. Their framework conceptualizes interfirm relationships as a recurring sequence of negotiation, commitment and execution. Each phase is governed by formal legal and informal socio-psychological processes and focused on attaining efficient and equitable (or fair) outcomes. The authors believe such developmental processes to be cyclical rather than sequential, and suggest that relationships are maintained 'not because they achieve stability, but because they maintain balance: balance between formal and informal processes' (1994: 112). During the negotiating period, partners develop joint expectations through a formal process of bargaining on terms and procedures. In the ensuing commitments stage, agreement is reached and a structure established on the terms and governance of the relationship. This structure can be either formally codified in a legal agreement or informally understood in a psychological contract. In the executions stage, these commitments are carried into effect. This cycle repeats itself when misunderstandings, conflicts or changed expectations prompt a process

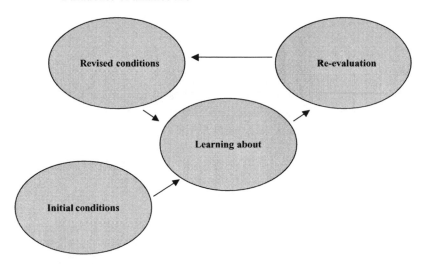

Figure 1.3: Teleological approaches: Doz (1996)

of renegotiation. In due course, the collaborative relationship becomes institutionalized. Their framework comprises a milestone improvement on linear models and provides a helpful focus on interactions between formal and informal processes. Doz (1996) proposed an alternative approach that views alliance evolution as yet another cycle of three sequential, interactive processes (see Figure 1.3). Based on a longitudinal and inductive study of technology development alliances, he inferred that:

Successful alliances . . . evolve through a sequence of learning-reevaluation-readjustment cycles over time, in which the impact of initial conditions quickly faded away. Unsuccessful alliances stumbled on the absence of learning, or on stunted learning, or, still, on successful reevaluation leading to negative readjustments as partners concluded they would not work together successfully. (1996: 64)

Initial conditions and outcomes are thought to be mediated by learning along various dimensions (the environment, tasks, process, skills and goals) in cycles that are both cumulative and progressive. As with Ring and van de Ven (1994), alliance process relies on ongoing partner assessments of equity and efficiency, in addition to adaptability. Doz concluded that, first, alliances do not evolve merely as implementations of an initial design nor do they evolve independently from initial conditions. Second, middle managers play a critical role in alliance process. As Doz notes:

Strategy content and outcomes are hard to understand without an understanding of how participants in the processes that generate these outcomes interact. (1996: 81)

Regardless of its apparent realism and practical appeal, however, this model may risk attributing too much of alliance effectiveness to learning and voluntary managerial intervention. Although these are undoubtedly important, they may account only for a part of a more complex process, and our understanding of alliances might be improved by relaxing any a-priori assumptions of symmetry, teleology, progress and manageability. The latter two are even more implicit in a subsequent process framework, which posits alliance evolution as mediated primarily by cumulative and progressive learning cycles (Doz and Hamel, 1998) (see Figure 1.4). Put differently, despite a helpful departure from life cycle approaches to iterative models, so as to allow for a greater degree of realism, the three frameworks alike appear to be driven, at least on the surface, by an interest in improving alliance performance through the realization of specific managerial tasks (Doz and Hamel, 1998; Leavitt, 1965). This characteristic is perhaps most clearly reflected in their common language. Existing process rhetoric typically entails a combination of various managerial tasks – 'negotiation', 'courtship', 'engagement', 'commitment', 'formalization', 'execution', 'implementation', 'learning', 're-evaluation', 'adjustment' – in addition to relying on normative statements such as 'would necessarily lead to', 'would require', 'will result in' and so forth. Management remains the agent of teleology, or the intelligence behind

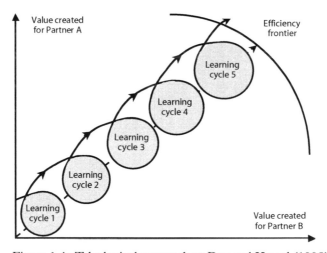

Figure 1.4: Teleological approaches: Doz and Hamel (1998)

alliance success. And it is this, a task orientation and assumption of progress, that best characterizes them as teleological. Teleological approaches to development and change implicitly assume an Aristotelian perspective on process as informed by 'final causes'. Aristotle did not go so far as to commit to 'backward causation' – or the notion of end states as exerting a causal pull on antecedent events – but retained a deep belief in purpose as governing process (Lear, 1988). He maintained that 'the deepest cause for things must be sought not in the beginning of things but in their end – their *telos*, their purpose and final actuality, that to which they aspire' (Tarnas, 1991: 61). Organizational entities, in the teleological perspective, are considered as purposeful and alert, but able to learn and adapt to changing circumstances. Using van de Ven and Poole's (1995: 520–1) definition of change, in a teleological sense, comprising a 'cycle of goal formulation, implementation, evaluation, and modification of goals based on what was learned by the entity', even the Ring and van de Ven (1994) approach shares these characteristics, even if they are more explicit in Doz (1996) and Doz and Hamel (1998). But, as Sydow and Windeler (1998) suggest, accepting the possibility of unintended consequences, due to either human frailty, misunderstanding or bounded rationality, would imply that alliance process must at least partly be the product of forces beyond managerial intent and control.

Evolutionary approaches

Different still is the evolutionary perspective, according to which entities must continuously compete for survival given a scarce resource base and a series of blind (or chance) variations. In contrast to life cycle and teleological approaches, the emphasis is now squarely on the environment as the principal motor of change, retaining only those entities that best fit its evolving structure. Among these evolutionary theories, as van de Ven and Poole (1995) acknowledge, there exist several variations, the most important of which include Darwinian and Lamarckian evolution, and S. J. Gould's 'punctuated equilibrium' variety. Differences amongst these are limited to rate of change and the inheritability of characteristics. Darwinian evolution, for instance, proceeds at a far slower pace than Gould's punctuated equilibrium, and retains fewer traits than the Lamarckian equivalent.

Within the alliance process literature, one finds a number of studies that share these characteristics, though they may speak to different levels of analysis. For instance, Koza and Lewin's (1998) 'co-evolutionary approach' applies well to individual alliances, whereas the contributions of Gulati (1993, 1995a, 1995b), Gulati and Gargiulo (1998), and Reuer,

Zollo, and Singh (2002) address process at the level of populations. Implicit in these treatments is the notion that alliance evolution (even of individual alliances) is driven predominantly by forces operating at the population level. Evolution is, in other words, fairly deterministic, with the environment as the principal change agent. Although this suggestion may disagree with Aldrich (1999) and van de Ven and Poole (1995), evolution thus appears relatively deterministic – at least from the perspective of the single alliance as member of a population – leaving relatively little room for voluntarism and idiosyncrasy (Child, 1972, 1997). Further, the assumption of natural selection would presuppose an evolution from relatively simple to fitter and more sophisticated phenomena, which may also render evolution progressive. McKelvey's (1997) suggestion that organizational evolution cannot be understood independently from a simultaneous evolution of the context in which organizations find themselves is relevant in this respect, and forms the basis for, for instance, Koza and Lewin's (1998) contribution.

Dialectical approaches

These generic categories of evolutionary theories parallel an evolving literature. Using van de Ven and Poole's (1995) impressive review of process paradigms as an intellectual scaffold, we find that the literature seems to have traversed three process paradigms (see Figure 1.5). A fourth

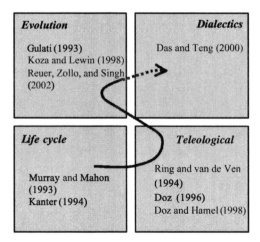

Figure 1.5: Four generic process paradigms: van de Ven and Poole (1995)

paradigm, dialectics, remains relatively uncharted, except for a recent contribution by Das and Teng (2000). In it, the authors suggest that our understanding of alliance instability and failure can be significantly improved by examining the internal tensions to which they are subject. Informed by the social philosophies of Marx and Hegel, theirs is a view of alliances as sites in which conflicting forces compete on three fronts: cooperation versus competition, rigidity versus flexibility, and short-term versus long-term orientation. This internal tensions framework helps explain why alliances are as vulnerable and unstable as they appear to be. True to its Hegelian origins, it allows these forces to compete until one gathers sufficient strength to dominate over the others, upon which the alliance will evolve into something new, or result in it being terminated. In fact, it is because these three tensions are uniquely present in alliances, as opposed to single organizations, that they are so prone to fail (Das and Teng, 2000: 85). This seems to provide a better explanation of alliance instability than do competing theories such as transaction cost theory, game theory, market power theory, and the resource-based view. However, Das and Teng say little about the possible virtues in having these internal tensions present in alliances. For instance, might it not be that competition secures efficiency where cooperation can fail to do so? Instead, they contend with those before them that instability is necessarily a 'bad thing', suggesting that this also explains why researchers have often taken them as 'a proxy for poor alliance performance' (2000: 78). Also, their theory is limited to three tensions to the exclusion of other equally legitimate, opposing forces – vigilance and trust, control and autonomy, planning and emergence, innovation and replication, exploration and exploitation, and justice and mercy, among others. One wonders whether incorporating these might not provide an even richer understanding of the instability and vulnerability of alliances? Finally, there is no explicit suggestion of these forces coexisting but potentially at different levels inside alliances – interorganizational, organizational, departmental or interpersonal levels. For example, cooperation may take place broadly between two businesses but competition may exist primarily with one or two individuals involved in this relationship. Or one may be confident of the abilities and integrity of a firm but vigilant of those of a particular actor. As with most forms of categorization, the boundaries of this two-by-two matrix are probably far less rigid than presented. For instance, there may well exist elements of teleology (e.g. planning) in a dialectical perspective on process as opposed to, say, blind variations (or chance) – the malfeasance, luck, and individual initiative that can characterize alliance life (Aldrich, 1999; Brunsson, 1985; March, 1981).

Alternatively, teleological and dialectical models may be incorporated within the framework of evolution for similar reasons (Aldrich, 1999: 200).

Despite helpful transitions from life cycle (linear) to teleological (iterative) to evolutionary (population-level) to dialectical (internal tensions) theories, however, this literature as a whole may have remained comparatively rational and atomistic in orientation, in focusing principally on discovering patterns or regularities in the potentially varied events that comprise alliance life. Alliances are defined by purposes, and their success by the degree to which they meet these purposes. By and large, they are assumed to evolve in a relatively deterministic and law-like fashion. To be sure, alliances have purposes; and when examining strategic alliances in stable and predictable environments, the above characterization may be relatively unproblematic. However, when considering alliances in potentially dynamic or unstable contexts, this approach risks leaving affairs unaccounted for. First, the strategic purpose of an alliance may well be liable to change, sometimes considerably, and thus may well be less constant and more variable than usually assumed. Besides, strategic agendas may exist at multiple levels, from the organizational to the individual, and may not necessarily be congruent with those of the alliance. This multiplicity of intentions is well recognized, though few proposals exist for coping with the necessary complexity it creates. To quote March and Sutton:

It is not clear that organizational purpose can be portrayed as unitary or that the multiple purposes of an organization are reliably consistent. It is not clear that a single conception of purposes is shared among participants in an organization. It is not [even] clear that purpose antedates activities. Nevertheless, talking about the purposes of organizations and evaluating comparative organizational success and failure in fulfilling those purposes are conspicuous parts of conventional discourse... Such comparisons become a basis... for writing history, and for stimulating arrogance and shame. (1997: 698)

Second, we may need to exercise caution in assuming progress. There may well be instances in which one stage is not necessarily an improvement on the one before, or in which a relationship 'regresses' from, for instance, a relatively sophisticated and trusting collaboration into a straightforward, less naive, buyer–supplier type relationship. Chapter 3 provides an illustration of this. Third, we may have to be equally careful in assuming management to be the primary force in alliance process, driving them progressively closer to predefined objectives. Alliances may well be impacted by events that are difficult to anticipate and manage in the traditional sense of being carefully planned and controlled. Things happen to it. Fourth, a strong rationality, whether assumed inside single alliances or at the population level, may be less successful in accounting for the relative disorder, heterogeneity, and unmanageability of alliances, and for the role of human agency in shaping their evolution. To evaluate the merits and consequences of this metaphysical attitude, we must ultimately look at the empirical world itself.

2   The context of drug discovery

There is a wonderful paragraph in Kary Mullis's *Dancing Naked in the Mind Field*:

In the early weeks of 1968 I submitted an article I had written to the foremost scientific journal in the world, *Nature*, published in London. I called it 'The Cosmological Significance of Time Reversal' and congratulated myself on its cleverness . . . I was a second-year graduate student in biochemistry at Berkeley. I had read a lot about astrophysics and had taken some psychoactive drugs, which enhanced my perceived understanding of the cosmos. Not very good reasons to think that an international journal of science would want to publish my views for the edification of their very knowledgeable readership. It was accepted. . . . Years later I invented the polymerase chain reaction (PCR). I was a professional scientist, and knew what I had discovered. It was not the speculations of a kid about the universe and time reversal. It was a chemical procedure that would make the structures of the molecules of our genes as easy to see as billboards in the desert and as easy to manipulate as Tinkertoys . . . I knew that PCR would spread across the world like wildfire. This time there was no doubt in my mind: *Nature* would publish it. They rejected it. So did *Science*, the second-most prestigious journal in the world. *Science* offered that perhaps my paper could be published in some secondary journal, as they felt it would not be suitable to the needs of their readers. [Screw] them, I said.(2000: 103–5)

Ironically, Kary Mullis was awarded the Nobel Prize in Chemistry in 1993 for his discovery of PCR. His experiences, amusingly retold in his strange and controversial but entirely autobiographical book, might well be the exception rather than the rule. It may also suggest, however, that it remains difficult to abstract the scientific enterprise from the social context in which it unfolds. Such was the observation also of Thomas Kuhn, philosopher of science, in publishing his divisive *The Structure of Scientific Revolutions*. Scientific research and measurement is paradigm-driven, concluded Kuhn (1970: 126).

Men whose research is based on shared paradigms are committed to the same rules and standards for scientific practice. That commitment and the apparent consensus it produces are prerequisites for normal science, i.e., for the genesis and continuation of a particular research tradition. (Kuhn, 1970: 11)

Kuhn compares our intellectual approach to the solving of a jigsaw puzzle. Puzzles, argued Kuhn, have preordained, fixed solutions. He suggested:

[Consider] the jigsaw puzzle whose pieces are selected at random from each of two different puzzle boxes. Since that problem is likely to defy (though it might not) even the most ingenious of men, it cannot serve as a test of skill in solution. In any usual sense it is not a puzzle at all. Though intrinsic value is no criterion for a puzzle, the *assured existence of a solution* is. (1970: 37, italics added)

Heirs to the Enlightenment, the natural sciences have prospered greatly and, in many instances, have contributed significantly to our quality of life. The past fifty years in particular have been marked by important scientific developments. It is difficult to imagine life today without the benefits bestowed on us by the scientific enterprise: Fleming's discovery of penicillin, the discovery of the 'double helix' structure of DNA by Wilkins, Watson, and Crick (with Rosalind Franklin's help),[1] the mapping of the human genome, Bayer's theorem, quantum mechanics, Einstein's theory of relativity, and the Nash Equilibrium, are among the first that come to mind.

This book would be incomplete without at least a preamble on the context of biotechnology research. This short chapter seeks to fill that void. I am conscious that this is an inherently risky proposition, as today's biotechnology context will need updating by the time this book reaches the bookshelves. Nonetheless, a context-sensitive theoretical perspective would seem to demand it. This chapter therefore discusses the present state of the drug discovery enterprise, the proliferation of cooperative activity in this field, and the moral questions raised by the introduction of genetic and genomic technologies. It also describes the serendipitous nature of medical research, specifically the development of therapies for humans, including anything from chemical library specialists and high throughput screening technology providers to genomic sequencing and gene therapy. It concludes with a contemporary illustration of serendipity, familiar to many – the discovery and development of Pfizer's controversial anti-impotence drug Viagra.

---

[1] Rosalind Franklin's research on X-ray techniques, first showing the helix structure of DNA, was shared (apparently without her consent) by her colleague Maurice Wilkins with Crick and Watson, enabling them to make their breakthrough discovery. Wilkins, Crick, and Watson were awarded the Nobel Prize for their contributions to science. Franklin died four years before, at age thirty-eight, and was never formally acknowledged as having played a potentially vital part in Crick and Watson's work on DNA.

The promise of biotechnology

A recent *TIME* special issue on the future of medicine commenced evocatively thus:

> Just as the discovery of the electron in 1897 was a seminal event for the 20th century, the seeds for the 21st century were spawned in 1953, when James Watson blurted out to Francis Crick how four nucleic acids could pair to form the self-copying code of a DNA molecule. (*TIME*, 11 January, p. 42)

Hopes of miracle cures for hitherto incurable diseases, however, are overshadowed by the moral dilemmas of cloning, altering and commercializing human genes, and marketing genetically modified organisms (GMOs). As Brian Appleyard coarsely remarks:

> Evolutionary theory and genetics have proffered an earthly heaven in which an understanding of our biological inheritance will unify us in an awareness of what we truly, scientifically are. (1999a: 39)

And elsewhere:

> Genetics is not just another technological development like the advent of antibiotics, computers, or space shuttles. It is not simply another phase in the spectacular progress of science marked by such theories as Darwinian evolution, quantum mechanics, or relativity. Nor is it merely a big idea like capitalism, communism, democracy, or fascism that changes people's views of the world. Rather, it is all of these things – a historically unique combination of philosophy, science, and technology that confronts humanity with the most fundamental questions, our answers to which will determine the human future. (Appleyard, 1999b: 3)

Promises, unthinkable around the turn of the twentieth century, have financed a myriad of small biotech companies, some of which have been highly valued, but most of which have yet to help bring a drug to market. The handful of victors – the Food and Drug Administration (FDA) approved at least fifty-two biotech products between 1994 and 2000[2] – help sustain those less fortunate or with product candidates too early in the pipeline to provide sustainable revenues. Indeed, disappointment is as epidemic as the hype associated with biotechnology. Novartis,[3] for instance, was, until recently, reported to have been scrambling to salvage a $1 billion investment into gene therapy focused on cystic fibrosis and cancer by putting on hold all but one of its human testing programmes involving two of its biotech partners, Genetic Therapy Inc. and SyStemix (Langreth and Moore, 1999). Nonetheless, between 1995 and 2000 the

[2] Ernst and Young Annual Biotech Report 2000.
[3] Novartis is the result of a merger between Sandoz and Ciba-Geigy AG in 1996.

FDA approved nearly three times as many biotech products as in the previous thirteen years combined – though this may in part be explained by the relative novelty of biotechnology and the long lead times (typically twelve to fifteen years) associated with drug development.

The biotech industry's growth rate, estimated in 1999 at 17 per cent,[4] is indicative of an immature and rapidly developing industry. Product sales are projected to reach $24 billion by 2006.[5] The US Department of Commerce recently ranked biotechnology among the top twelve emerging technologies thought to present particularly good economic potential (Sapienza and Stork, 2001). In Europe there were 1,036 biotech startups at the end of 1997, the vast majority of which are privately held, employing around 39,000 individuals. This represents an increase of 60 per cent over the previous year, according to Ernst and Young's (annual) 1999 survey. Investment in biotech research and development has risen by 20 per cent during this same period to Ecu 1.71 billion. By comparison, a similar growth marks the pharmaceutical industry. Of the twenty-five largest corporations (by market capitalization) listed in the *Financial Times* 'Global 500' index for 1998,[6] six are pharmaceuticals – representing a higher concentration of market value than any other industry in that coveted top tier – which, taken together, boast a market capitalization of just over $700 billion. At least ten major deals have been negotiated since 1993. Ciba-Geigy merged with Sandoz, in December 1996, to create Novartis in a deal worth in excess of US$30 billion; Glaxo Holdings merged with Wellcome, in May 1995, in a deal worth US$14.3 billion; and Roche Holding took over control at Corange, in March 1998, at a cost of US$10.2 billion. GlaxoWellcome and Bristol Myers Squibb drew up plans for the world's biggest ever merger, only for this strategy to be rendered obsolete by the creation of the $180 billion pharmaceutical colossus GlaxoSmithKline in December 2000. In much the same way, Pharmacia, itself the product of a fusion of Pharmacia and Upjohn, merged with Monsanto that same year, and recently announced its intention to merge with Pfizer. Pfizer, likewise, incorporated Warner-Lambert. Astra and Zeneca merged to form AstraZeneca, Hoechst Marion Roussel and RPR united to create Aventis, and American Home Products absorbed American Cyanamid. Such consolidation activity, especially when viewed in combination with the increase in sales force resources, testifies to the importance of scale economies, among other alleged benefits (Taggart, 1993; Yeoh and Roth, 1999). Assisted

[4] Growth rate is estimated as follows: 1999 sales by biotechnology companies/1998 sales of the same × 100% (source: Ernst and Young Annual Biotech Report 1999).

[5] Ernst and Young Annual Biotech Report 1999.

[6] *Financial Times* Survey, 28 January 1999.

by the gradual harmonization of the regulatory processes for authorizing new medicines, drug companies were able to shrink the time it takes to achieve global market coverage from well over eight years to only four years (Yeoh and Roth, 1999: 640). In addition to resultant economies of scale, consolidation is propelled also by a slowdown in the flow of new drugs from biotechnology partners, a significant number of drugs that will go off-patent within the next three years, and the expectation of increased regulation of collusive behaviour by the US government in its pharmaceutical industry (Martin, 1999). It now costs approximately $800 million to bring a drug to market, a figure twice that of 1987 (*The Economist*, 13 July 2002: 51), requiring 5,000 chemical compounds to be screened to produce one commercially viable, approved drug.

In the USA, where biotechnology was first commercially exploited, there exist in excess of 1,300 biotech firms, around 300 of which are publicly listed on the NASDAQ exchange (Green, 1997). As of late 2000, a handful of these companies, including Abgenix, Human Genome Sciences, and Millennium Pharmaceuticals, boasted a bank balance of $1 billion or more, sufficient to grant them financial independence and better their bargaining position vis-à-vis their pharmaceutical foes. Many others, regardless of geographic location, have fared rather less well, their share price performance being contingent primarily on announcements of collaborations with big pharmaceuticals (in the absence of commercially viable products), the discovery of promising lead compounds, patent applications, feedback from clinical trials, and FDA and European Medicines Evaluation Agency (EMEA) assessments. UK-based British Biotech may again serve as an insightful example. In February 1998, its share price enjoyed a fifty-two-week high of 285 pence, only to collapse to 92 pence upon the announcement that the EMEA had ordered the firm to conduct a second 1,500 patient Phase III clinical trial of Zacutex, its treatment for acute pancreatitis. Prior to that, the Oxford-based biotech firm reported a drop in turnover of 96 per cent, in the second quarter of 1997, due to the premature termination of a partnership agreement with GlaxoWellcome for the development of the arthritis and bowel disease drug BB-2983. A second share flotation in July 1996 ended in disappointment with only half its shareholders exercising their 143 million rights to new shares, in spite of the fact that a second main drug prospect, Marimastat, had entered Phase III clinical trials. Bad fortune struck yet again. Disappointing results from this pivotal Marimastat Phase III trial, published in February 1999, drove the share price lower still. When its director of clinical research was dismissed and publicly criticized British Biotech's product and clinical strategy, investor confidence seemed to have reached an all-time low. Indeed, it is little wonder that Wall Street refers to biotech shares as 'story stocks', reflecting the notion that their value is derived not from products, sales or resources, but information which, in turn, shapes expectations (Werth, 1994).

Although the pharmaceutical industry has been consolidating, the same cannot be said for biotechnology. Alliances have prevailed instead – an exception being radical new efforts by GlaxoSmithKline, AstraZeneca, Aventis, Novartis, and Pfizer to slice parts of their research programmes into competing biotechnology-like companies that will compete for resources in much the same way smaller alliance partners have traditionally done (Pilling, 2001). These re-engineering strategies are relatively novel and the virtue of this approach is yet to be established. For the most part, however, pharmaceuticals have made a serious commitment to biotechnology-based collaborations. Pfizer, for instance, has increased its spending on external collaborations threefold, since 1993, to an expenditure of US$80 million in 1996. Novartis has dedicated up to one-third of its resources to external collaborations. In fact, the top fifteen pharmaceuticals are thought to account for 50 per cent of existing collaborations with biotech firms, each of which has an average value of US$40 million. Indeed, in 1996 Roche's portfolio alone included seventeen such alliances (BioWorld, 1997).

The increasing interest of pharmaceuticals in biotechnology partnerships has helped compensate for a reduction in venture capital investments. Though by far the largest source of cash in 1996, venture financing dipped to US$2.5 billion in 1997. In fact, specific investments in biotechnology increased by only 2.2 per cent, compared to an overall venture capital funding increase of 34 per cent (Gove, 1998). Investments by large pharmaceuticals in their biotech partners, on the other hand, grew significantly to US$4.5 billion during that same period (Hatlestad, 1998). The most active pharmaceuticals will typically have thirty to forty ongoing alliances with smaller biotech partners. R&D investment is clearly seen as an important source of competitive advantage (Dierickx and Cool, 1989; Henderson and Cockburn, 1994; Yeoh and Roth, 1999).

The vast amounts poured into biotech firms afford pharmaceuticals a window on emerging technologies and flexible processes, whilst granting the startup firms the means to gaining legitimacy within the pharmaceutical industry. The latter is well illustrated by Werth (1994) in narrating Vertex's collaboration with the Japanese pharmaceutical giant Chungai:

The room erupted. More than the money, which was crucial, the announcement rang with deliverance. Boger [co-founder of Vertex] had promised everyone he hired that Vertex would be better than other companies: They were the original buyers of his story. And yet the constant dire need for money had discouraged many of them. They worried privately whether they had made the right choice and whether Boger was to be believed. Now, it dawned on them – some for the first time – that Boger's optimism, his aura of glowing success, was justified. Suddenly, they were much closer to being a drug company and getting richer than their own work indicated. Corporately, if not scientifically, the company had legitimized itself much sooner than even Boger had expected. (1994: 160–1)

These investments, however, have remained limited to strategic alliances and have, for the most part, not resulted in consolidation activity (Loizos, 1998), though some expect mergers and acquisitions to be the dominant trend in future years (e.g. Hayward, 1998). According to Loizos (1998), a combination of characteristics is responsible for this apparent lack of consolidation. First, only an estimated two out of every hundred biotech companies are profitable, leaving those that remain as potential cash drains and therefore unattractive takeover targets. Also, it is difficult to value a biotech startup company, particularly one that is focused on research. Lead times are long and the drug discovery process fraught with uncertainty, and, rather than acquiring a high-risk business, pharmaceuticals may instead seek to license particular technologies or chemical libraries, or pursue a real options strategy with respect to biotechnology investments. Similar to financial options, a simultaneous investment by a pharmaceuticals company into a portfolio of biotech startups will allow it to defer a more serious financial commitment until one biotech partner demonstrates potential, for example, by producing a lead compound which the pharmaceutical company can enter into clinical trials.

Universities are increasingly seen as the incubators of biotechnologies, becoming the new 'silicon corners' of technological sophistication. Trading their proverbial ivory towers for new business incubators, universities appear well on their way to becoming an increasingly powerful force in today's economy. Educational institutions like Harvard, MIT, Stanford, Oxford, and Cambridge have all been associated with startup biotech firms. Kendall Square, MA, appears to have become the new silicon valley of biotechnology. Many biotech firms emerged as a result of scientists at academic institutions becoming more entrepreneurially minded (Barley et al., 1992), though they often lacked the management or production experience necessary to commercialize the emerging technology (Powell and Brantley, 1992). Oxford University, for example, has sought to swap its 'dreaming spires' for 'silicon spires' (Goldberg, 1999), generating such spin-offs as PowderJect Pharmaceuticals and Oxford Asymmetry International (now Evotec-OAI). Though universities are often beneficiaries of such ventures (e.g. the University of Alabama at Birmingham had, by the end of 1999, already earned more than US$10 million in royalties and licensing fees from faculty discoveries), the implications of this development are not limited to just academe. A recent study by the Milken Institute in Santa Monica, CA, suggests that high-tech activity may explain 65 per cent of the variance in economic growth among metropolitan regions during the 1990s (Goldberg, 1999: 21). The sprouting up of research parks surrounding universities is testimony to this development.

A brief history

The scientific basis for biotechnology stems from the efforts of James Watson and Francis Crick, two Cambridge University researchers, to deduce the structure of the DNA molecule, resulting in the famous discovery of the 'double helix' in 1953. That heredity is controlled by genes located on chromosomes and made up of DNA molecules had already been established by molecular biologists earlier that century. These DNA molecules store genetic information. DNA is transcribed and translated into proteins, enzymes and other biological molecules which determine the observable characteristics (or phenotype) of living organisms. All organisms possess RNA, ribosomes, and other cellular machinery needed to read, transcribe, and translate the DNA information that comprises the genetic code. Diversity is thus a function of different types and combinations of expressed genes, which determine an individual organism's genetic makeup and phenotype, in a process of coevolution with the external environment.

In 1973, Herbert Boyer of Stanford and Stanley Cohen of the University of California in San Francisco developed a technique now known as restricted enzyme-based DNA recombination (RDNA). This technology allowed them to cut, paste, and recombine fragments of DNA and introduce them into a bacterial cloning vector. These bacteria subsequently manufactured proteins encoded by the foreign DNA, thus allowing scientists to turn bacteria into cheap manufacturing facilities for the production of particular proteins normally associated with different species. An example of this is the development of human insulin to treat diabetes.

Two years later, in 1975, George Koehler and Cesar Milstein, of the British Medical Research Council, developed a technology to produce monoclonal antibodies, an effort which secured them the Nobel prize in 1984. Their technology allowed them to fuse antibody-producing white blood cells with tumour cells, forming immortalized hybrid cells (or hybridomas) that could survive for longer periods outside the human body (or *in vitro*) and produce highly specific antibodies against distinct infectious agent antigens. The discovery of these two technologies, RDNA and monoclonal antibodies, and the more recent development of protein engineering became the corner stones of biotechnology.

On a commercial level, in 1976 the US Patent Office granted the University of California and Stanford University the rights to Boyer and Cohen's RDNA technology. In that same year, Guy Swanson, a venture capitalist, persuaded Stanley Cohen to establish the biotech firm Genentech. At its first public offering on 14 October 1980, its stock soared from US$35 per share to US$89 per share within the first hour of trading, establishing a new record for Wall Street, and spawning a period of intense speculation in biotech equity and an avid interest of venture capitalists in acquiring a stake in startup companies. At least 155 such biotech firms were founded in less than two years, in the USA alone (Barley et al., 1992). Amgen, being one of them, boasted a market capitalization of US$66 billion at the end of 2000, and three products on the market – unusual for a biotech firm – generating annual sales of nearly US$3.2 billion (van Brunt, 2001). The industry has since proliferated, inspired by promises of miracle cures and visions of vast personal fortunes.

Biotechnology remains an intrinsically ambiguous and diverse practice, transcending traditional disciplinary boundaries by drawing from, and combining, natural science disciplines as varied as genetics and chemical engineering (Hayward, 1998). According to Powell and Brantley (1992) it has been a competence-destroying innovation – that is, requiring the mastery of a new discipline – in that the scientific basis of biotechnology (primarily immunology and molecular biology) is significantly different from the traditional organic chemistry knowledge base of the more mature pharmaceutical industry. It is also a highly transnationalized activity, and yet, ironically, it appears embedded in local and national environments whose system and culture of innovation is pivotal to developing technologies (Hayward, 1998).

Biotechnology has elicited a wide public response as interest groups have called attention to issues of accountability, ethics, and security. The controversy stirred up by the Roslin Institute and PPL Therapeutics's joint manufacturing and subsequent reproduction of Dolly the Sheep – created in 1997 by cloning a cell taken from the udder of an adult ewe and hence named after Dolly Parton – serves as a useful illustration. Dolly was the only healthy survivor among nearly 270 artificially created foetuses. Reflecting on the Dolly experiment, Appleyard muses:

With Dolly the sheep there was the promise that we could try our lives all over again. Human cloning, apparently coming ever closer, was the symbolic apotheosis of the society of consumption and the dematerialised self. We could buy a replay of our lives – press stop, rewind and then play. (1999a: 40)

In 1999, Dolly was diagnosed as having aged too rapidly, being about six years older than she ought to be, which has led to concerns about the prospects of transferring age-related characteristics when genetically manipulating cells.[7] Across the Atlantic, scientists at Advanced Cell Technology, a Massachusetts-based biotech firm, have experimented with creating a herd of cattle genetically modified to be immune to bovine spongiform encephalopathy (BSE, 'mad cow disease') and able to produce milk that closely resembles human milk. Additionally, experiments are underway to grow hearts, lungs, livers, and kidneys carrying human genes in pigs and produce bulls that father only female offspring. Will there be any long-term effects of consuming such genetically modified milk products? Will genetically modified organisms upset the balance of populations in natural ecosystems? Will patent laws result in a few large farming corporations controlling key crops? News coverage of genetically modified foods, particularly since 1999, has been extensive, not least due to public fears over any unexplored consequences of genetic manipulation. Not only have the public reacted by destroying fields of experimental GMO crops, but investors are reluctant to raise their stakes in GMO technologies. Axis Genetics, for example, was placed into administration in September 1999 after failing to attract a needed £10 million to finance operations. Although they featured a strong patent portfolio, including two key technologies for producing vaccines in fruits and plants, the investment community remains wary of being too closely associated with GMO crops (Cookson, 1999).

But the moral questions get more disturbing. Given the theoretical ability of genetic engineering to correct foetal defects, who will decide what a 'defect' is? Has society, by officially classifying such diseases as depression and ADHD (attention deficit–hyperactivity disorder) as a disability, taken conditions with biological as well as psychosocial bases and ruled that biology should dominate? Are we thus medicating for conditions that may be, at least partly, under the control of individuals (Fukuyama, 2002)? Are we at risk of falling prey to the ambitions of early eugenicists, which in Nazi Germany escalated from forced sterilizations to mass genocide, under the ethical aphorism that we ought not merely to love our neighbour but should extend this to future generations (Gray, 1999)? On the other hand, would it be unfair to deny infertile couples, or those suffering from a hereditary disease, access to their own genetic offspring? Would it be appropriate to clone from the body of a car crash victim in order to create, say, a genetically identical child? Should private companies be allowed to hold patents on particular genes so as to

---

[7] Dolly was born with shortened telomeres, affecting her potential life span.

commercialize particular genetic treatments? Is it ethical to develop genetic tests for conditions for which there is no known cure? Should a person whose genetic profile shows potential problems pay higher health insurance rates than someone whose profile does not?[8] Francis Fukuyama, in his provocative *Our Posthuman Future: Consequences of the Biotechnology Revolution* (2002), warns of the subtle dangers of interfering with human nature. Where we may have been unhappy with our natural endowments in the past, we usually sought to better ourselves through education and work. This moral imperative, however, may be deflated by the seductive potential to improve ourselves and our descendants by an artificial shortcut. It corroborates our nature-defeating search for perfectibility. Biotechnology, Fukuyama reasons, thus risks blurring the line between treating serious illnesses and catering to vanity and self-improvement through medical intervention. And his arguments force us to rethink the very idea of 'being human' – what does it really mean? As eloquently put by an anonymous contributor to *The Economist*:

The very idea of engineering our genes tugs us violently in opposite directions. It promises release from inherited afflictions and raises the spectre of manmade monsters. It represents a triumph of human curiosity and technical daring, but tempts us also towards arrogance and folly...Before long, it is feared, direct modification of genes could start to loosen our grip on what it is to be human. Need a person have two biological parents? Should a crossbred ape-man have civil rights? We have no ready answers. Faced by such puzzles, it can seem that we are creating a science that will one day exhaust our capacity to tell right from wrong. (*The Economist*, 16–22 March 2002: 83)

Alan Colman, Research Director at PPL Therapeutics and intimately involved in cloning Dolly the Sheep, now warns of the ethical problems and risks associated with cloning human beings. He surmises that it might prejudice the upbringing of the cloned children and deprive them of genetic privacy, that the activity will be unsafe and inefficient, and that the benefits it produces so marginal, and the risks so high, that human cloning cannot be condoned. Oxford University professor Richard Dawkins, on the other hand, has gone on record stating that human cloning should be pursued if only out of sheer curiosity.[9] The controversial physicist Richard Seed, who wishes to be the first to clone a human being, believes that cloning will become 'the first serious step in becoming one

---

[8] Interestingly, this question was posed by *TIME* in a recent poll. Whereas 55 per cent of respondents thought it reasonable that smokers should pay higher insurance rates than non-smokers, only 8 per cent found it equally reasonable to charge more to persons with certain genetic profiles (*TIME*, 11 January 1999: 59).

[9] Dr Alan Colman and Professor Richard Dawkins featured in an Oxford Union Society debate on the proposition 'This House believes that the cloning of human beings is unethical', on 4 June 1998.

with God' (Unsworth, 1998). Similar efforts are planned by Severino Antinori, Panos Zavos, and an obscure sect called the Raelians.[10] The sheer possibilities of genetic engineering and biotechnology in general have evoked emotional responses on both sides of the argument – one that is increasingly dominated by questions of ethics rather than of technological capability. At the same time, the short-term pressure on biotech startups to raise sufficient capital to fund their operations (burning rates can easily add up to US$30,000 per month for a start-up like Vertex, or US$75 million per year for a larger firm like British Biotech) too often dominates issues of morality and social good (Werth, 1994).

Despite predictions of it becoming the basis for a new techno-economic paradigm, biotechnology is not yet, according to some, as sophisticated as microelectronics and information technology (cf. Hayward, 1998). To date, the discipline has generated relatively few commercially viable products. It is plagued by a lack of cash inflows to continue to support processes that are lengthy, unpredictable, and fraught with scale-up production and downstream processing problems and difficult clinical trials. Such industry traits require firms to be flexible and financially well endowed so as to take advantage of its promises, for 'fortune favours the prepared mind', as the French microbiologist Louis Pasteur observed in the 1850s. Preparation, alas, is expensive and, as a result, collaborations are commonplace. Partly in an effort to forestall a merger, acquisition, or bankruptcy, biotech firms have entered into partnerships with pharmaceuticals to build strategic bridges and secure funding whilst giving the latter a window on novel technologies and flexible research processes. 'Science proceeds mostly from an abundance of materials, not understanding,' interjects Werth (1994: 153). And, compellingly, elsewhere:

Scientists, curiously, talk a lot about luck. As murderously as they work, as dedicated as they are to rigour, as much as they may believe in their own perfection, they concede that great scientific careers are almost always favoured by something else: great timing of an unseen hand connecting the observer and the observed. Pasteur's oft-used remark about fortune encapsulates the view, almost universally shared among scientists, especially in the drug industry, that they'd rather be lucky than good. (1994: 210)

Serendipity illustrated: Viagra[TM]

The drug discovery process can be fraught with serendipity. Pfizer's creation of Viagra, an unexpected but lucrative discovery, helps illustrate this

---

[10] Details on the Raelians and their cloning efforts can be found on their website: www.clonaid.com

property.[11] A first research programme into hypertension, commenced by an in-house team in 1985, was redirected to combat erectile dysfunction. Within a few years of starting the programme it became clear that the lead compounds for hypertension were causing biological activity through an enzyme that is found in the vascular smooth muscle and blood platelets. As a result, the programme's focus changed towards developing a drug to combat angina by relaxing the blood vessels, thus stimulating the blood supply to the heart muscle. Pfizer scientists were interested in finding a compound that would inhibit the enzyme phosphodiesterase, responsible for breaking down cyclic guanosine monophosphate (cyclic GMP), an enzyme whose release results in vasodilation. If the levels of cyclic GMP could be artificially raised, by inhibiting the enzyme, the blood supply to the heart would increase as coronary blood vessels are dilated and platelets prevented from sticking together.

In 1989, Pfizer scientists identified a compound, sildenafil citrate, which they entered into trials in 1991. Clinical trials are required for drug approval and are intended to test for toxicity (Phase I) and efficacy (Phases II and III). Pfizer's first clinical trial tested for toxicity, using healthy male volunteers, and moved from a single dosage to administering multiple treatments over a seven-day period. With this early phase still ongoing, it was granted permission to proceed with Phase II using angina patients, having demonstrated the drug was sufficiently safe. The drug was subsequently administered to patients suffering from severe heart disease but only proved moderately efficacious. Trial results were disappointing.

However, clinicians running the ongoing Phase I seven-day safety studies had learned of some interesting side effects to the drug. Trial volunteers on high dosages of the drug had reported frequent and sustained erections. Yet, despite encouraging developments in the scientific literature disclosing the involvement of cyclic GMP in generating and maintaining erections, too little was known about the mechanism behind this phenomenon. Pfizer decided to commit 1,500 individual scientists and US$340 million to the project and, in due course, repeat Phase II clinical trials using impotent men. This time the efficacy was beyond doubt. Viagra was approved by the Food and Drug Administration (FDA)

---

[11] One of the best known historical illustrations of serendipity in drug discovery is probably Alexander Fleming's discovery of penicillin in 1928. He was actively involved in a project to identify the microbe that caused the 1918 'flu epidemic (killing around 22 million people worldwide – nearly twice the number killed during the First World War), when a green mould drifted through the window of his London-based hospital laboratory and landed into a petri dish whilst he was on holiday. Upon his return, Fleming noticed that the green mould had destroyed one of his cultures. This mould became the basis for the development of penicillin (Werth, 1994).

on 27 March 1998. European approval followed in September of that year.

Viagra had generated revenues of US$300 million by 8 May 1998 and is expected to provide constant revenues of well over US$1 billion per year. By June 1998, only months after FDA approval, it had already been prescribed to 1 million American men and generated a vast black market in Brazil. It is expected to provide a return to normal sexual activity for 100 million impotent men worldwide.

The development of Viagra helps us appreciate the serendipitous nature of the drug discovery process. Most biotech firms need financial resources to sustain long periods of research whilst having no marketable products to provide a cashflow stream. Pharmaceutical firms, on the other hand, want to benefit from new technologies and flexible research processes. According to Klaus Ebert, Head of Scientific Support at Boehringer Ingelheim GmbH:

The partnering process will continue, since many of the technologies emerging in the next decade will come from small companies. Our main aim is to get access to competitive technologies, further strengthen our technological basis (e.g. genomics, therapeutic proteins, combinatorial chemistry or antisense) and to use certain core technologies which can be targeted at many indication areas. (Ernst & Young Annual Biotechnology Report, 1996: 37)

This view is endorsed by George Poste, formerly Head of R&D at SmithKline Beecham:

The pace and scope of technological change is so dramatic and costs are escalating so rapidly that no-one can be self-sufficient. (Coopers & Lybrand Annual Report, 1997: 3)

and by Jurgen Drews, President of Global Research at Roche Holdings:

The tools of innovation are rarely in the hands of one company, therefore to access them you must collaborate to assemble the critical elements. (Coopers & Lybrand Annual Report, 1997: 3)

Three empirical studies

This chapter sought to provide an introduction to the field of biotechnology research. Of particular relevance are the proliferation of collaborative activity between pharmaceutical and biotech companies, where self-interest seems best served through cooperating, the importance of access to, and protection of, unique resources to sustain a competitive advantage, the rapid technological changes within the biotechnology field, and the inherent serendipity[12] of drug discovery. As a rule of thumb, only one out of every 5,000 drug candidates discovered in laboratories will eventually be commercialized (Arnst, 2001). Indeed, particularly because of these latter two characteristics, the evolutionary path and outcomes of biotechnology research alliances (specifically collaborations between new biotech firms and pharmaceutical companies) appear unpredictable, allowing them to take off into directions that were not anticipated at the formation of the relationship.

The next three chapters contain detailed accounts of three such alliances. The cases have been anonymized upon the request of informants, and any resemblance to existing corporations is unintentional. Each narrative retells the lived experience of an alliance between a biotechnology company and a much larger pharmaceutical, and draws on the detailed accounts of those that participated in them. They are all different, and none of the collaborations unfolded quite as anticipated at their formation.

To ease their reading and afford some sense of organization, each case has been sliced three ways. First, there is a general narrative outlining the evolution of the alliance from its inception to either its dissolution (in one case) or the end of the observation period (in the two remaining instances). Following this narrative is a more detailed discussion of four specific features – its social makeup, strategic rationale, activities, and operating rules – as well as its contributions and specific context.

The distinction between these features is necessarily artificial but seems intuitively helpful, for the first four comprise the answers to very elementary questions: *who* is involved (social makeup); *why* does the alliance exist (strategic rationale); *what* is being done (activities); and *how* is this being done (operating rules)? It seems reasonable to expect these to become relatively institutionalized over time: although the operating rules of an alliance might well change over the duration of the relationship, this is unlikely to happen very frequently or else there would be no stable platform on which to develop the collaboration. Any game requires rules for the game to take place. One might make arbitrary concessions but these must remain relatively rare, for if every rule were to be revocable then

---

[12] Although serendipity is referred to mostly as a positive, albeit unpredictable, development, this need not be the case. Medical history contains several examples of negative serendipitous developments. One of these has become the subject of much recent debate and a controversial book by Edward Hooper. In his *The River: A Journey Back to the Source of HIV and AIDS*, Hooper suggests that AIDS was introduced accidentally during vaccine trials in Africa during the 1950s and 1960s. The vaccine in question, 'CHAT' (designed to fight polio), is thought to have been grown on tissue taken from chimpanzee kidneys, hence allowing for the HIV virus to be transferred to humans (The Economist Review of Books, *The Economist*, 13–19 November 1999: 3).

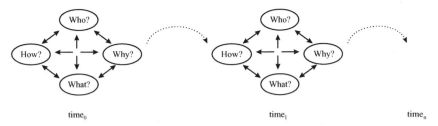

Figure 2.1: Alliances as evolving structures

one would not have a game at all. And we can probably assume a similar degree of stability for its strategic rationale(s), activities, and social makeup. Intuitively, at any rate, there appears to be a sense of relative stability about them. Two further assumptions underlie this framing exercise. First, every alliance can essentially be described as a given configuration of these four features, at any point in time (see Figure 2.1). In other words, it can usefully serve as a generic device to narrate its evolution. This approach is entirely descriptive, not normative, and relatively theory-neutral. Second, each of the four is likely to be ubiquitous as well as somewhat ambiguous. Strategies may well be found to exist at different levels – that of the alliance, the organization, the laboratory, and the individual – and may or may not be fully congruent. Some are explicit, others implicit. There is no expectation of there being a single, universally held strategy to inform the collaboration. And the same may be true for its other features. Social makeup refers, at a macro-level, to the organizations involved; at a micro-level to specific individuals. Operating rules may be formalized and explicit but can also be tacit and unquestioned, existing primarily as memory traces, perhaps as embedded in particular research cultures. Examples of these may include a Popperian approach to drug discovery, gentlemen's agreements, the natural reciprocation of favours done, real options approaches to biotechnology investments, implicit cost–benefit calculations, and the legitimacy-granting ability of established pharmaceuticals. Yet, despite being less often articulated, these provide the raw materials for sense-making and the legitimization of human behaviour. Research activities, in turn, may include formal activities, as specified in the agreement, but others as well, particularly for a science that is too new to have been formally specified.

Social makeup

Human actors engaged in an alliance serve as resources, the more senior of whom enjoy the ability to coordinate the activities of others whilst possessing a degree of control over various tangible resources. These actors can also serve as an important source of information on firms as well as individuals as collaborators, on their capabilities and reliability (Gulati, 1993). They constitute its social makeup. Turpin (1993) and Inkpen and Beamish (1997) linked the absence of a stable social makeup to the phenomenon of 'corporate amnesia', whereby past lessons, partner-derived knowledge, and mutual intentions are forgotten as the social composition of the alliance changes over time. The social capital contributed by actors involved in alliances provides opportunities to appropriate various other resources, whilst shaping and constraining the set of actions available to them (Burt, 1992). Interpersonal relationships can be particularly meaningful given the moral perils that arise out of the unpredictability of partner behaviour and the potential for free-riding and opportunism (cf. Galaskiewicz and Wasserman, 1989; Gulati, 1998; Hamel, Doz, and Prahalad, 1989; Harrigan, 1986; Killing, 1982; Kogut, 1988b). Their social makeup can change, for instance, as a result of the involvement of a new individual, the departure of a problematic one, the acquisition of one partner organization by a competitor or the violation of a tacitly held agreement.

Comments contributed by informants in the pilot phase[13] of this research project attest to the role of interpersonal relationships in biotechnology collaborations, albeit anecdotally. 'Once the infrastructure for a particular alliance is in place,' suggested one, 'the people make it happen. In fact, people will often override technological failure.' Yet when this social makeup is altered, whether purposefully or serendipitously, the results can be damaging in terms of efficacy and efficiency. As recalled by another:

When Glaxo took over Wellcome, we could no longer make sense of them. People had moved around and had no clue as to what was going on. It can easily take a year before that is sorted out.

And a third:

If the key players or champions of a partner firm leave, that can affect the likelihood of a repeat alliance. A change of ownership can be a real killer.

Moreover, provided that those engaged in the collaboration can demonstrate due diligence, relationships might survive even when projects fail or targets remain unmet. As contributed by the CEO of a very successful biotech firm in the UK:

---

[13] Please refer to the appendix for a detailed discussion on my data sources and methods.

What is important in such cases is to help save the face of your champion at your partner firm. He stands to lose most and you need to protect him, especially if you want to continue the relationship or ensure future collaboration.

Strategic rationale

The strategic rationale for an alliance serves principally to legitimize the activities of those involved in it. As Gulati reminds us: 'firms don't form alliances as symbolic social affirmations of their social networks but, rather, base alliances on concrete strategic complementarities' (1998: 301). The theories discussed in the previous chapter tendered various explanations for strategies of cooperation. Whereas most alliance partners will be able to provide concrete explanations for them, they themselves, and the individuals engaged, may well pursue their own agendas alongside those of the alliance. This opens up the possibility of occasional misunderstanding, operating inefficiencies, and conflict.

Activities

The content of an alliance, being legitimized by stated strategic rationales, finds expression in the everyday pursuits or projects of those involved in it, and guidance in contractually determined scientific targets or milestones. The latter appear more fluid than one might have thought, in that they can often be renegotiable, subject to regular reviews by a coordinating body (or steering group), and likely to change with emergent discoveries, access to new technologies, and ongoing progress assessments. Many biotechnology-based alliances will tend to function on the basis of negotiated milestones, only some of which generate financial payments. Others may be funded on a full-time-equivalent (FTE) basis, any cash receipts to the biotech partner of, say, a large pharmaceutical being contingent on the number of scientists assigned to the joint project.

Operating rules

Finally, the governance structure and operating rules of alliances include systems of authority and communication, formal or otherwise, workflow, and the use of agreed-upon technologies and processes. In other words, *how* is the *what* accomplished? What control mechanisms appear most relevant given the purpose, pursuits, and social makeup of the alliance? Various taxonomies exist within the literature on what are essentially different governance structures (e.g. Faulkner, 1995; Garrette and Dussauge, 1990; Kanter, 1989). But beyond governance structure, what *informal rules* may guide the interaction between collaborating individuals?

Given the rapid developments in science and in technology, and the relatively uncertain nature of drug discovery, formal contracts are thought to inevitably chase informal agreements. Consequently, they will need to allow for some degree of flexibility and, in practice, are frequently updated as one approaches the contractually-stipulated ending date of the agreement to guide the future exploitation of joint technologies and allocate downstream royalty payments.

Alliance performance and contributions

The gains from collaborating can be tangible (e.g. milestones achieved) or perceptual (e.g. an amicable working relationship) and measured with respect to two criteria: the *accomplishments and perceived success* of the actual collaborative relationship and, perhaps more crucially, the *contribution* of the alliance to individual partner firms. The activity of measuring performance in biotechnology-based research alliances can be difficult, particularly if research objectives are broadly defined (e.g. 'to discover a drug candidate against infectious diseases'). Lead discovery and technology development, each of which is an intrinsic part of the drug discovery process, are inevitably serendipitous. As Werth recalls in chronicling the history of the pharmaceutical startup Vertex:

Far from the orderly, data-based process of iteration and reiteration, the selection of Vertex's first clinical candidate illustrated another Vertex dictum: *The ultimate reward for research may turn up elsewhere than intended.* The key is to draw the right lessons, be astute, act decisively, do the proper experiments. (1994: 416; italics added)

A substantial part of the development costs of a lead compound is often spent on eliminating routes of inquiry. Hence, in research-based alliances even failure to identify a lead compound or apply a specific technology may constitute useful knowledge. It is progress but in a Popperian sense.

This might help explain why some alliances survive despite failing to attain the objective(s) that prompted their formation in the first place. Success, in a strict sense, may remain painfully absent but progress present. And as long as both partners can, and are willing to, continue to justify their ongoing investments inside their own organizations – perhaps by reasoning that if they are to collaborate with anyone on this research project their partners are the best people to work with, or because proof of principle was established, or even because dissolving the alliance would cause significant embarrassment – and providing they can afford to continue, they may do so. The third case serves as a particularly interesting illustration in this respect.

Coevolutionary developments

Likewise, the collaborative process can be either fuelled or thwarted by parallel developments within individual partner firms. Mergers and takeovers make for telling examples, as they may render ongoing alliances less important strategically in the newly created context. As one senior research scientist explained:

Takeovers by large pharmaceuticals can disturb the alliance. Xenova has experienced this twice, when two of the biotechs they were collaborating with were taken over by larger firms. Genzyme took over Pharmagenics to form GMO, specialising in oncology. And Roche took over Genentech. Given that Roche have their own natural products involvement, the link with Xenova became less important. As a result, Xenova's partnership was perceived to be less of a priority than it had been.

The publicized controversy surrounding the proposed Telecom Italia alliance with AT&T provides a relevant example also, albeit in the context of quite a different industry. The announcement by the Italia chairman Gian Mario Rossignolo on 9 April 1998 that they were dropping the collaboration in favour of a deal with Cable and Wireless surprised AT&T executives and industry analysts alike. Apparently, a turf war between the flamboyant Rossignolo and government-appointed Tommasi di Vignano resulted in the forced resignation of the latter, the departure of many senior managers, and the undoing by Rossignolo of much of Tommasi di Vignano's work, including the much-anticipated AT&T alliance.

Industry and competitive dynamics

Last but not least, the life of collaborations appears contingent on a co-evolving external environment and, some argue, cannot be understood independently of it (cf. Koza and Lewin, 1998; McKelvey, 1997). For instance, long lead times associated with running screens against natural products libraries as compared to synthetic libraries have rendered the former increasingly unattractive to pharmaceuticals. Similarly, an otherwise successful cooperative relationship may be rendered irrelevant by a change in the competitive environment, for example when a competitor announces a breakthrough in the same area. Or a research project can be negatively impacted by the failure of a similar project carried by a competitor or reported side effects of comparable medicines and decisions by regulatory authorities.

Each case study concludes with a brief thematic discussion. Many of the issues highlighted here have previously featured in the alliance literature and may be familiar. This thematic discussion is repeated in Chapter 6 but across the case narratives.

And it is to these three stories that we must now turn.

3 Through the looking glass 1: Rummidgen and Plethora
1994–8

Are we where we wanted to be four years ago? No, we're not. Are we pleased? Yes, we are.

(Green, Plethora, March 1998)

When, in April 1994, Plethora's Gregor Green and Professor Edward Carr from Woodstock University, UK, met at an official luncheon, hosted by Woodstock Innovation (a wholly owned company of Woodstock University created to fuse university-based research and business), Professor Carr suggested his company (Rummidgen) could provide Plethora with the combinatorial chemistry capabilities it had been looking for. Ensuing from that encounter, Carr hurriedly faxed a series of papers on combinatorial chemistry to Derek Lodge who, at the time, knew little about this pioneering technology. Having only recently been appointed as Managing Director of Rummidgen, Lodge briefed through the articles as best as he could, in preparation for a formal meeting with Plethora the following morning. That very next day the alliance was agreed in principle. Rummidgen was to become one of several collaborations pursued simultaneously by Plethora as part of a portfolio strategy code-named 'PlethoraGen', given that most were intended to capture advances in human genomics, and cell and molecular biology.

Signing of the formal agreement was delayed as Plethora awaited approval by its various internal committees, and due to the pharmaceutical's intentions to announce several alliances simultaneously. Whilst anticipating the formalization of the collaboration, Rummidgen recruited Jon Coe to head up a new laboratory, Oxygen, created as a joint endeavour between Plethora and Rummidgen to facilitate the development of specific solid phase combinatorial chemistry capabilities. Plethora promised to contribute US$5.5 million to that development although the new subsidiary would remain wholly owned by Rummidgen. In addition, the biotech company received another US$3.5 million from 3i, the venture capital firm, upon securing the collaboration.

Jon Coe was interviewed by Green (Plethora), Richard Lewis (Plethora), and Nigel Hornby (Plethora) in October 1994, reflecting the active participation of both firms in setting up the subsidiary company. He was formally offered the job in November and due to start on the 1 January 1995. By then, however, the alliance agreement had still not been signed and was to be delayed by another four weeks. During this waiting period, Rummidgen, and the newly recruited Coe, began to construct a special laboratory at its subsidiary company, certain that Plethora would ultimately deliver on its promises. When, ultimately, a formal, two-year contract was signed in February 1995, Coe spent the ensuing four months building up this research facility by recruiting fifteen scientists and making capital investments in sophisticated chemistry equipment. Plethora transferred some of its basic combinatorial chemistry technology to Oxygen. In June 1995, Coe delivered its first library of compounds to Plethora, well ahead of its expectations, allowing Plethora chemists the opportunity to champion the collaboration within their own organization.

The initial strategic justification for the collaboration was that of *lead optimization*. The alliance had been set up as a 'fee-for-service' agreement (i.e. a contract research alliance) in which hits provided by Plethora were optimized by Oxygen in making libraries, including benzoxazepinones and prostaglandin, whilst developing new chemistry technologies. In terms of governance, it was coordinated by a steering committee and two 'gatekeepers' to manage its operations on a day-to-day basis. From the start, Rummidgen devoted much time and effort to the joint programme, so much so that, one day, Plethora telephoned Coe suggesting that his laboratory 'shouldn't work its scientists so hard'. The pharmaceutical seemed to have difficulty keeping up with the output of its biotech partner. Besides, rumours of scientists voluntarily working throughout the night and even on weekends, at Rummidgen, compared rather poorly to Plethora's commitment and levels of productivity, and resulted in some tension early on in the alliance.

The abrupt and unexpected departure of Plethora's Richard Lewis, in mid-1995, resulted in the involvement of Mark Amis, a senior chemist at Plethora, who rapidly made himself unpopular with those at Rummidgen. Not only was his perceived arrogance not appreciated, but his reluctance to champion the alliance within Plethora is likely to make any future collaboration difficult to justify. The department for which he was responsible within Plethora competed directly with the collaboration in terms of its focus on chemistry technologies. Indeed, his view was that the joint project should have been carried out in-house in the first place, and he was unwilling to defend the alliance within Plethora.

In June 1996, just over a year into the relationship, Plethora significantly redirected the collaboration from *lead optimization* to *lead discovery*. It now demanded the generation of compounds that could be screened in-house by Plethora against particular targets. Refocusing the collaboration towards pure discovery took three months. Simultaneously, Plethora suggested that its biotech partner proceed with this discovery process using a mixtures approach rather than one focused on developing and screening single compounds. For Oxygen, this implied adopting a research philosophy that stood in stark contrast to its traditionally academic approach to, but also their commercial interest in, new chemistry technologies. Indeed, its scientists were convinced that the industry had wisely moved away from mixtures, considering them cheap, nasty, and ineffective. It took until December 1996 for Rummidgen to persuade its pharmaceutical partner to abandon mixtures in favour of single compounds.

By 1997, the working relationship had become more akin to a collaborative effort (i.e. a collaborative research alliance). Plethora had been flexible in allowing certain targets to be renegotiated, particularly in the early months. Given that drug discovery processes are inherently serendipitous, the pharmaceutical had been understanding and patient when targets were not met, even tolerant in allowing Rummidgen to pursue spin-off projects that, to it, seemed promising. After intense negotiations the collaboration was extended for one year in May 1997. As Lodge commented on this development in a news release:

It is an important endorsement of our capabilities that Plethora has extended this major collaboration. We have now established the leading, international, service-based company in combinatorial chemistry with an impressive client list headed by Plethora. (Rummidgen, April 1997)

Rummidgen, having rapidly evolved from a relatively insignificant biotech startup into a profitable and reputable firm, now demanded a 20 per cent increase in funding above the sum agreed with Plethora two years earlier. Plethora conceded, but reluctantly. This negotiating tactic by Rummidgen, however, despite bringing in extra revenues, may well have signalled a first turning point in the relationship. As its CEO, with the benefit of hindsight, acknowledged:

This was the child turning around and slapping the parent . . . They fed back to us saying that they had never renegotiated terms ever. It did change the nature of our perceptions of each other and probably ensured that we didn't continue beyond the third year. (Lodge, Rummidgen, March 1999)

To the surprise of the biotech partner, shortly after the extension had been signed, one of its key scientists, Karl Amis, resigned to take up

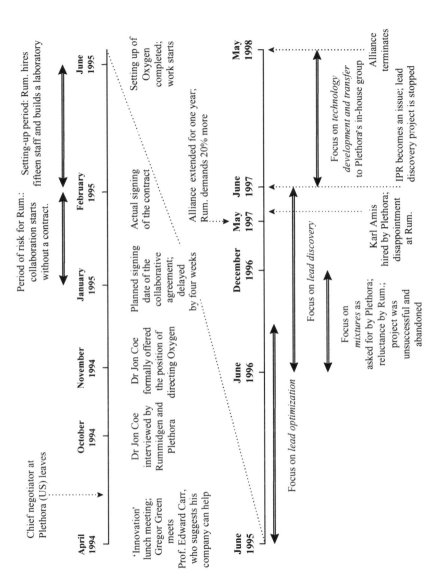

Figure 3.1: Chronology of the Rummidgen–Plethora alliance: 1994–8

a financially lucrative post with Plethora. The pharmaceutical was un-apologetic even though individuals at Rummidgen and Oxygen felt an unwritten rule – a 'gentlemen's agreement' – had been breached and the spirit of the contract violated. This action evoked particularly unpleasant emotions at both partner firms, expressed in the felt embarrassment of one senior Plethora scientist, Gregor Green, and the ensuing distrust by key individuals at Oxygen and its parent company.

They were shocked because they don't see us as equals. If you have a slave you don't ask him whether he feels good today. You just tell him to go and do some-thing. I told them we felt offended, that they had lied . . . and they were shocked . . . I would fire each one of them. If any asked me for a job I would say: 'never in a million years'. (Lodge, Rummidgen, April 1998)

Plethora subsequently refrained from hiring any more scientists from its biotech partner, although Lodge claims that its headhunters continued to approach key individuals, including his righthand man, Coe. Shortly after this apparent breach of trust, in June 1997, Rummidgen published a CD-ROM containing a catalogue of structures of prostaglandin molecules. This marketing effort was legitimized by its explicit strategy to position itself as a world-class biotech partner and, although the formal alliance agreement prohibited the biotech company from marketing and selling compounds produced on behalf of Plethora, it did allow for the man-ufacture of similar structures. Despite Rummidgen's efforts to try and secure Plethora's approval prior to making the library available to third parties, senior scientists at the pharmaceutical's California-based head-quarters acted surprised and dismayed by their publication.

As an immediate, but unintended, consequence of this publication, a conflict on intellectual property rights ensued, driven by scientists at the parent company. Whilst Plethora's Cambridgeshire (UK) office appeared comparatively sanguine, it became obvious that Plethora (US) was to be-come more directly involved with the alliance. More precisely, the conse-quences of Rummidgen's actions were twofold. First, the lead discovery project was ended at once, even though it had been very successful in identifying interesting compounds, as Plethora had become worried that it was providing too much sensitive disease target-related information to its biotech partner. Second, Plethora's UK-based subsidiary increased its efforts to develop an in-house group designed primarily to render the Oxygen alliance obsolete. Instead, the strategic focus of the collaboration was now squarely on the development and transfer of chemistry tech-nologies. The working relationship returned to being a 'fee-for-service' type arrangement, marked by little or no further joint initiatives, no information on disease targets, and Plethora appropriating technologies developed by Rummidgen.

During this third year of collaboration, Oxygen scientists worked along-side Plethora's in-house group to develop a general body of knowledge in combinatorial chemistry. Although technology development and transfer had always been a part of the formal contract, such a singular focus had not been envisioned in the original negotiations. Moreover, Oxygen scientists were sceptical about the capabilities of Plethora's in-house group and its reasoning concerning the efficiency with which Plethora could replicate the efforts of its biotech partner.

I think it is a crazy decision on their part. In the strategic sense it is the worst possible thing they could do. They haven't got the right culture. A production department should be focused on making many compounds very quickly and yet they have stuffed it with technology developers. Also, they would merely be an internal service provider. What is the penalty for not providing that internal service? Nothing! (Lodge, Rummidgen, April 1998)

The alliance was dissolved in June 1998. At the time, neither partner intended to pursue an extension to the existing agreement although, as both partners agreed, there clearly are tangible measures of success in lead optimization, lead discovery, and technology development, and the potential of the collaboration appeared not to have been exhausted. As Rummidgen's Chief Operating Officer commented:

Often the technical performance of a collaboration can end up being ignored due to the politics of it. (Keilor, Rummidgen, April 1999)

Who, why, what, how?

The ensuing discussion elaborates on the narrative, making extensive use of statements, quoted verbatim, by those closely involved with the collaboration. It adds detail to this description, but without making this chapter necessarily and intolerably repetitive. Given that the strategic justification for an alliance and its subsequent activities are so strongly interrelated in practice, it is somewhat difficult to provide a discrete discussion of each without this becoming repetitive as well as tedious. And for our purposes this may not really be necessary. Thus both are discussed under the heading 'strategic rationale'. This approach is identical for all three cases.

Strategic rationale

Combinatorial chemistry is a suite of technologies that allows for the rapid production of compounds that can subsequently be put through screens. Solid phase chemistry is one such technology in which compounds are created on microscopic resin beads – a science in which Plethora had little expertise prior to the alliance. Collaborating with Rummidgen allowed its scientists to learn about the technologies involved and, at a later stage, to apply this learning in-house. As Plethora's Director of Research, Phil Yancey, explained to a Woodstock Innovation Society audience:

What particularly attracted us to Rummidgen was that, unlike the American combinatorial chemistry companies, they aren't simply in the business of selling us combinatorial libraries and keeping the technology totally to themselves. We can internalize the technology being developed by Rummidgen and use it in-house as needed.

The explicit motives for the collaboration changed substantially twice during its three-year existence. As Hornby (Plethora) admitted: 'we haven't been consistent; we have been modifying our objectives over the three-year period' (April 1998). From June 1995 to June 1996, Oxygen scientists were involved in *lead optimization*, taking hits from Plethora and optimizing them by generating chemical libraries and developing combinatorial chemistry technologies. "That was particularly exciting,' recalled Coe:

We were working not only with interesting chemistry, but the biology was interesting too. And, I think, that was an ideal way of getting started in the collaboration. (Oxygen, April 1998)

A first change of strategy

To the biotech firm's surprise, in June 1996, Plethora decided to change the focus of the alliance from *lead optimization* to *lead discovery*, where the emphasis became one of producing large quantities of compounds for screening by the pharmaceutical.

I have pulled Nigel Hornby's [Plethora] leg when he said there was a strategic evolution in Plethora's requirements and I would respond by telling him 'I would call it a lurch'. From a small company's point of view, Plethora makes a decision and then suddenly the whole weight of the company comes upon you to enforce that decision. (Coe, Oxygen, April 1998)

The sheer abruptness of this change in emphasis seems characteristic of the asymmetrical power relationship between the two partner firms, particularly in the early days. This is, in fact, quite common in alliances between large pharmaceuticals and much smaller biotech startups. Plethora's vast financial resources helped foster a dependency relationship, as appears evident by its reluctance to discuss Plethora's strategic priorities, instead catching its biotech partner 'unawares'. Likewise,

Rummidgen's subsequent acquiescence to Plethora's demands, despite strong feelings of discomfort, seems indicative of an asymmetrical power relationship.

Looking at the move from optimization to discovery we weren't happy. The trouble with these changes is that Plethora goes through a lot of thinking about these things. As a partner, what you get is overnight. You don't get any part of the discussions that have gone on. You get the solution. That was unsubtle and uncomfortable. (Lodge, Rummidgen, April 1998)

Aside from the pharmaceutical's financing of the collaboration, rendering it the dominant partner, its organizational culture was increasingly viewed by Rummidgen's scientists as arrogant and insensitive, despite Plethora's explicit and much publicized objective to become '*the* preferred partner for collaborations' (as publicly stated by Yancey in 1996). The implementation of Plethora's first change of strategy was gradual, moving from a state in which discovery was only marginally important towards a situation in which around 90 per cent of time and resources were dominated by a lead discovery research programme three months later. Coe, responsible for the day-to-day operations of the alliance, appeared fairly sanguine about the development:

I smiled. As long as the collaboration was developing it was a good thing, from my point of view. It meant that we not only got skills in lead optimization but also in lead discovery. I knew the business well enough to know that we needed to have lead discovery under our belt – we had to prove it and do it because that was where our future outside of Plethora lay. So secretly I was quite glad. (Oxygen, April 1998)

This shift in strategy, however, also resulted in Plethora's proposal of a correspondent shift from a focus on single compounds to working with mixtures. In other words, a new rationale was to go hand in hand with a change in 'doing research', based on a philosophy the biotech company found difficult to appreciate.

Making mixtures was contrary to our business philosophy. Mixtures were cheap, nasty, and didn't work. The whole industry was moving away from mixtures and Plethora wanted to get back into this area. We had evolved past this stage and to be told to go back into it is like being told to go back to kindergarten. So we politely resisted for quite a while until it seemed inevitable that we had to do it. We did it, and in good grace to be fair. It was one of those things that if we had not done it we would not have been able to argue passionately that mixtures are not the way forward. And I think Plethora accept that now. When I joke with Nigel Hornby [Plethora] about this, he will respond, 'Yes, guilty, put the cuffs on me. We were wrong and you were right.' (Coe, Oxygen, April 1998)

Lodge suggested likewise:

We were forced to be more production oriented which was not only more mundane, but wasn't bringing us the value we had expected. (Rummidgen, April 1998)

Lodge and Coe argued with Plethora scientists that using mixtures that are inherently difficult to characterize would be a poor choice of technologies. Under the existing agreement, Rummidgen was not entitled to any royalties on compounds identified as having produced biological activity but, instead, obtained rights to use the technologies developed. This helps explain their voiced reluctance to proceed with mixtures as it would not generate the technology value expected by the biotech. Ultimately, the partners settled for a compromise in which Oxygen dedicated a team of three scientists, led by Karl Amis, to the project. Plethora allowed for experimentation with the technology to make the process more stimulating and intellectually demanding whilst being less production oriented. Karl Amis and his team put together 10,600 compounds in mixtures of twenty compounds for screening by Plethora. Although the project was considered to have been carried out superbly, the research team never

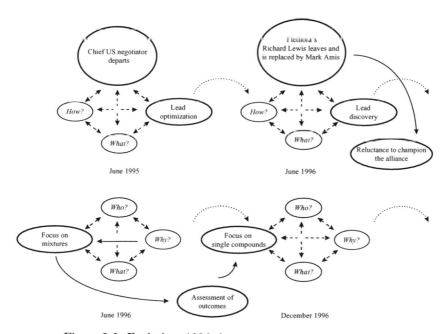

Figure 3.2: Evolution: 1994–6

received detailed feedback from the pharmaceutical partner, except being asked for a de-convolution of certain mixtures that required the manufacture of 160 single compounds. Within six months, the collaboration was redirected towards a single compound research programme. Three months later, Karl Amis left Oxygen to take up a lucrative post with Plethora – a controversial step that was to have a fairly significant impact on the working relationship.

A second change of strategy

As a consequence of a subsequent dispute on intellectual property rights, relating to the marketing of a CD-based prostaglandin library, Plethora decided once again to shift the nature of the collaboration, this time from *lead discovery* to *technology development and transfer*. This second change in the strategic justification for the collaboration, in June 1997, appears to have been triggered by an unintended, but nevertheless significant, consequence of Rummidgen's decision to market this virtual library under the impression that Plethora would not object. But it did. In contrast to Plethora's first change of mind, this one took immediate effect and was driven primarily by a group of influential scientists at Plethora's parent company in Malibu, California (USA). Though Oxygen did send a prototype copy to Plethora's headquarters in California, inquiring if they would oppose this virtual library of structures being distributed, it claims to have received no written response. It appears that California scientists may have failed to examine the catalogue carefully, although Rummidgen argues that permission was granted verbally by William Bryson, one of Plethora's more senior Malibu-based scientists. However, upon discovery of the virtual library having been made public, a group of Plethora scientists working on a prostaglandin project at the parent company protested and took action.

They were furious. How dare we sell compounds similar to the ones we have made? We told them we were allowed to do it under the spirit of the contract and we had sent them the structures in advance, and they had said 'Yes, you can sell them, we don't have a problem with it.' All of this blew up into a major row. (Coe, Oxygen, April 1998)

Given their involvement in an unrelated prostaglandin project, they had intended to patent these structures, and felt that those catalogued by Rummidgen were too similar and, hence, their publication was in violation of the collaboration agreement. Incidentally, in May 1999, these same Malibu-based Plethora scientists applied for, and were granted, a patent on these prostaglandin structures. However, the patent makes no mention of Rummidgen as the co-inventor of these structures which, according to the terms of the legal agreement, it should have done. Hence, they themselves now clearly violated the contract. Rummidgen confronted Plethora's Gregor Green with this violation but, rather than filing a formal complaint with the patent issuer, decided that it might be more beneficial in the long term if, according to Lodge, they tallied up 'brownie points' with Plethora, leaving them indebted to the biotech firm for undefined future purposes.

Having become worried about possible violations of intellectual property rights, the parent company started to exert more influence over the collaboration. It soon became obvious that Plethora no longer wished for its biotech partner to have information on specific targets nor on its philosophy of doing lead compound discovery. Instead, it chose to concentrate its efforts on building an in-house facility for combinatorial chemistry.

We went through a period where we knew Plethora was going to set up this group and we argued and campaigned very hard for them not to do so – that we should do it instead. But this whole Plethora (US) driving Plethora (UK) thing prevented us from putting in a fair pitch, I think. It was a case of 'I know it makes sense for you to do this, from a technological point of view, an outsourcing point of view, and a we-believe-you-can-do-it point of view, but all of that counts for nothing if Plethora feels that the IPR is not 100 per cent under their control.' (Coe, Oxygen, April 1998)

Hornby, Plethora's 'gatekeeper' of the collaboration, first conceived the idea for the development of this in-house research group and justified Plethora's initiative:

The technology was the main objective of the collaboration. The objective for the in-house group is making libraries. The collaboration is a means to an end. (Plethora, March 1998)

To which a Rummidgen bench scientist responded:

It has changed the whole collaboration, the way we work in general. When the collaboration started it was recognized that we were developing technology that was transferred to Plethora, but it was a long time before we actually went about transferring technology in an organized way, in June 1997. (Biddlecombe, Rummidgen, May 1998)

This new development also made the delivery of specific outcomes uncertain.

It has been difficult from our point of view because if you're doing lead discovery work there is a recognizable deliverable there ... When you move to technology development the whole pace of work slows down ... On technology development

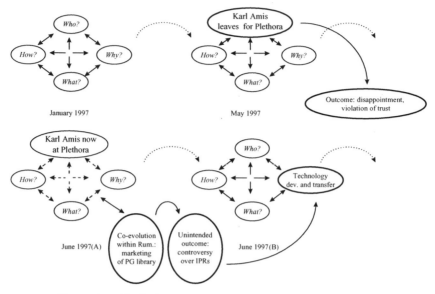

Figure 3.3: Evolution: 1997

you can get lucky or through clever science you can do wonderful things. But if the chemistry doesn't work out it looks bad for us and that was something that has made us slightly nervous about exclusively looking at technology development. (Biddlecombe, Oxygen, May 1998)

In sum then, the relationship progressed through three distinct strategic phases, in as many years, as Plethora substantially altered the stated 'why' of the collaboration. These transformations were not without discomfort and have generated mixed feelings among those individuals involved with the collaboration. The second change of strategy proved the most significant in that it was preceded and instigated by an unpleasant controversy surrounding the ownership of intellectual property and legitimate uses of technologies, which subsequently helped produce an increasing sense of distrust.

Operating rules

Oxygen was set up as a wholly owned subsidiary of Rummidgen to facilitate a combinatorial chemistry collaboration with Plethora, allowing it to prepare separate financial records and be managed as a distinct entity. It is not a typical joint venture in that Plethora owns no equity in either Oxygen or its parent company Rummidgen, and in that the former continued to exist once the alliance had been terminated.

As is generally the case with Plethora's alliances, the Rummidgen collaboration was governed formally by a steering committee, consisting of four representatives of each partner organization. This group met quarterly to discuss progress on short-term objectives, resource allocation, time scales, technology transfer issues, ownership of intellectual property, and ideas for new approaches, technologies, and projects. Every six weeks Plethora received a formal technical progress report, prepared by Paul Biddlecombe and Ulrich Eco, two Oxygen bench scientists closely involved with the joint project.

Under the formal agreement, Plethora received royalties on sales by Rummidgen (Oxygen) using technology developed during the alliance. The biotech partner received no downstream royalties on lead compounds it identified but is entitled to use the body of knowledge generated in future collaborations with third parties.

The deal structure should reflect the risk to Plethora – for example, if the collaboration gives us technology which is useful in the early stage of the discovery process, there is still a very long way to go, and a huge amount of expense before a sales product results. The payoff for our collaborators should in part reflect the risk we're carrying. (Yancey, Plethora, 1996)

The original contract, however, did not anticipate any significant changes in the cooperative relationship, and proved less useful when the alliance was redirected twice. Moreover, the controversy surrounding the intellectual property rights to the prostaglandin library was due in part to the unfamiliarity of Plethora's Malibu-based scientists with the contractual arrangements. On reflection, Cambridgeshire-based Plethora scientists acknowledge as much.

Following this event, it became obvious that Plethora's California-based parent would set the agenda, changing the nature of the working relationship by virtue of its obsessive protection of chemical targets, rendering any future prospects for continued collaboration less likely and making it increasingly difficult for the biotech to mature as an independent and profitable organization. These developments were perceived as completely irrational by the biotech partner.

I think they have an irrational fear of loss of confidential information. Plethora suddenly started developing very unfavourable commercial terms – so unacceptable that we cannot work with them. For instance, they require total ownership of all intellectual property which, for a company like ours, means we don't have a future. (Lodge, Rummidgen, April 1998)

This attitude became increasingly obvious, particularly at the quarterly meetings.

Plethora stipulated performance targets, under which we could continue to work with them, which were not achievable. And we said: 'Well, did your internal group achieve them?' They said: 'That is not the point,' upon which I responded: 'Is there anybody in the world who can achieve this? Then why are you asking us to do something that nobody else in the world can do and that you cannot do yourself? It is a totally unrealistic target.' They said: 'Well, get back to us when you can do it.' (Lodge, Rummidgen, April 1998)

As these statements aptly illustrate, the cooperative venture, in what was to be its final year, had evolved into one increasingly characterized by a 'fee-for-service' attitude, suspicions of opportunistic behaviour, and a felt lack of trust.

On a less formal level, although Coe (Rummidgen) and Hornby (Plethora) considered themselves alliance champions, coordinating its daily operations, each was critical of the other for being insufficiently influential to make key decisions. This lack of autonomy and ensuing inability to deliver on promises became the root cause of various confrontations between Coe and Hornby, requiring 'off-the-record' mediation by Green (Plethora) and Lodge (Rummidgen).

Gregor and I have tried to work at this by making sure that Nigel [Hornby] is more consistent and also by encouraging Jon [Coe] to listen more critically. (Lodge, Rummidgen, April 1998)

Over the duration of the alliance, Coe's portfolio of collaborations increased substantially to include various other pharmaceutical partners, leaving less time for the Plethora collaboration. 'We don't get the same exclusivity and attention as before,' complained Hornby (Plethora, March 1998). Informal dialogues between Coe and Hornby took place regularly and served primarily to exchange personal views on the success and future of the cooperative relationship. Usually in the form of informal telephone conversations and email messages, these are thought to have accounted for as much as 90 per cent of all interpartner communications.

Frustrations of bench scientists at the biotech partner with the way the alliance operated also became increasingly apparent. Although Oxygen scientists were required to provide six-weekly technical reports to Plethora, they tended to receive little or no feedback in return.

We were producing all these compounds that were sent off to Cambridgeshire or California and wouldn't really hear a hell of a lot back again. From a motivational point of view that is not enough. (Biddlecombe, Rummidgen, May 1998)

Likewise, there was an expectation of more involvement of the pharmaceutical partner by means of a secondment programme which never materialized and 'caused a bit of a disappointment for a lot of people' (Eco, Oxygen, May 1998).

Social makeup

People, not the institutions they work for, make successful collaborations. Institutions can get in the way, but ultimately it's the people who are key to success. (Yancey, Plethora, 1996)

Although Yancey's public presentations have come to be regarded with some scepticism by senior managers at Rummidgen, there is agreement on the prominent role of interpersonal relationships in collaborations. Their significance to the evolution of cooperation becomes apparent when considering several key events. First, Lodge and Coe both assumed a certain degree of risk when entering the alliance in the absence of a signed agreement. Lodge put his trust in Gregor Green, a senior Plethora manager, rather than in the pharmaceutical per se. As Lodge explains:

Who are you placing your faith in? At that point you need someone you can phone and say: 'Gregor, I trust you, what do you believe?' It has to be someone you can trust and whose judgement you value. Up to that point he had already proven to be straightforward, very reliable, and believable. Gregor told me the collaboration wasn't yet certain, but way over 95 per cent certain. And I trusted him. I wouldn't trust Plethora. (Rummidgen, April 1998)

Green, reflectively, concurs with this:

I used to have long conversations with Derek and have dinner with him and tell him not to panic for everything was going to be OK. And he had to trust me on that and actually hired Jon Coe before the deal was signed ... Those early stages required quite a big risk on Derek's part and he put quite a lot of trust in me. (Plethora, March 1998)

In contrast, Coe, taking a personal career risk, felt confident that Plethora as a reputable pharmaceutical would deliver on its promises. He explained his rationale thus:

No one promised me anything; there was nothing in writing. It was hoped Plethora would sign in January but last minute hold-ups took it into February. I just knew they would perform. Plethora is very professional. It is almost like the Bank of England: if you cannot trust Plethora you cannot trust anybody. (Oxygen, April 1998)

Second, the replacement of Plethora's Richard Lewis, who left to take up a post with rival pharmaceutical Glaxo, by Mark Amis impacted quite significantly on the effectiveness and geniality of the cooperative relationship. Amis's perceived arrogance and failure to champion the alliance within Plethora became increasingly obvious and was a source of irritation at Rummidgen and its subsidiary, Oxygen. Said Chief Operating Officer, Keilor:

I don't think the guy is a very constructive guy, he is an arrogant guy. There were times when I just wanted to smack him in the gut . . . I've never come across someone I have disliked so much in this industry. I really found it very difficult. Arrogant swine! . . . Richard Lewis was very good, and I wonder how different it might have been had he stayed on. (Rummidgen, April 1999)

Third, though bench scientists generally appeared more sanguine and more satisfied with the working relationship than their CEO, Derek Lodge, they were cynical towards the behaviour of their pharmaceutical partner. This cynicism appeared rooted in what was seen to be an act of 'poaching', when their colleague Karl Amis was hired by Plethora.

When the collaboration started there was a gentlemen's agreement – nothing on paper – that if we had an application from anyone at Plethora or if Plethora had an application from anyone of us, that person's CV would be returned. This was either between Gregor and Derek, or Nigel and Jon, or Mark Amis and Jon. But that didn't happen. (Biddlecombe, Oxygen, May 1998)

Plethora's Mark Amis rationalized the decision thus:

I do not see how we could have done things differently. I don't think they know to this day that Karl Amis had a job offer with another company. And we could never tell them that because of confidentiality . . . It's a hard world. (Plethora, June 1998)

Rummidgen, however, saw things rather differently:

They claim that due to ethics they could not discuss Karl Amis's situation. But in the real world people do. Gregor or Mark could have called us privately. To stand back and say that ethics prevented us sounds absurd. I think this was a rationalization of their action. I don't think they even realized how offensive we found their behaviour. (Lodge, Rummidgen, March 1999)

Not only did it reflect poorly on Plethora as a collaborator but it created an environment of distrust between the more senior individuals.[1]

---

[1] As a side issue, it is interesting to note that recently Plethora was confronted with a similarly unpleasant experience, though on a much larger scale. Plethora has filed a lawsuit in a Michigan court against its take-over target Xtreme Biogen, arguing that it was grossly misled by Xtreme Biogen's president Rick Cobein. Apparently, when Plethora president Harold Thompson, in November 1999, asked Mr Cobein about rumours of a possible merger between Xtreme Biogen and American Cosmetics, he was allegedly told that an announcement of a merger would not happen for 'several months'. The deal, however, was announced two days later.

I think this hurt Jon [Coe] disproportionately because he felt that the guys [Nigel Hornby and others] understood his problems, yet they just sat there through lunch without mentioning anything. And then Karl Amis comes in on Monday morning and says 'I'm going.' This was when trust broke down at the scientific level. Jon felt exposed here. He didn't understand why someone couldn't have cuddled him and said 'You're losing somebody,' before letting Karl Amis break the news. (Lodge, Rummidgen, May 1999)

This particularly unpleasant consequence transpired shortly after a steering group meeting, when Lodge and Coe discovered that despite individuals from Plethora having known about Karl Amis's impending departure, they had been instructed not to disclose this.

It was the starting point of the deterioration of our relationship with Plethora; a feeling here that perhaps they were never expecting to collaborate with us in the longer term. They were setting up to do this themselves and one good way of doing this was to hire our people. (Lodge, Rummidgen, April 1998)

Plethora admitted it was at the time recruiting capable scientists to staff its in-house facility, yet argued that Karl Amis intended to leave Oxygen in any event and was considering a lucrative offer from another pharmaceutical. Hence, employing him would appear the best strategy given such circumstances, even if it implied violating an unwritten rule. Although several Oxygen scientists have since applied for similar positions, Plethora have not made any formal offers.

Fourth, shortly after the initial negotiations had been completed and a contract drafted, in late 1994, Plethora's chief head office negotiator of the collaboration agreement resigned. The consequences of his departure became most apparent when Malibu-based scientists expressed their dissatisfaction with the manner in which the contract dealt with the ownership and use of intellectual property. None of the existing California-based Plethora group had been involved with the original negotiations and alliance formation and, hence, they failed to appreciate and understand the fundamental ideas behind the agreement, one of which was to allow Rummidgen to grow its business on chemistry technologies developed during the collaboration. Moreover, senior Plethora scientists appeared reluctant to 'champion' the alliance. Several, including Green and Yancey, were approaching retirement and there seemed little incentive to risk generating controversy within Plethora over a single partnership in a portfolio of many.

This is a family row caused by an uncle that isn't really known to either of us. And until the uncle either dies or is replaced by another uncle the prospects for a future collaboration appear bleak. (Coe, Oxygen, April 1998)

Towards the end of their negotiated extension, a further prolongation of the collaboration became increasingly unlikely. As for Rummidgen, Plethora would have had to admit that it made serious misjudgements, particularly with respect to the establishment of the in-house production facility to replace the alliance. This Plethora was unlikely to do. 'It would be too much of a loss of face,' suggested Lodge. Plethora insisted that the internalization of combinatorial chemistry capabilities had been part of its collaborative strategy from the start, though it was apparently not at all clear to the biotech partner that this was to become the only focus of the alliance.

Fifth, an unusually important element in biopharmaceutical collaborations, particularly for biotech firms, is their ability to enhance or damage one's reputation. Reputation is widely considered to be a key strategic resource in the biotechnology field. Rummidgen's negotiations with a prominent IT services provider nearly broke down when it received a very unfavourable reference provided by a senior Plethora scientist which apparently had included the comment: 'Rummidgen rip us off, they cheat us' (Lodge, April 1998). Interestingly, the opinion of one senior manager had been considered to represent the collective view of Plethora. Mark Amis (Plethora) acknowledged that certain Plethora scientists feel this way and admitted to there existing 'negative vibes about Rummidgen'. Having been fortunate to rescue this new alliance, Lodge explains:

Fortunately, I have some friends at a high level with that company [the IT services provider] who told me that it happened. I think the normal way business works, if I did not have those relationships within that company, the IT firm would have walked away. That's what I would do. But they actually called us up and said: 'We don't believe this because we know you anyway, but you should know that that's what they [Plethora] are saying.' (Rummidgen, April 1998)

He, nonetheless, recognises there are certain individuals within Plethora (for example, Gregor Green) that he trusts would render a positive endorsement if asked.

Contributions and performance

Realizing the importance of early success, Coe delivered the first plate of compounds in June 1995.

Particularly in the early days it is important to show something demonstrable, say a plate of compounds. Even though it may be slightly cosmetic it allows them to walk around the company saying, 'Look at this, and we only signed the agreement a short while ago.' Nobody cares what the compounds are at that stage but everyone gets a feeling that something is really happening. (Lodge, Rummidgen, April 1998)

During the three-year period, Oxygen generated several libraries for Plethora, particularly in the lead discovery phase. Delivery became considerably more difficult in the final year of cooperating when the alliance was focused purely on new technology development.

Your hands are very much tied by the chemistry. Even if you're the best scientist in the world, there will be types of chemistry or ideas that will never work because there is something fundamentally flawed about them. (Biddlecombe, Rummidgen, May 1998)

'From the chemist's point of view, they can lose confidence a little bit in their ability if they are faced with something tough,' adds Eco (Oxygen). An early technology development, a silicon link-up, has proved beneficial and, at one point, there were talks of a joint publication.

Organizational *learning* was always an underlying, tacit objective for both partners and appears to have manifested itself in four areas. First, the collaboration was initiated by Plethora to allow its scientists, through a biotechnology partner, to learn about combinatorial chemistry technologies and solid phase chemistry. 'And in that sense we have learned a lot,' admitted Hornby (Plethora, March 1998). Second, Plethora was able to assess the feasibility and generate the confidence levels needed to internalize this technology using an in-house facility. At the level of the individual, learning is reflected in the personal development of scientists as they broadened their skills and knowledge base. Third, the partners appear to have influenced the strategic thinking of one another. Plethora came to recognize the limitations of drug discovery using mixtures rather than single compounds. Rummidgen, through Plethora's insistence on the large scale manufacture of compounds, has recognized this to be a legitimate and unmet need within the pharmaceutical industry. And, finally, each has learned more about the negotiation and management processes of biotechnology research alliances. Rummidgen now demands downstream royalties on lead compounds it helps to identify. For instance, recently Bayer acceded to £7 million in milestone payments for each Rummidgen compound that completes clinical trials plus subsequent royalty payments if it enters the market, on top of a fixed fee of £9 million.

As regards the evolutionary path of the collaboration, it appears not to have developed quite as anticipated during the formation phase in 1994. 'We have heard informally since then that Plethora did not believe we would do it. We've been told that they thought this was money being thrown away,' recalls Lodge (Rummidgen). Plethora, however, acknowledges having received good value for its money.

Are we where we wanted to be four years ago? No, we're not. Are we pleased? Yes, we are. The reason is that science has developed beyond our anticipation. (Green, Plethora, March 1998)

Further, the evolutionary path of the collaboration appears characterized by a punctuated equilibrium structure, rather than a life cycle or teleology, whereby periods of relative stability are interrupted by short periods of instability and change.

Coevolution of partner firms

Rummidgen's development over the formal three-year relationship has been impressive and well beyond that predicted by Plethora.

What we had not anticipated is the way in which their business has taken off. They have grown in size, in number of chemists, and they have enlarged their repertoire and toolbox, if you like, with new technologies, way beyond that which we anticipated. (Green, Plethora, March 1998)

Its subsidiary, Oxygen, grew from the recruitment of Coe, in 1995, to nearly seventy-eight scientists at the end of 1998. Subsequent to the Plethora collaboration, Rummidgen established alliances with a diverse range of pharmaceutical companies. Its first public offering, in March 1998, raised nearly £20 million. The implications of such rapid, organic growth appeared twofold. First, some senior Plethora scientists questioned whether their investment was dedicated purely to the collaboration or used as seed capital instead.

We've often wondered whether they were spending all of their time on just Plethora work or were using our money to do other things. The way we set our collaboration up, it was very loose in terms of what they would deliver . . . Basically they used us as seed money to grow their business. (Mark Amis, Plethora, June 1998)

Also, as its portfolio of alliances increased, the Plethora collaboration may have become increasingly less pivotal to the future of Rummidgen and senior Plethora scientists felt they were given insufficient attention.

I think for the first year I thought Oxygen would play a big role in our future. What happened was that we discovered they weren't the right people for us because they were doing business with so many other companies. (Mark Amis, Plethora, June 1998)

From an organizational culture perspective, Plethora was at times characterized as arrogant, contemptuous, and insensitive by its biotech partner. These traits were most evidently reflected in the sudden changes of strategy imposed on Rummidgen without prior dialogue, and the unapologetic recruitment of a key scientist. Some have linked Plethora's arrogance to the concurrent approval and marketing of its much-publicized drug Pipfler, particularly as Nigel Hornby had been on the original development team as well as being the gatekeeper for the alliance.

I think Pipfler was becoming a real product for Plethora and, though this might sound odd, I think we have seen the organization change as a result of that. Nigel Hornby [Plethora's gatekeeper of the Rummidgen alliance] discovered it. The whole organization changed. It was as if they had won the lottery... They simply became more arrogant. (Lodge, Rummidgen, March 1999)

More subtly, however, resentment may have arisen as a result of Rummidgen's success as a biotech startup and, upon it going public, the rapid increase in personal wealth of those with equity ownership or options on equity in the firm. By 31 December 1998, its chief executive, Derek Lodge, had accumulated share options worth nearly £6,000,000. Gareth Keilor, Chief Operating Officer, had share options worth over £800,000.[2]

When the company [Rummidgen] went public, they [individuals at Plethora] knew about the options Coe held and the value these represented. I think this created some jealousy... Part of the problem may have been them sitting there and thinking: 'We are making these people rich,' in a way that they couldn't become rich... They were looking at it: 'He's going to be a millionaire, and he is going to be a millionaire'... I wonder if this was not a major element that damaged the relationship. (Lodge, Rummidgen, March 1999)

On an interpersonal level, some individuals working within the biotech firm felt they were insufficiently appreciated and respected by Plethora scientists.

Mark Amis took no notice of me at all when I was alone, very little notice when I had fifteen staff under me, and much more notice now I manage seventy staff. Mark is very status ridden. (Coe, Oxygen, April 1998)

Changing strategic priorities within the partner organizations may have influenced the cooperative relationship in several ways. First, Plethora's strategy of developing an in-house facility for combinatorial chemistry research appeared an obvious motive for redirecting the *raison d'être* of the

---

[2] These figures are based on computations using the 1998 Rummidgen International plc Annual Report and Financial Statements, and using the 31 December 1998 share price. These figures have not been adjusted for the striking price of the options.

alliance towards an emphasis on technology development and transfer. Second, Rummidgen's extraordinary success as a partner to the pharmaceutical industry, evidenced by announcements of alliances with various large pharmaceuticals and a successful stock market flotation, appears to have generated suspicions by Plethora of Rummidgen using its funding as seed capital to grow its own business.

This quite successful collaboration, despite having apparently not exhausted its potential, was dismantled due to reasons that may have been neither purely economic nor financial. Nor were they entirely within managerial control. Rather, concerns about intellectual property rights, the personal ambitions of a small number of senior individuals, and the unintended consequences of certain decisions made a further extension difficult to justify.

You can have a wonderfully successful technical collaboration, but they [Plethora] have not thought about extending it when things went a little sour. And there must be people within Plethora saying: 'Well, we've got all of this . . .', and then someone else might say: 'Yes, but they stole from us and we hate them,' and then that's the end of it. (Keilor, Rummidgen, April 1999)

Thematic discussion

The process of reconstructing the cooperative relationship between Plethora and Rummidgen generates a set of observations on its process dynamics and evolution. Summarized, these are as follows.

Predictability

The evolutionary path of this biochemistry-based alliance would have been extremely difficult to predict for a number of reasons. First, the day-to-day reality of collaborating contained a number of surprises and crises that may have been difficult to anticipate, including the recruitment of Karl Amis and the departure of several individuals. Second, the sheer speed of technological progress within the biotechnology sector made it difficult to foresee what research techniques and processes would be available within the next few years and, hence, rendered the content of the alliance less predictable. Third, the serendipity of biochemistry-based discovery research, which applies equally well to technology development processes, contributed further to this unpredictability. Finally, the evolution of this alliance was, it appears, shaped in part by unintended outcomes. The recruitment by Plethora of Karl Amis, and the controversy surrounding the prostaglandin library, may serve as good illustrations of this property.

Evolution

The evolutionary path of this particular alliance seems most akin to a *punctuated equilibrium* view, where longer periods of relative stability are interrupted by shorter periods of instability and change. This observation seems consistent with Gray and Yan's (1997) findings of a study of US–Chinese joint ventures, and Gulati's (1998) expectations of alliance evolution.

Longevity

Longevity does not appear to be a particularly useful measure of success, at least not for this particular alliance. Even with sentiments of frustration and disappointment, both partner organizations considered the joint programme as having been successful, given its tangible accomplishments. Rummidgen was able to leverage the alliance to gain legitimacy in the pharmaceutical industry, to successfully negotiate several substantial collaborations, and, ultimately, to bring the firm to the stock market by means of an initial public offering (IPO). Plethora, in turn, gained access to various promising chemical compounds and state-of-the-art combinatorial chemistry technologies that it was able to bring in-house. Yet, while the potential of the collaboration did not appear to be exhausted, the alliance was not extended (again) in 1998. This observation on longevity as a measure of success is at variance with some alliance studies (e.g. Lynch, 1993) whilst consistent with others (e.g. Hamel, 1991; Hamel, Doz, and Prahalad, 1989).

Change and reaction

A change in one of the four institutionalized features of this alliance has, at times, prompted compensatory or retaliatory changes in others. For instance, the unexpected departure of the chief Plethora (US) negotiator left Rummidgen without a champion to rationalize and defend its decision to publish the chemical library. This, in turn, resulted in a conflict over intellectual property rights – which conceivably could have been avoided – and a retaliatory change in the strategic focus of the alliance from lead discovery to technology development and transfer. At the same time, it reverted the nature of the partnership from a collaborative to a 'fee-for-service' type arrangement. In other words, an unanticipated change in the social makeup of the alliance ultimately resulted in a transformation of its explicit strategic justification.

Second, the departure of Richard Lewis brought about the introduction of Mark Amis as his replacement. Amis, sensing that his in-house chemistry unit was competing directly with the alliance and threatened by it, failed to champion the collaboration within Plethora. This conflict of interest, which arguably could have been avoided with some foresight on the part of Plethora's management, illustrates clearly the coexistence of potentially incompatible strategic agendas at different levels in the organization. Not only did the working relationship become more cumbersome as a result, but Amis's lack of commitment impeded any future extension. Once again, a change in the social makeup of the alliance appears to have impacted significantly on its performance and potential.

Third, the decision by Plethora to recruit Karl Amis and, particularly, its apparent violation of a socially-binding agreement, and its contemptuous treatment of the issue, resulted in a lack of trust felt by senior Rummidgen collaborators in their Plethora counterparts. A renewed vigilance, in other words, was the retaliatory response to Plethora's defiance of trust-based features of their relationship.

Fourth, the decision by Rummidgen to publish a select group of chemical structures, as part of their marketing strategy, was interpreted by US-based Plethora scientists as a violation of the collaboration agreement (although this remains disputed by the biotech firm to this day). In retaliation, Plethora (US) persuaded its UK subsidiary to redefine the strategic justification of the alliance (from discovery to technology development and transfer) to the extent that Rummidgen would no longer have access to specific drug targets pursued by Plethora.

Incidentally, these examples may also illustrate the degree to which actors draw on tacit social rules to make sense of a changing environment, and to legitimize their behaviour. For instance, Mark Amis's perception of the alliance as being in direct competition with his chemistry department may become easier to comprehend when examined from the viewpoint of an ambitious chemist trying to 'climb the corporate ladder' within a relatively bureaucratic organizational structure. His unconstructive stance regarding Rummidgen was, in his view, almost certainly legitimate. It certainly was seen as significant given the authority vested in him by Plethora. His conduct, in turn, may have informed these rules by contributing to the ultimate transformation of the alliance into a straightforward 'fee-for-service' technology transfer relationship, whilst limiting the possibility of extending the joint programme in future years.

Similarly, with the vacuum created by the departure of the chief negotiator, US-based Plethora actors could no longer draw on his experience and recollection of the negotiations to rationalize what appeared to be an intellectual property rights violation. Not surprisingly, they felt justified in their accusations. They, in retaliation, sought to change its strategic rationale by focusing it squarely, and opportunistically, on technology development and transfer. Moreover, they may have helped rationalize Plethora's subsequent treatment of Rummidgen (possibly including its decision to recruit from its biotech partner).

Interpersonal relationships

The collaborative process appears to have been quite strongly contingent on the nature of the interpersonal ties between specific individuals. Derek Lodge (Rummidgen) and Gregor Green (Plethora), for instance, mediated regularly to resolve operational difficulties, cope with frustrations, and pre-empt more serious problems. Additionally, the pre-contract collaboration appears to have been based in large measure on the continued reassurances by Green to Lodge, and Lodge's reliance on them, rather than on, say, Plethora's reputation per se.

Trust

Indeed, character-based trust appears to have played a significant role in the collaborative relationship. The actual cooperation began four weeks prior to a signed written contract, and included the recruitment of Jon Coe and the creation of a subsidiary company, Oxygen. Derek Lodge (CEO) sanctioned each of these actions based primarily on the frequent assurances by Plethora's Gregor Green. Two years into the alliance, the relationship deteriorated significantly upon Plethora violating a 'gentlemen's agreement', an implicit understanding that neither partner would use the collaboration as a recruitment exercise. In other words, Plethora violated that which had been taken for granted by Rummidgen, defying a deep-seated, moral rule, with considerable consequences.

Learning

The value of the alliance to both partners appears to have been derived in part from mutual learning processes. Plethora utilized it to learn more about combinatorial chemistry and its potential for drug discovery. It subsequently internalized this technology. Rummidgen came to recognize the legitimate need in the pharmaceutical industry for the large-scale manufacture of chemical compounds, despite this being more production-oriented and less stimulating intellectually. Each comprises an example of what Child and Faulkner refer to as *strategic learning* in that, in each case, it provided a better understanding of the criteria and conditions for organizational success (1998: 285). Other learning processes that relate more specifically to the transfer of technologies, first from Plethora to Rummidgen and later from Rummidgen to Plethora, are more like Child and Faulkner's (1998) *technical* learning.

Industry context

The narrative suggests that this alliance was not immune to a well-known phenomenon in pharmacology: the 'not-invented-here' (NIH) syndrome. This essentially expresses the reluctance of scientists to accept anything not made in-house, whether a drug candidate, a technology or a process. Mark Amis's lack of enthusiasm for adopting contributions from the joint project serves as a good example. Given his responsibility for an in-house chemistry unit, he believed the collaboration should not have happened in the first place. To quote one of Amis's collaborators:

I think he did not want to be doing this collaboration; that he should be doing this in his department. With many, many things he just tried to make things as difficult as possible... Plethora like to think that they are doing it themselves – that's the key thing. They have this stack of money, and the chemists... I think there is a lot of NIH in the way they did things. (Keilor, Rummidgen, April 1999)

Reputation

The reputation (or legitimacy) that results from collaborating can be an important factor in attracting future partners (cf. Gulati, 1995a). This type of information can, however, be disseminated by individuals who may not have first-hand experience with the actual relationship but act instead on hearsay. Such was the case here, when a senior Plethora scientist provided a derogatory reference to one of Rummidgen's prospective IT partners. Yet, provided such individuals occupy sufficiently senior positions, their views can be taken to represent those of the organization. In this particular instance, Derek Lodge's (Rummidgen) strong personal ties with a senior manager at the prospective firm helped neutralize the impact of the reference. Without it, this new collaboration would probably have failed to materialize.

Real options strategy

Plethora's strategy of pursuing several alliances simultaneously (code-named 'PlethoraGen') appears consistent with the literature on *real options theory* (e.g. Copeland and Keenan, 1998; Kogut, 1991; Mitchell and Hamilton, 1988). A fugitive from the field of finance, it posits that multiple investments in biotech firms generate a portfolio of options that can, but need not, be exercised (by increasing resource commitments) at the leisure of the pharmaceutical at some future time. As Plethora acknowledged, even if just one biotechnology alliance proves successful, the monetary rewards will usually easily render this portfolio strategy worthwhile.

We will return to these observations in Chapter 6.

4 Through the looking glass 2: Cambiogen and Plethora
1995–9

> If you come out of the collaboration with more knowledge than you had when you went in, even if you haven't achieved the objective, the alliance may still have been successful . . . it is learning that renders it successful.
> (Green, Plethora, March 1998)

A joint programme between Plethora and Cambiogen, both successful companies in their own right, was the unusual outcome of a much less significant partnership of Plethora and Myco Pharmaceuticals, in early 1995. Myco, founded in 1992, specialized in anti-fungal research (mycology is the scientific study of fungi) and had entered into various collaborative research efforts with academic institutions until 1993, when it opened up its own laboratories in Cambridge, Massachusetts. Having received substantial funding from The National Health Institutes, Myco began to actively search for pharmaceutical partners and approached, amongst others, Plethora. A strategic alliance was negotiated and active collaboration began on 1 March 1995, although the formal agreement was backdated to 1 January. Plethora decided to purchase a 20 per cent equity stake in its biotech partner. The primary objective driving the collaboration, which was to remain unchanged throughout the next four and a half years, was to search for a broad-spectrum drug for treating fungal infections in humans. Myco was, at the time, one of the most prominent research groups worldwide in fungal genetics. Whereas the pharmaceutical industry was close to having exhausted traditional approaches to targeting fungal infections, Myco appeared to provide a new research approach, using unique technologies to identify genes in yeast that, when interfered with, could prove lethal to the yeast and, by implication, to the fungi. The potential gains from the discovery of such a drug are evident when one considers that fungal infections, usually the result of a weakened immune system, are thought to contribute to a significant number of deaths among older people as well as patients dependent on chemotherapy treatments and drugs that suppress the immune system.

During the spring of 1996, Myco joined efforts with Perseptive Biosystems to create ChemAnalysis Pharmaceuticals. In an effort to extend its capabilities beyond the anti-fungal programme to incorporate anti-bacterial research, Myco merged its technology for drug discovery using microbes as model systems (fungus-based research) with Perseptive's chemistry technologies. The new name, ChemAnalysis Pharmaceuticals, sought to reflect these newly acquired capabilities. Additionally, Myco was to gain royalty-free licences to all present and future Perseptive technology for application in drug discovery. Perseptive was granted a 42 per cent equity interest in the newly positioned biotech firm in return for access to its technologies and some physical space. By forming an alliance, Myco was able to combine its own expertise in molecular biology with Perseptive's strengths in chemistry.

A second change in ownership (social makeup) happened barely a year later, in January 1997, when ChemAnalysis announced its takeover by Cambiogen Pharmaceuticals,[1] in an equity transaction worth around US$89 million.[2] Just prior to the announcement, in mid-1996, Plethora had informed ChemAnalysis of its intention to extend the collaboration agreement for another two years, based on its satisfaction with the way the programme was advancing. Also, in December 1996, ChemAnalysis Pharmaceuticals had filed an application for an IPO of 2.5 million shares at US$11 to US$13 apiece, which would have given it a market capitalization of US$111 to US$131 million.

The takeover proved timely. Just prior to it, ChemAnalysis and Plethora had met off-site in Cape Cod, Massachusetts, to take stock of the joint effort. After two years of collaborating, the partners had essentially completed their target-based screens with little to show for it in terms of tangible accomplishments, except some learning. Cambiogen's genetic and genomic technologies, however, now provided access to an entirely new range of possible experiments, thus preventing a stalemate situation from occurring, by radically changing their approach to drug discovery research.

At the time of the takeover announcement, Cambiogen's chief business officer, Ray MacCarthy, explained their strategic justification thus:

This represents the major move of forward integration for 'Cambiogen research' to become 'Cambiogen pharmaceuticals'.

Under the agreement, existing ChemAnalysis shareholders (including Plethora) were given a total of 4.8 million unregistered Cambiogen shares,

---

[1] For accounting purposes, the transaction was recorded as a purchase by Cambiogen of ChemAnalysis. Hence, I refer to it here as a takeover, though most alliance agents view it as a merger, it having been much more amicable than a takeover would imply.
[2] *BioCentury Extra.*

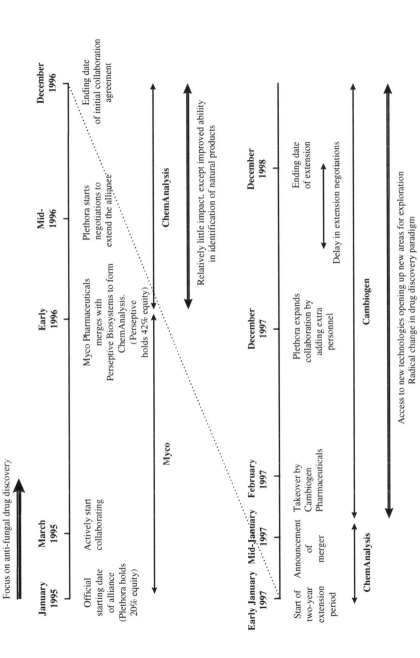

Figure 4.1: Chronology of the Cambiogen–Plethora alliance: 1995–9

representing 17 per cent of the company, in exchange for their ChemAnalysis equity stake. Perseptive Biosystems, as one of its largest shareholders, received 1.6 million shares. In addition, it was given a US$4 million payment in settlement of a promissory note and repurchase of previously issued warrants.[3]

'There is a remarkable synergy between our companies,' commented Mark Webber, Cambiogen's CEO.[4] Indeed, the strategic fit between Cambiogen and ChemAnalysis becomes apparent when one considers their latent contributions. Cambiogen Pharmaceuticals contributed a broad base of genetic and genomic technologies, including human family studies and gene cloning capabilities as well as RADE (rapid analysis of differential expression) technology. This unique science allows for the identification of expressions of genes that may be involved in certain diseases using high throughput molecular biology. Further, Cambiogen provided a focus on chronic diseases, including obesity, asthma, cancer, and those related to the central nervous system (CNS), to complement ChemAnalysis's traditional emphasis on fungal and bacterial diseases and its expertise in the genetics of micro-organisms. Given that fungal and bacterial diseases are generally more quickly taken into clinical trials than are chronic diseases, the merger was to fill an important vacuum in Cambiogen's pipeline of potential drugs. Finally, when combined, the companies were to enjoy more than US$300 million in committed funding from pharmaceutical partners, cash reserves of US$70 million (which, at the then-current burn-rate, would last them at least four years) and a workforce of around 350.[5]

The impact of this second merger was clearly more significant, as scientists from both companies commented:

Because of the broader remittance and because Cambiogen was a significantly larger organization than ChemAnalysis and was already a public company with alliances with five or six pharmaceutical companies giving additional economic resources, we now had a whole series of technological capabilities, including molecular biology, robotization, automatization, all of which were simply not available at ChemAnalysis. (Ridley, Cambiogen, June 1998)

It changed our alliance in that their new technologies became available to us and thus opened up some additional areas that we had not anticipated. (Rand, Plethora, March 1998)

One of the new technologies available to the joint research was *transcript profiling*, facilitating the array of genes into a transcript. Cambiogen's expertise with transcript profiling using mammalian systems (i.e. using

[3] Press release, Cambiogen, 11 February 1997.
[4] Press release, Cambiogen, 20 January 1997.   [5] *BioCentury*.

mammals) made it a lot easier and quicker for the collaborative effort to create similar transcript arrays in the yeast and fungal area. Partially as a result of being able to access Cambiogen's genomic technologies, research processes changed dramatically, significantly reducing lead times from 'validated target' to 'clinical candidate'. Further, given that Cambiogen was, at the time, considerably larger than ChemAnalysis and already publicly traded, it provided the Plethora collaboration with access to more resources, in terms of financial and scientific capabilities, and an already experienced collaborator, endowed with a portfolio of several ongoing alliances.

Equally significant was the distinct entrepreneurial culture that Cambiogen brought to the collaboration. Whereas Myco was a more traditional company with a pragmatic orientation on delivery and profitability, Cambiogen appeared far more academically oriented, as stated by two of its scientists:

In terms of culture, the two companies were on opposite sides of the spectrum, one might say. I think the Cambiogen culture was more academic, more freewheeling, more loose. The people at Myco and, later, ChemAnalysis were very business-like, concerned with the bottom-line, very driven by specifics in the alliance. The Cambiogen culture was a lot more open, trying to look for synergies, providing a much more integrated approach. (Copeland, Cambiogen, January 1999)

One of the core values of Cambiogen is that nothing is impossible . . . We encourage a philosophy of 'forget for the moment if it is going to be practical, just think. If the outcome would be so outrageously good that it is worth pursuing that line of thought, we will find a way to do it.'[6] (Ridley, Cambiogen, June 1998)

The process of fusing these distinct cultures appears to have been relatively free of difficulties, given the flexibility, tolerance, and commitment of both partner organizations towards the joint research. Targets were negotiated on a give-and-take basis and Cambiogen became increasingly more focused on specific targets and deadlines, which pleased Plethora. Plethora benefited also from Cambiogen's flexible and innovative approach to research and its speed of decision-making facilitated by a flat management structure, unlike its own typically rigid, bureaucratic processes.

By 16 December 1997, Plethora and Cambiogen had agreed to expand the scope of their joint research programme for the remainder of its term by adding extra personnel to it. The original group of sixteen (in 1995) increased to twenty full time equivalents (FTEs), dedicated solely to

---

[6] This observation is consistent with one of Cambiogen's core value statements, which reads: 'We believe nothing is impossible' (*Boston Business Journal*, 5–11 December 1997).

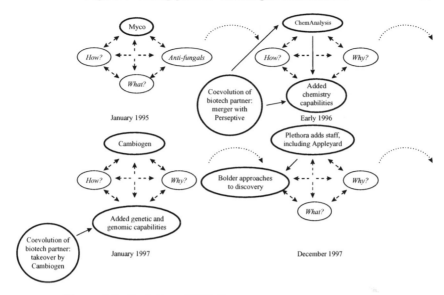

Figure 4.2: Evolution: 1995–7

the Plethora collaboration. 'We are excited about the additional commitment that Plethora has made to our anti-fungal programme,' commented Alan Crane (VP of Business Development at Cambiogen) publicly upon the announcement.[7] Plethora's decision to contribute more resources to the programme signalled an attempt to exhaust as much of its potential as possible during what was then thought to be its final year.

We were coming to the end of the third of four years and while it was clear that significant things had been achieved, the feeling was that with a few additional resources to implement these new ideas, the final year could be really impressive. [Plethora's] middle managers were responsible for this and wanted Plethora's senior managers to feel this had been really beneficial. (Ridley, Cambiogen, June 1998)

As illustrated above, the more senior individuals stood to lose personally, in terms of prestige and power, if the alliance they helped negotiate failed to produce measurable achievements and thus failed to champion them within their respective organizations. In this particular instance, although the extra effort still failed to provide the elusive anti-infectious lead compound, Plethora collaborators were able to persuade their US-based headquarters to extend the joint programme for a further two years – but not without difficulty.

[7] Press release by Cambiogen, 16 December 1997.

Who, why, what, how?

The ensuing analysis elaborates on the narrative. It makes extensive use of statements, quoted verbatim, by those closely involved with the joint research programme. In each case, these appear to have expressed a shared experience rather than a unique, one-off affair (unless this is clearly indicated). As before, the analysis seeks to show how alliance evolution can be studied as a process of reconfiguration of its various institutionalized elements.

Strategic rationale

In contrast to the Rummidgen collaboration, the strategic justification driving the Cambiogen alliance remained intact throughout the four-and-a-half year period, namely the identification of a broad-spectrum anti-fungal drug. Fungal infections, as a disease group, are widely considered to be an extremely difficult target with a relatively low success rate.

It is now recognized that broad-spectrum anti-fungal research is a damn difficult thing to do. I mean, it's one of the hardest areas of research . . . one of the most difficult areas to be involved in. (Copeland, Cambiogen, January 1999)

Many companies have worked on anti-fungal research and yet the bottom line, if you look at what we have in the clinic today, is very miserable. (Pirsig, Cambiogen, May 1998)

Given such sheer complexity, performance is assessed primarily using sub-goals or targets, sometimes referred to as 'technical milestones', given that they do not normally trigger payments. These were negotiated by Cambiogen and Plethora at quarterly steering group meetings and generally required Cambiogen to screen a specified number of compounds for biological activity against the disease target. Even if no biological activity was reported, that knowledge itself was considered relevant and seen as contributing to the success of the alliance. Over the duration of the joint programme, the nature of each milestone was characterized by the following: first, given the different organizational cultures of Cambiogen and Plethora, each set of targets constituted a compromise solution, reflecting concessions made by both the commercially oriented Plethora and the more academically inclined biotech partner. For instance, as Green explained:

I can think of one particular set of targets that some people at Cambiogen were very enthusiastic about and people at Plethora thought wasn't the best idea they had had. And the decision was made that we include a group of targets that we [Plethora] care about and some that they [Cambiogen] care about, whether we think they are going to work or not. It is a compromise. 'If it's important to you, do it.' If someone [Cambiogen] really cares about some particular targets, we [Plethora] tell them to conduct the experiment and let the science decide. (Plethora, March 1998)

This experiment was but one of six projects undertaken by Cambiogen but abandoned after three months due to lack of results, as previously agreed with Plethora. The relationship had become one of 'give-and-take', marked by reciprocated tolerance, flexibility, and mutual respect.

Second, the merger and takeover each contributed new capabilities to the collaboration. The merger with Perseptive Biosystems to form ChemAnalysis Pharmaceuticals added chemistry technologies to an alliance driven primarily by molecular biology. A subsequent takeover by Cambiogen Pharmaceuticals contributed genetic, genomic, high throughput and profiling technologies, and robotization and automation to the joint programme. The latter, in particular, appears to have impacted profoundly on the alliance. Such was the view of both companies:

The merger with Cambiogen had a very major impact on the alliance . . . It allowed us to utilize or integrate new technologies into the programme, and led to a very major change in the way we search for drugs today . . . What took us three years in the programme we can now accomplish in one. (Pirsig, Cambiogen, May 1998)

There are now techniques applied in the programme that would have simply not been available without the merger of ChemAnalysis and Cambiogen. And those are beginning to yield results that everyone is excited about, and had the merger not taken place, none of this would have happened. (Ridley, Cambiogen, June 1998).

Third, and more generally, both the scientific field (e.g. through the Yeast Genome Project and the US Human Genome Project) and relevant genomic technologies have evolved more rapidly than either partner could anticipate. As commented on by both partners:

The alliance has taken off in directions which we could never have anticipated four years ago. Science just moves so quickly. You have to respond to the changing scientific environment. (Green, Plethora, March 1998)

When we started, the yeast genome project was only about 60 per cent done – since then it has been completed. A lot of the genetic technologies have improved a lot, so what used to be very difficult is very easy today. (Pirsig, Cambiogen, May 1998)

In sum, whereas the overarching strategic justification remained unchanged, even in the face of one merger, one takeover, and a rapidly evolving science, the actual bench research that drove the collaboration incrementally closer to this objective changed profoundly as a result.

Operating rules

Unlike its alliance with Rummidgen, Plethora purchased a 20 per cent equity interest in Myco Pharmaceuticals. This stake has since eroded with each merger. Its governance structure, however, was akin to Plethora's other research-based alliances and remained unaffected by either. Payments from Plethora to Cambiogen were based on a negotiated number of FTEs dedicated to the joint research projects, triggering a payment of US$250,000 per FTE. This number of FTEs was reassessed at quarterly meetings by a coordinating body, appropriately named the 'Plethora–Cambiogen Steering Group' (PCSG), which met regularly to discuss progress and re-establish priorities in view of new scientific and technological developments. These meetings brought together five individuals from each organization – a mixture of scientists and business developers – and took place over two days. More frequent videoconferences were scheduled fortnightly to allow collaborating scientists to interact and discuss progress on, or difficulties experienced with, specific milestone targets. Though re-evaluated quarterly, these targets were set at the beginning of each year. Summaries from these fortnightly interactions, which tended to last for two hours at a time and were restricted to scientists, were presented at PCSG meetings. Those concerned with business development issues met outside the steering group meetings on an as-needed basis, primarily to ensure that the contractual agreement continued to cover the science practised and its post-alliance use, and to help resolve emergent misunderstandings. In the words of the Head of Research:

It is good to separate the science from the business. If there is going to be a misunderstanding that needs to be resolved, it is better that business people resolve these issues and let the scientists continue being friends and working together. (Green, Plethora, March 1998)

This sharp division between bench scientists and those on the business end of the collaboration became most obvious during the extension negotiations of late 1998. Although the scientific group had prepared for an extension to be finalized six months prior to the 31 December deadline, the New York-based legal department failed to gain agreement on intellectual property right issues and was concerned by the potential threat Cambiogen could pose as a future competitor. Moreover, Cambiogen was a very different company from Myco, with much greater bargaining power, which resulted in intense negotiations on cash payments and, particularly, post-alliance rights to technologies and downstream royalties. 'Cambiogen don't come cheap,' commented Green (Plethora, May 1999). The six-month deadlock was ultimately resolved through the intervention of senior Plethora management who, apparently, did away with much of the contractual material drafted by their lawyers as it proved too constraining for the day-to-day collaboration and the flexibility required for it to function effectively.

Communication between alliance agents, formally and informally, was usually considered very satisfactory.

The collaboration has led to very open and frank discussions and the development of very close relations . . . We have opened the lines of communication such that anyone can communicate with anyone. (Pirsig, Cambiogen, May 1998)

You must over-communicate and undersell your results. If your partner says it's brilliant, it is probably OK. If you think you are communicating at about the right level, then you're probably not communicating well enough. (Green, Plethora, March 1998)

An estimated 50 per cent of all inter-partner communications and information exchanges were completely informal and facilitated primarily by email correspondence and telephone discussions.

We have the daily calls. We are thus in very close communication. Information flows very effectively and we have really learned to make sure that the few thousand miles between us do not create a barrier to the exchange of materials, information or anything. (Pirsig, Cambiogen, May 1998)

With respect to the issue of control, Plethora remained the hand that fed the collaboration and provided the institutional framework for its governance.

It is always clear that the decision about what is going to be a good drug discovery is Plethora's. So Cambiogen can propose a series of projects and targets but the Plethora people will say that 'No, we don't want to do that because historically people have never found a decent compound against that class of target' . . . Plethora calls the tune. (Ridley, Cambiogen, June 1998)

But Cambiogen apparently became quick to adapt.

We have become tuned to their [Plethora's] expectations in terms of operating procedures, what kinds of things would be acceptable and what wouldn't . . . very early on. (Copeland, Cambiogen, January 1999)

Plethora, however, seemed to consider any reference to control as hardly relevant.

You are using a word ['control'] that is hardly relevant, because there is so much consensus here. An alliance will only work if it is delivering something to both parties. (Green, Plethora, March 1998)

Certain dimensions of control were much less explicit. As appears common in many biotech collaborations, both organizations cooperated on the basis of an implicitly held 'gentlemen's agreement' with respect to the recruitment of those scientists active in the alliance.

It is one of those things where you know that active recruitment isn't something you should do... It is like Common Law, it is not written down but you know what you should and shouldn't do ... it would not be kosher. (Ridley, Cambiogen, June 1998)

Although never formalized in the contractual agreement, it was understood that neither organization could act predatorily in using the other as a breeding ground for new recruits. Despite this understanding, however, Cambiogen did make offers of employment to two Plethora scientists, one of whom had been intimately involved with the joint programme, yet surprisingly without damaging the cooperative relationship too seriously.

One had left the company [Plethora], so I recruited him. Another left Plethora because of reorganization there. It was all done with discussion and understanding with Plethora. If it would have caused any adverse effect on our relations, we would not have pursued it. Before we completed the process, we discussed it with people at Plethora. If there had been any bad feelings, we would not have gone ahead with it. (Pirsig, Cambiogen, April 1999)

Robert Gray, in May 1998, became the first ever scientist to leave Plethora for a biotech partner. Although the pharmaceutical had recently made an offer of employment to a young scientist at Rummidgen (see Chapter 3), not until now had Plethora understood the psychological impact of such practices.

There was a bit of 'Hmmm... that's not very nice.' It was interesting to see the film played from the other side. (Green, Plethora, May 1999)

Social makeup

The nature and character of the social ties that spanned the organizational boundaries of Plethora and Cambiogen appeared marked by mutual satisfaction and relative stability.

What made this excellent was actually the creation of a team that, first of all, developed very close interpersonal relations. There was a chemistry right from the beginning... to the point that many of us are just good friends. (Pirsig, Cambiogen, May 1998)

Plethora's sentiments concerning the quality and amicability of the co-operative relationship were strikingly similar. 'The personalities involved haven't felt threatened by either side' (Rand, Plethora, March 1998).

We really have shared ownership . . . They [Cambiogen] are more of an extension of Plethora, where we can see what they are doing, we understand it, we work as a team. (Mark Amis, Plethora, June 1998)

Good interpersonal relationships seemed especially significant in a science as complex and unpredictable as anti-fungal research, in terms of having the potential to help carry a joint programme, and the individuals involved in it, through times of great uncertainty. This became apparent during the negotiating period for extending the alliance, when Plethora (UK) was unable to renew its commitment for six months due to severe delays in constructing the contract at its US parent. Gray, having just 'jumped ship' from Plethora to Cambiogen, played a crucial role as liaison between the two organizations, using his personal contacts within Plethora to repeatedly update and reassure Cambiogen.

Chris [Plethora] and I were able to have some very frank conversations. We don't need to hide behind the company line. We can just be honest with each other as to where things stood. That really helped, because I was able to gain an insight from him as to where sentiments at Plethora lay; where there was strong support for the collaboration, where there was maybe less strong support for the collaboration, where he thought Cambiogen's demands for the new deal were reasonable, which demands would just never be met under any circumstances . . . and I communicated those insights to the staff here. (Gray, Cambiogen, May 1999)

Moreover, such frank communication helped pre-empt the misunderstandings usually associated with organizational and scientific complexity and serendipity.

Scientific problems are inevitable. So when that happens, the interpersonal relations will have to kick in. (Copeland, Cambiogen, January 1999)

Fortunately, we mostly met or exceeded expectations. But if we could not do it, or had difficulties, it was displayed very clearly where those difficulties are. I think this is greatly appreciated on both sides and has really turned out into very close relations. (Pirsig, Cambiogen, May 1998)

This social interchange was expedited by an informally organized secondment programme between Plethora and Cambiogen, in which individuals could opt to spend a short period of time within each partner organization. From Plethora's perspective, this opportunity may have been motivated by a secondary agenda, namely to help internalize specific technologies proprietary to Cambiogen, much as they did with their other partner, Rummidgen.

There really are two [benefits]. First, there is that of learning some of the technology that we don't have in-house and bring it back to Plethora. Second, it helps in the team building – it really makes a difference if you can talk to people face to face . . . Spending time with them and getting to know them makes things run much more smoothly. (Rand, Plethora, March 1998)

This motive may help explain why Plethora, over the collaborative period, sent more scientists to Cambiogen than vice versa, exploiting this secondment opportunity.

As regards the stability of the relationship, although both the merger and takeover had some influence on its social makeup, particularly in terms of size and diversity, this impact seems to have been fairly trivial. Plethora and Cambiogen and, prior to that, ChemAnalysis were careful to leave the core anti-fungal research team in place on both sides of the joint programme. As Cambiogen expanded, however, as a consequence of both its takeover of ChemAnalysis and its expanding portfolio of pharmaceutical partners, some individuals were assigned larger responsibilities, leaving them with less time for Plethora. In an effort to maintain the momentum that had been achieved with Plethora, Cambiogen involved and trained others to assume some of the operational responsibilities, apparently with reasonably good effect.

Some of the senior people now were given responsibility for other alliances also and thus had less time to spend on the Plethora collaboration. Because of that, other people were brought in by Cambiogen to take on that role and that has worked out quite well. So I don't think we have lost out at all. (Rand, Plethora, March 1998)

It is hard to see how we have lost out. Certainly, the key players have been present throughout and have more or less been there all the time. Their overall responsibilities have become broader and they are not solely focused on the Plethora alliance but have taken on, and trained, new people. (Green, Plethora, March 1998)

In contrast to the involvement of new individuals at the operational level, which seems to have had little influence on the cooperative relationship, a more significant change was generated through the active involvement of Roderick Appleyard, Head of Microbiology at Plethora, in late 1997. Appleyard contributed an unusual degree of boldness and resourcefulness to an otherwise conservatively minded Plethora crew. Given Plethora's continued dominance in setting objectives and determining research approaches, his influence on the steering group opened up new avenues for doing research in legitimizing non-traditional, riskier approaches to mastering this difficult scientific area. As one Cambiogen scientist explained:

A positive turning point, I think, was when Roderick Appleyard joined. I noticed that prior to that point it was a very conservative group in terms of the selection of targets and the kinds of approaches that were taken. When he joined the group there was more of an opportunity to take risks and go for some of the new approaches and technologies, new solutions to the problem. I think that marked kind of a change in the relationship . . . It kind of got us where we are today . . . a lot of novel approaches that we would not have taken in the past. (Copeland, Cambiogen, January 1999)

Almost as important was the departure of Cambiogen's Bill Schmier, in October 1997.

He was, to some extent, disruptive in not being a team player but an agenda setter, right in the middle of meetings. He didn't sit down and build strategy, but came with an agenda which was totally unexpected and diverted the meetings not in the most positive way. (Pirsig, Cambiogen, April 1999)

Prior to another high profile collaboration in late 1997, with Monsanto, Schmier had been actively involved in the steering group. However, given his much increased responsibilities after the highly public Monsanto alliance, he proved less helpful and less able to help coordinate the collaboration. 'It was time for him to move on,' suggested Green, reflecting the opinion of several steering group members at each partner organization.

Perhaps the most significant event in the collaborative relationship was the painful delay in negotiating the last two-year extension. Although the social makeup of the project group remained mostly intact (bar the recent move of Gray), Cambiogen's perception of the Plethora collaborators changed quite dramatically during this six-month process. It became increasingly apparent that the ultimate control of the collaboration, and the decision to recommit to it, lay firmly with Plethora (US), leaving individuals at Plethora's UK subsidiary (the 'real' partner for all practical purposes) effectively disarmed.

We have worked hard to try and regain that same level of trust that we had before the negotiations, and I am not sure you can ever get back to that level, especially when something has been that much of a trauma for people . . . It was a significant part of people's lives. I understand that Grahame [Plethora] was really, really exhausted at the end of it. And so was Anna [Cambiogen]. You can't put people through something like that and then expect people to return to a normal relationship. That just doesn't happen. (Gray, Cambiogen, May 1999)

Despite a significant toll on the morale of, particularly, the Cambiogen collaborators, the merger and takeover did not significantly alter the strategic rationale or operating rules of the alliance. At least, these events did little to delay the working relationship. This does not, however, imply that the individuals involved in the collaborative research cannot influence its evolutionary potential and effectiveness. The involvement of Roderick Appleyard (Plethora), for instance, encouraged the joint team to pursue more innovative ways in anti-fungal research. Likewise, Bill Schmier (Cambiogen) failed to function well within the steering group and temporarily constrained its potential. Finally, Robert Gray (initially with Plethora and later with Cambiogen) served a crucial role as a liaison between the partner organizations throughout the months of uncertainty whilst Plethora (US) was reworking the extension agreement.

Although one might expect individuals at Plethora to bond less quickly with Cambiogen scientists than with those at Rummidgen, given the sheer physical distance between them, the converse appears to have happened. Whereas the Rummidgen collaboration was channelled primarily through two individuals, the Cambiogen alliance was designed to be more transparent, through regular videoconferencing and multiple individuals interacting simultaneously. Besides, individuals at both Plethora and Cambiogen interacted much more frequently at a social level than did their counterparts at Rummidgen. 'Within the Cambiogen alliance, people are constantly thinking, "What can we do outside of the steering group level?"' (Green, Plethora, May 1999), and subsequent social activities included various exotic dinners and sporting events.

Contribution and performance

Given the sheer unpredictability of drug discovery, performance measurement is usually shrouded in ambiguity. Measures of alliance success appear to have been of two types. First, performance was measured against specific targets set at the beginning of every year and subsequently reassessed and reprioritized on a quarterly basis. By far the clearest indicator of success would have been the identification of an anti-fungal lead compound. More than four years of collaborative research, however, failed to come up with a good candidate drug.

As for technical milestones, many but not all were met. Rapid advances in biotechnologies, genetics, and genomics appear to have rendered several targets obsolete before their due date.

Have all milestones been met? If you look at the original work plan, no, they haven't been met. If we had met all of these milestones set four years ago, we wouldn't be doing the most sensible things now. (Green, Plethora, March 1998)

I guess if I was to look at what we are doing now versus what we wrote in the proposal initially, then I think the original plan now probably contributes 20 per cent of the total work...So we've continuously adapted things. (Gray, Cambiogen, May 1999)

It is perhaps not surprising that the collaboration took off in directions that could hardly have been anticipated during the negotiations in early 1995.

If you roll back the clock and ask what did people expect to get from it when it started compared with what they actually got, it may be that they haven't. Given the sheer number or the nature of the things that have been discovered, their expectations have not been completely met. But in a different sense their expectations have been fully met because there are a number of highly technical difficulties that needed to be overcome and were overcome in a very professional way. Even though it may not necessarily give you what you expected, your respect for that partner is substantially increased. You realize that if you are going to work with anybody in this field, these are the people you should be working with. (Ridley, Cambiogen, June 1998)

The latter part of this observation incidentally also sums up Plethora's assessment of the cooperative relationship. In the absence of having achieved the overriding strategic objective, its twofold extension was rationalized in part by Cambiogen having successfully performed a number of screens and, to a significant extent, the achievement of much less tangible measures of performance. This was perhaps a success of different sorts.

There are multiple definitions of success. How well do people work together? Have you worked together to solve problems? Are you both committed to the end point? Are you both taking responsibility for getting to that point? Is there open communication? Do you trust each other? Those sorts of things. (Green, Plethora, March 1998)

Cambiogen has alliances with ten different companies ... Out of those ten, we probably think of the Plethora anti-fungal relationship as our best collaborative relationship, in the sense that the team work ... is strong, the coincidence of opinions on what needs to be done, it has been a very good cooperative dealing ... If you were to ask people which alliance they enjoy most, quite a few will say the Plethora relationship. (Ridley, Cambiogen, June 1998)

In fact, some scientists identified so strongly with the research programme that the quest for an anti-fungal 'superdrug' became a personal one, as one scientist illustrated:

One of the bad things is that we haven't succeeded, that we haven't come forward with more targets – this is a kind of personal defeat for me personally. I want to succeed. I want to come up with something that will help the relationship. (Copeland, Cambiogen, January 1999)

Although not all targets (or technical milestones) were met throughout the joint programme, many routes of inquiry were eliminated as a result. Within a predominantly Popperian research tradition, this is quite acceptable, as scientific knowledge is thought to progress largely incrementally by disconfirming hypotheses. Thus, when viewed in a learning sense, the collaboration was undeniably successful.

We've combed through all the traditional areas of fungal research. We have visited those pretty thoroughly, eliminating many paths of inquiry. The initial assumptions were that if we were to revisit some of these areas, perhaps with additional knowledge on the genetic side and some target validation knowledge, and bring in the novelty of the Plethora library to some of the targets, that we would succeed. I think that assumption was wrong. (Copeland, Cambiogen, January 1999)

If you come out of the collaboration with more knowledge than you had when you went in, even if you haven't achieved the objective, the alliance may still have been successful . . . Even if you have learned how not to do something – it is learning that renders it successful. (Green, Plethora, March 1998)

It has been successful in the sense of having learned a hell of a lot about target discovery and some new technologies . . . It has really made us competitive . . . whereas without them we wouldn't be. (Amis, Plethora, June 1998)

Plethora came to appreciate the benefits of flexibility and speed of response, facilitated by a relatively flat managerial hierarchy and an entrepreneurial spirit. It successfully internalized some of Cambiogen's genetic technologies. Cambiogen, on the other hand, learned to be more pragmatic, and less driven purely by intellectual curiosity, in its target selection.

In contrast to the Rummidgen alliance, the relatively stable evolutionary trajectory of the collaboration can be explained threefold. First, the nature of the deliverables sought at Cambiogen was very different from those pursued at Rummidgen. Rather than Plethora dictating objectives to its biotech partner, Plethora and Cambiogen *together* reached consensus on worthwhile pursuits. Second, as this process generated multiple projects within the same collaboration it served as a levelling device on its evolutionary path and performance, as disappointment with one project could often be offset against success in another. Third, in stark contrast to the Rummidgen alliance, this particular collaboration was not felt to be competing with any in-house research unit. Rather, it was in Mark Amis's own interests that this Cambiogen alliance should succeed, for any accomplishments would produce new work for his in-house chemistry group. The two complemented each other far better than the Rummidgen alliance ever did.

Coevolution of partner firms

The coevolution of the biotech partner, from Myco to ChemAnalysis to Cambiogen Pharmaceuticals, is clearly one of the more unusual features of this case. It has been described in some detail and further elaboration is probably unnecessary. Plethora's recent marketing of Pipfler, the hugely successful angina drug, seems not to have had quite the same impact on the alliance as it had for Rummidgen, except in raising expectations for future drugs, including anti-fungals. Cambiogen gained in credibility as a biotech partner to the pharmaceutical industry. It successfully negotiated at least four major alliances since its involvement with Plethora, all of which easily outstrip the Plethora alliance in size. 'We are getting better at it,' declared one Cambiogen scientist, 'we're not rookies anymore.'

The most significant threat to a continuation of the collaboration was Plethora's delay in agreeing to an extension of the collaboration. This appears to have been caused in large measure by its fear of creating in Cambiogen a powerful future competitor, particularly given the latter's explicitly stated objective of becoming a fully fledged pharmaceutical. Even if an extension had failed to materialize, Cambiogen would have retained certain rights to using the technologies and targets developed during the collaboration, whether unaccompanied or in collaboration with another pharmaceutical.

If Plethora had not renewed the collaboration, we [Cambiogen] would have been in a position to just pursue it [anti-fungal research] as aggressively as we can with any company... We would have walked away with all the targets, all the screens, everything in our hands. (Pirsig, Cambiogen, April 1999)

This anxiety, combined with the awareness that Plethora stood to lose the product of more than four years of joint learning about anti-fungal research, eventually persuaded Plethora that the potential benefits of extending the project were worth the risks. Indeed, transcript profiling currently appears to be yielding results in terms of target discovery and provides exciting avenues for taking the cooperative programme forwards until its next deadline. Indeed, as discussed with Cambiogen, unless the collaboration produces a promising lead compound, it will be terminated at that time.

Thematic discussion

As before, the process of reconstructing this alliance generated a number of observations on its evolution, social makeup, performance and success, as discussed here.

Evolution

When Plethora negotiated a joint research programme into anti-fungals with Myco Pharmaceuticals, it could not have foreseen the merger with

ChemAnalysis and subsequent takeover by Cambiogen Pharmaceuticals. The evolution of this particular alliance would have been difficult to predict. This unpredictability was augmented by the rapid scientific advances in genetic and genomic technologies, the sheer difficulty of doing anti-fungal research, and, more broadly, the serendipity of drug discovery.

Success

Equally unpredictable appears the eventual success of this joint programme. Significantly, it was deemed to be successful without having accomplished its central objective. In as opportune an environment as biotechnology, confirmed 'cul-de-sacs' (hypotheses that were tested but rejected) are considered relevant and indicative of success. Moreover, learning about new approaches to research and to the challenges of collaborating, as well as the transfer of knowledge on specific genetic and genomic capabilities, can form a yardstick for measuring success and failure. This is in addition to the agreeableness and effectiveness of day-to-day working relationships.

Change and reaction

As illustrated in Figure 4.2, changes in any one of the four institutionalized features of this alliance may occasionally trigger retaliatory or compensatory changes in others. For example, what started out as a molecular biology programme into anti-fungal research expanded to incorporate chemistry capabilities and, once more, to include genetic and genomic technologies. Even if the merger had but a relatively marginal effect on the alliance, the subsequent takeover by Cambiogen proved far more consequential. Indeed, without it the collaboration might well have turned into a stalemate scenario with little incentive to continue. Both partners had exhausted their range of technologies, and executed every possible experiment, with no lead candidate in sight. Cambiogen, as a 'white knight', came in useful, by providing access to a new set of capabilities and vastly different approaches to doing research. Thus, each of these events involved a change in the social makeup of the alliance (the *who*), which subsequently prompted complementary (rather than retaliatory) changes in its activities (the *what*) and research approach (the *how*).

Second, the merging of two distinct organizational cultures and the access to new sets of technologies opened up new avenues for anti-fungal research. Although Plethora acknowledged that Cambiogen is a very different company from Myco, they agreed to extend the collaboration twice, and neither its continuation nor its performance appears to have been constrained.

Third, in stark contrast to the Plethora and Rummidgen research programme, the alliance with Cambiogen complemented, rather than competed with, one of Plethora's in-house chemistry groups. Ironically, Mark Amis was closely involved in each. In fact, it was in Amis's own interests that this Cambiogen alliance should succeed, as any learning or lead compounds would transfer directly to his in-house chemistry group for optimization. As before, one sees how human agency may be able to exercise a quite significant impact on an interfirm relationship. A change in the social makeup of this particular alliance, with the involvement of Roderick Appleyard, legitimized and empowered a bolder approach to risk taking in target identification. This, in turn, informed structure by changing the risk profile of some of the targets pursued within the joint programme. Interestingly, Mark Amis's attitude towards the Cambiogen alliance contrasts sharply with that towards Rummidgen. To help contribute to the success of the collaboration made a great deal of sense, as any compounds resulting from the alliance fed directly into his chemistry facility. Amis's championing of this particular alliance is legitimized by this complementarity. Further, individuals at Plethora seem to have relied on the fiercely competitive context of drug discovery research to mediate their actions. Faced with Cambiogen's rapid expansion as a biopharmaceutical firm, senior Plethora managers seemed reluctant to extend the collaboration, apparently concerned that they might help create yet another competitor in an already very competitive industry.

Finally, the narrative provides examples of other tacitly held structures that actors rely upon to inform their interactions. Those particular to this case included certain interpretative schemes (e.g. taking your partner's proclamations with a 'grain of salt'), moral codes of conduct (e.g. relying on a 'gentlemen's agreement'), and resources (e.g. Plethora as the 'sugar daddy' of this programme). However, though they may draw on these institutions, they need not be constrained by them, as Cambiogen's decision to hire two Plethora scientists serves to demonstrate.

Industry context

The case illustrates the impact of a rapidly evolving science. Although the overarching objective remained unchanged throughout the documented four-and-a-half-year period, the individual targets (sometimes referred to as 'technical milestones') set at the beginning of every year became repeatedly outdated and had to be renegotiated at quarterly steering group meetings. Their short shelf-life, and the sheer difficulty of anti-fungal research, added to the complexity of performance assessments.

Social makeup

Although the network of collaborating individuals expanded with the merger and takeover, this appears to have had little influence on the relationship. This apparent stability might reasonably be explained by the conscious efforts of both organizations to preserve the core group of collaboration scientists and, when these were gradually assigned larger responsibilities, have them introduce and train others to take over some of the operational elements. One exception was the active participation of Roderick Appleyard, a senior Plethora scientist, who, by virtue of his influence on the steering group, helped move the collaboration towards riskier and more innovative approaches. The introduction of a new actor (the *who*) resulted in new approaches to joint research (the *how*). Hence, although a change in its social makeup can trigger retaliatory changes in other institutionalized practices, this clearly need not be the case.

Legitimacy

A strategic alliance with the reputed pharmaceutical Plethora provided Myco Pharmaceuticals, a biotech startup, with a route towards legitimacy within the industry. In this respect, it is little wonder that ChemAnalysis (previously Myco) proved an attractive takeover target to Cambiogen Pharmaceuticals, as the merger included the active participation within an ongoing Plethora alliance.

We will compare Cambiogen's experiences with those of Rummidgen in Chapter 6.

5 Through the looking glass 3: Bionatura and Pflegum Courtal
1992–9

It is in the lap of the gods as to whether, in that large reservoir of natural products, there happens to be one so effective against biological targets that it goes on to become a drug.

(Annan, Bionatura, April 1998)

When, in the early 1980s, Pflegum Courtal decided that drug discovery using natural chemicals was a technology of the past, the firm followed in the footsteps of rival firms by divesting its natural products chemistry division. When, a decade later, several pharmaceuticals once again turned to natural chemistry discovery in search of novel drugs, Pflegum Courtal sought to establish a research-focused alliance with a biotech firm, through its research division Proton, so as to regain a foothold in a type of chemistry that searches for drug candidates using natural products alone. Nature, it is thought, contains the necessary remedies to fight everyday diseases – one merely has to locate the right compounds for the right disease targets. Natural products chemistry is thus fundamentally different from the more common synthetic chemistry, whereby chemical compounds are tailor-made in laboratories. At the time, Bionatura was one such company amongst various other providers, including PanLabs, MycoSearch, Amgen and in-house departments at Glaxo, SmithKline Beecham, Merck and Pfizer. As collaborating with another major pharmaceutical seemed unattractive, Bionatura emerged as a leading candidate given its advanced edge natural products chemistry capabilities and its dire need for financial resources.

Whilst an initial four-year collaboration agreement was signed with Bionatura Discovery on 1 January 1992, negotiations began as early as 1990, with some joint work on AIDS as a drug target towards the end of 1991. As explained by a member of the negotiating team:

If we wait for our lawyers to get everything done, it [the collaboration] can die on the vine – the project can become old before the papers are signed. What we do is make reversible contributions that would not be devastating in any case,

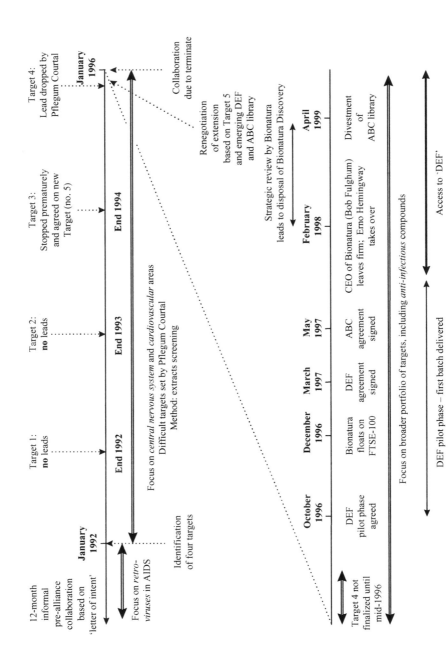

Figure 5.1: Chronology of the Bionatura–Pflegum Courtal alliance: 1991–9

that are necessary for the well-being of the project and get the project started, so that we're scientifically ready to roll as soon as the papers are signed. (Boteach, Proton, May 1998)

This pre-alliance joint focus on retro-viruses in AIDS, based solely on a 'letter of intent', was altered to cardiovascular targets and the central nervous systems (CNS), which were to be screened against Bionatura's ABC library, upon formalizing the agreement. The original four-year contract was structured around four specific screens, approximately one for each year of the collaboration, and called for Proton to pay Bionatura on a per-screen basis. Neither the first nor second target resulted in the identification of a lead compound. The fourth was plagued by operational difficulties. Research towards the third target, in early 1994, started off well but the effort was abandoned by Proton and replaced by a fifth target, for reasons that were never entirely clear to individuals at Bionatura. Musil, Bionatura's Head of Research, comments:

I think they had lost faith in that target and wanted to change their minds and do something else in place of that to complete it. So we went out of the bounds of the initial contract, if you like, to allow a fifth target to replace that. So we were quite flexible about that. (Musil, Bionatura, April 1998)

Bionatura's resilience was tested yet again when, in early 1995, Proton became more interested in anti-bacterial targets and asked Bionatura to screen one of their bacterial enzyme targets in place of the fourth, and problematic, target agreed upon at the formation of the alliance. By the time negotiations began for an eighteen-month extension, in late 1995, the collaboration had failed to deliver any of the sought-after lead compounds and Bionatura barely broke even on the financial arrangement. A potential compound, named AM-DB7, had emerged from the last screen but, despite having demonstrated anti-bacterial activity, was abandoned by Proton, as it was apparently not potent enough, could not be optimized, and was insufficiently selective. Pflegum Courtal's research division, however, did state that it was willing to escalate its commitment, based partly on its amicable working relationship with Bionatura over the past three years but, perhaps more significantly, on the 'proof of principle' established by the discovery of the AM-DB7 compound. As commented by a senior scientist at Bionatura:

Had this compound not been discovered, it is doubtful that the alliance would have been extended. Evelyn Murdoch [Pflegum Courtal's commercial director for licensing, alliances, and outsourcing] told me as much. (Annan, Bionatura, 23 June 1999)

Despite disappointing results, the partners agreed to an eighteen-month extension period, but on very different terms. Whereas Bionatura effectively tried repeating (or reproducing) the 1992–6 collaboration agreement, Proton (Pflegum Courtal) insisted on putting the ABC library through a much larger number of screens without having to pay on a per-screen basis (as was the case in the original agreement). Under these new operating rules, Proton was to be supplied with a library of natural product samples, which they could put through an unspecified number of screens in-house, in parallel with their own library of synthetic chemicals.

In contrast to synthetic discovery processes, natural products chemistry suffers from unusually long lead times. In the absence of purified natural chemicals, natural products chemistry uses a selection of organisms to create broths to test for biological activity. When such activity is observed, a lengthy process of de-replication and purification then seeks to link this activity to one particular compound that can be isolated and replicated. However, the average two- to three-year lead times became increasingly unacceptable to the pharmaceutical industry in general, and Proton (Pflegum Courtal) in particular. As explained by the two most senior scientists, one from each partner organization:

There had been all sorts of technology developments in the area of high throughput screening, screening hundreds of thousands of samples in a very short time frame. To have to wait months or years to find out what these active compounds are is not what people want to do anymore. And this rang home to us not only by Proton, but by other collaborators and potential collaborators as well. (Musil, Bionatura, April 1998)

Bionatura has been forced through our pressure and others to adopt a style of research that is now competitive with those other tools that are now available. I think people are still genuinely interested in natural products. But it's got to be done in a way that is competitive and early enough in a project to have an impact. (Boteach, Proton, May 1998)

Under pressure to compete with synthetic and combinatorial chemistry processes, Bionatura, in mid-1996, increased its efforts to develop a technology, using existing capabilities and resources, to significantly shrink lead times and reduce costs. Proton proved instrumental in this search by suggesting the development of a purified library of compounds as a by-product of natural products discovery processes. The resultant library became known as DEF, and contained a collection of purified natural chemicals that could be screened rapidly alongside synthetic libraries, enabling the screening process to proceed faster and more efficiently. The

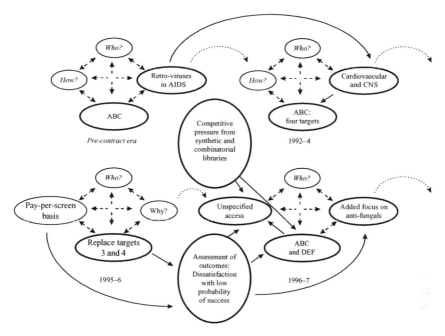

Figure 5.2: Evolution: 1991–7

project's £10 million price tag was designed to be funded by a consortium of four pharmaceuticals, to reduce the cost of access to each.

You've got a project that you think will revolutionize the way natural products is done, but it is expensive and you are a small company. You go to your partners and say, 'Look, you've got a long-term vested interest in natural products. Will you be interested in investing in this as a consortium if we bring down the cost to you to 25 or 20 per cent of the total?' And this is what we did. (Annan, Bionatura, April 1998)

Both Pflegum Courtal and rival pharmaceutical Pharmagen took advantage of this opportunity, contributing about £2 million each in equity, though Bionatura's CEO, Bob Fulghum, tried repeatedly, but without success, to increase Pflegum Courtal's contribution. As explained by his colleague:

I believe Proton was very active in developing our DEF concept. But what they weren't quite so forthcoming about was funding it as intensively as we would have liked. We did ask them initially for quite a bit more money than they agreed to provide, so we are still not out of the woods funding this project, by a long way. But I think the project exists because of Proton. (Annan, Bionatura, April 1998)

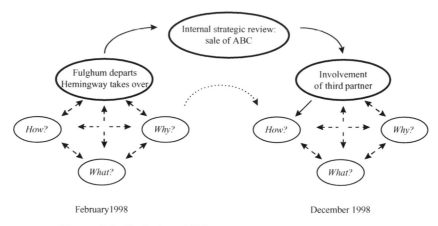

February 1998   December 1998

Figure 5.3: Evolution: 1998

A DEF pilot phase contract was agreed upon in October 1996 and called for isolating 500 DEF compounds from a sample of seventy micro-organisms and thirty plant-extracts within 210 days. Beating this deadline by two months, the pilot batch was successfully delivered by Bionatura and a formal DEF agreement signed, in March 1997, with Pflegum Courtal (Proton) and, soon afterwards, with rival firm Pharmagen. The ABC agreement was extended in May 1997, for the second time, for another eighteen months. The alliance now consisted of a two-tier structure, featuring two collaboration agreements that ran in parallel, though DEF's increasing popularity soon rendered it responsible for the bulk of all inter-partner transactions, with the ABC project accounting for the remainder. More recently, however, following a strategic review during 1998 by Bionatura, instigated by its new CEO, Erno Hemingway, the further development and manufacture of its DEF library were scaled back.

By December 1998, the cooperative relationship had been extended twice, had evolved into a two-tier collaboration based on distinct technologies, and was viewed as largely successful by both partners. Yet the collaboration had failed dismally in generating tangible accomplishments, bar two joint publications and two joint patent applications as a result of the 1992–6 period. Cooperation appears to have been sustained for well over seven years (eight years, when including the pre-contract collaborations), primarily as a result of Bionatura's unique natural chemistry capabilities, Proton's felt need to access such technologies, mutual respect, strong interpersonal relationships between collaborating individuals, and the hope that the discovery of a lead compound was just around the corner.

Who, why, what, how?

As with the previous two case studies, the discussion that follows expounds on the narrative. It extensively uses verbatim statements by those closely involved with the collaboration to illustrate the felt experiences by many, rather than merely the unique experiences of the individual.

Strategic rationale

When several major pharmaceuticals, including Pharmagen and Pflegum Courtal, sought to reverse their decision, in the 1980s, to diversify out of natural products chemistry, an alliance with Bionatura appeared an excellent strategy to regain a foothold in this technology. It would provide access to natural products capabilities without necessitating large, and largely irreversible, resource commitments. This overarching strategic justification for the collaboration has remained unchanged, namely to find a lead compound using natural products chemistry technologies that Pflegum Courtal can develop and take into clinical trials. As explained by the pharmaceutical:

That's why we're here . . . There has been a flagging interest in natural products. I think there may be opportunities that exist that other companies might miss due to the difficulty of doing natural products discovery . . . Half of Merck's income comes from natural products discovery compounds, even though 10 per cent of their research money goes into that . . . That [the Merck experience] played a big part in our decision. (Boteach, Proton, May 1998)

There are a further two issues worth considering when examining Pflegum Courtal's strategic interests. First, the most senior scientist at Proton, Stephen Boteach, had previously been employed at the pharmaceutical giant, Merck. Merck is relatively unique within the pharmaceutical industry in that it has successfully taken several highly profitable drugs to market, all of which were derived from natural products chemistry discovery. Merck, in the 1940s, was the first company to bring an effective natural-products-based drug to market – Streptomycin, a drug designed to combat tuberculosis. It was discovered in the infected gizzard of a chicken that had died of the disease. Merck scientist Selman Waksman, who discovered the compound, spoke in defence of natural products chemistry when accepting the Nobel Prize in 1952. In his acceptance speech, he paraphrased a verse from the Biblical book of Ecclesiastes: 'Out of the earth shall come thy salvation' (Werth 1994). Unsurprisingly, therefore, Boteach remained a firm defender of natural products chemistry. His confidence in natural products discovery, despite its relatively low success rate, appears to have played a significant part in justifying the alliance to the parent, Pflegum Courtal.

Second, Pflegum Courtal's strategic interest in Bionatura's capabilities appeared ratified, not unlike Pfizer's, by a real options approach to drug discovery alliances. As suggested by one of the negotiators:

All the drug business is a gamble. You are served with a budget . . . where do you put it? What are your best bets? (Boteach, Proton, May 1998)

Such a predatory approach is not at all uncommon in biopharmaceutical research and, if anything, reflects the inherent serendipity of the drug discovery enterprise.

The four targets given to Bionatura at the start of the collaboration had essentially been those that Proton had previously been unsuccessful with. It was understood by both partners that these were difficult targets and, hence, it was not entirely surprising that Bionatura's efforts proved equally dismal. However, the low probability of successful discovery, combined with comparatively long lead times using its proprietary ABC library, became increasingly unattractive to Pflegum Courtal.

It is an expensive collaboration and we need to get something worthwhile out of it. I was under the impression in our first round of studies, as we basically got nothing that generated a programme out of it, that we really had to change our format, because it was clear that we could not go on in the format we used. (Boteach, Proton, May 1998)

Forced to compete with synthetic and combinatorial chemistry discovery processes, and to increase the probability of success in discovery, Bionatura and Proton proceeded together, in mid-1996, to develop the DEF concept. This proved perhaps one of the most significant joint efforts in a relationship which otherwise remained dominated by the pharmaceutical partner. Using a consortium strategy, Bionatura was able to reduce the initial investment to its partners to 20 per cent of the £10 million set-up cost, though it was never able to attract the two additional partners to Pflegum Courtal and Pharmagen, required to recoup the investment.

In sum, the joint research programme coevolved within, and responded to, the dynamics of a very competitive environment, as well as the changing needs of its partner organization. It developed the DEF library in an effort to remain competitive. Bionatura was flexible in allowing its pharmaceutical partner to deviate from previously agreed-upon targets. The now two-tier cooperative relationship has moved concurrently beyond its initial focus on cardiovascular and CNS targets to include anti-infectious diseases as a target group; a focus which it retains today, alas, still without any palpable accomplishments.

Operating rules

The actual cooperative relationship, based on a 'letter of intent', was started well before any contractually binding agreement existed. When a subsequent contract was agreed, it stipulated four screens to be performed by Bionatura on a pay-per-screen basis, with significant downstream rights to royalties for Bionatura if any of the screens produced a compound that subsequently became a drug. Lured by the prospects of vast fortunes, Bionatura, by January 1992, had ambitiously negotiated the marketing rights in Europe for any potential drugs, at the expense of larger cash payments up-front. The disappointment experienced by both partners during the first collaborative period (1992–6) caused Proton to be dissatisfied with the small probability of discovery provided by the very limited number of screens Bionatura could perform, and faced Bionatura with the financial consequences of barely breaking even on their cash receipts from Proton. Whilst negotiating the first extension of the joint programme, Proton, in late 1995, pressured its biotech partner to vastly increase the probability of success in discovery through the development of the DEF concept, allowing the pharmaceutical to run this library of purified natural products complementary to its synthetic library. Bionatura, in a notable change of negotiating tactics, now demanded more cash up front and fewer royalties on successfully identified compounds. As it explained:

The thinking at Bionatura has changed since the early days. Bionatura would much rather have a little bit more up front and not be too worried about the downstream rights. (Musil, Bionatura, April 1998)

Constrained by a lack of resources, the biotech firm was forced to become more short-term focused and sacrificed potentially high, but uncertain, returns on successful drugs for the security of having sufficient resources to fund its operations.

In contrast to this post-1996 change in its operating rules, allowing Proton to run an unlimited number of screens from an ABC library sample, the governance structure of the alliance remained unaffected. As with most joint programmes, a steering group, including senior members from both organizations, was set up to review progress and prioritize activities on a six-monthly basis. These meetings alternated between the UK, where Bionatura was based, and the USA, home to the pharmaceutical. Much more frequent communications took place using Internet-based technologies. A secure interpartner database system, used for transmitting details of chemical structures and sensitive information about specific targets, was made accessible through the Internet. Additionally, telephone conference calls between the partner organizations were loosely scheduled on an as-needed basis, and communications remained relatively informal throughout the seven-year period. Internally, Bionatura met regularly, on a monthly basis, to review progress and update its scientists on new developments with respect to the joint programme.

Both partners appear to have valued the flexibility of the working relationship, as is evident in their tolerance when agreed-upon deadlines proved difficult to meet. Although evidence of Proton's failure to strictly adhere to the agreement is quite easily identifiable (e.g. the pharmaceutical twice changed its mind on a target and exceeded the quantity of chemical samples provided and DEF quota on several occasions), Bionatura also admits to a leniency in meeting deadlines.

Time lines have always been pretty 'bungee-like', from their point of view and ours. They have been late in delivering assays and we have accommodated that... They changed horses from screen 3 to screen 5 for some deprioritization we didn't understand, and we produced the same work for the new project as we would have done for the old project had it continued. (Annan, Bionatura, April 1998)

Similar views were entertained towards performance measurement, for neither firm appeared keen on tallying debits and credits in any formalized manner. Put bluntly by the director of licensing and collaborations at the pharmaceutical parent firm, 'Nobody is counting... These are not things we pay attention to.' This view was reiterated by a senior Proton scientist:

The whole purpose of the agreement is to have a successful collaboration and to have something worthwhile. No one is going to be rewarded for just ticking items off a list. It is discovery which is going to make things worthwhile. That really drives the collaboration. (Boteach, Proton, May 1998)

Of course, when one appears the main beneficiary of a collaborative relationship, as seemed the case with Pflegum Courtal, it would seem less important, perhaps even counter-productive, to produce formalized assessments of fairness in terms of an equitable apportioning of resource commitments, risks, and rewards. The felt asymmetry by Bionatura, primarily in terms of its inability to negotiate more favourable financial terms and Proton's ability to manipulate the agreed-upon content of the relationship, has already been addressed and merits little more discussion. They are relatively well reflected in the following comments by scientists from both organizations.

Our pain would be the lack of what we would have discovered had we stayed with them... who knows what that is... maybe it's nothing. They are going to be missing one of their major corporate partners and reasonable source of support and the prospect of a drug candidate if anything comes out of this . . . the big thing for them is that it is notoriously bad to announce the end of a collaboration with someone who has been a major partner. (Boteach, Proton, May 1998)

We would obviously be gutted if they [Pflegum Courtal] decided not to continue with us. (Atkinson, Bionatura, May 1998)

Social makeup

The alleged 'success' of the cooperative relationship was due in part to a strong and enduring interpersonal chemistry between collaborating scientists. Individuals continued to operate as if within the same organization, expressing a shared identity and sense of ownership in the collaboration. Said one junior bench scientist:

I really like working with them. When phoning them up it is just like phoning someone within Bionatura. They are very open about things and very keen to get our input into what we think about samples going through and stuff. (Atkinson, Bionatura, May 1998)

And elaborated upon by the Director of Alliances and Licensing at Pflegum Courtal:

Even if there is a coincidence in the scientific interest, if there isn't good interpersonal chemistry, it is going to be doomed to failure. You cannot stress that enough. In all the collaborations that we have had that have been successful, this is one of the unifying themes. (Murdoch, Pflegum Courtal, April 1998)

It is perhaps significant, therefore, that the relationship appears to have remained stable despite the departure, and subsequent replacement, of several key individuals. For instance, towards the end of 1992, Jerry Burn, a bench scientist, left Bionatura, to be replaced as the 'gatekeeper' of the alliance by Jack Tolkien. Tolkien was subsequently replaced in late 1994 by Bob Musil, when the former was promoted to Head of Pharmacology within Bionatura. Neither departure seems to have had a very significant effect on the continuity of the joint programme. This could, however, have been the consequence of deliberate attempts by Bionatura to preserve these interpersonal relationships as much as possible. Tolkien remained a guest at the dinner table at steering group meetings, even though he no longer had any formal role in the alliance. Such practices may well have helped provide a sense of continuity for those individuals most intimately involved with the alliance.

Further, one might have expected the unexpected departure of Bob Fulghum (Bionatura's founder and CEO, who was quickly replaced by Erno Hemingway), in February 1998, to have impacted more significantly on the alliance than it did. As Musil explains: 'He was the founder of Bionatura...And to a lot of people in the pharmaceutical industry, Bionatura and Fulghum were the same thing.' Fulghum, however, had assumed responsibility primarily for the commercial aspects of the collaboration and, having detached himself from its day-to-day operations, had become irrelevant to the daily life of the alliance. This indeed may well be the most plausible explanation for the apparent lack of impact caused by the departure of so senior a manager. Moreover, and more subtly, Fulghum may not be sorely missed. At least not from Pflegum Courtal's point of view. The following comments, contributed by a senior manager inside the pharmaceutical parent, are telling:

He was a real pain in the neck . . . He always wanted more money. We call him 'the whiner' and I am very happy we don't have to deal with him anymore. He was just constantly whining . . . He was quite feminine in that way. I really didn't like him . . . One of our secretaries does a wonderful imitation of him because he calls so frequently to whine about why this is not enough . . . oh, it was just pathetic . . . None of us have really bothered to find out why he's gone. (Pflegum Courtal, April 1998)

I always thought he was a bit schizo really. He had a really nasty temper. He could be very nasty; vicious really. I can remember the last conversation I had with him. He accused me of the most vile things. He accused me of lying to him . . . you don't do that sort of thing. (Pflegum Courtal, April 1998)

Such comments also reflect on the different approaches of scientists and business developers towards the core purpose and management of strategic alliances. For instance, these comments were contributed by a senior manager responsible for negotiating the terms of the alliance agreement. His interests were clearly more commercially oriented than would be those of the scientists at Proton, its research division. Whereas Proton's attitude is much more akin to that of a biotech firm, Pflegum Courtal appeared patronizing, even predatory, in its treatment of Bionatura. The following comments may help illustrate this:

You will find, in our agreement, lots of rights – marketing rights – retained by Bionatura. And this is so ridiculous, as if they are ever going to use them . . . We have always tried to limit the damage done by their retained rights . . . and so what we tried to do was put language in the agreement that would say 'OK, you have marketing rights in this country, but only under specific circumstances.' So you set some very high hurdles for them and *hopefully they will never be able to reach them* . . . *We want to keep them out.* We don't want them to be part of our copromotions. (Pflegum Courtal, April 1998)

They are the big guys with the money. We are the little people who are supplying them with a service because we need that money to run our company. (Atkinson, Bionatura, May 1998)

On various occasions, Pflegum Courtal was able to exercise its dominance over Bionatura either by driving a hard bargain or by exploiting the joint research programme. For instance, due to its familiarity and involvement with the development of the DEF library, the pharmaceutical chose to invest only the bare minimum of £2 million, despite repeated attempts by Bionatura to secure more financial support. What is more, although Bionatura would have much preferred cash, and made this clear to its pharmaceutical partner, the investment was paid for in two instalments with equity, on Pflegum Courtal's insistence. Second, Bionatura barely broke even on the initial four-year collaboration while Proton changed two targets on its own initiative. Third, the pharmaceutical was allowed to overrun agreed-upon quotas without penalty, on several occasions. And it admitted as much:

The contract sets certain limits on the number of samples or amounts of materials that should be sent. If we get down to the point where they say 'We already sent you 1 milligram and you cannot have any more,' we would be in big trouble. So we just call up and say 'We are doing this and could you send us more?', and the answer is always 'Yes.' (Boteach, Proton, May 1998)

Despite such concessions being interpreted by Proton as a manifestation of a 'true' and mutually beneficial partnership, there seems little evidence that this attitude is reciprocated. Indeed, although individual scientists appear to have cooperated in an open, affable, equitable, give-and-take manner, the pharmaceutical, backed by its financial muscle, remained the dominant force in negotiating extensions and deciding on major transactions. Recognizing this asymmetry, Annan resolved:

No, I don't think it is symmetrical . . . there have been points in the initial collaboration when we asked for extra money towards a fifth target and it wasn't actually forthcoming. You then have to face a choice: are you going to be flexible to try to nurture the longer term relationship, or do you say no? (Bionatura, April 1998)

A final observation on the social character of the joint programme is perhaps appropriate. It concerns the tendency towards short-term achievements, although these ironically remained absent, due to the personal ambitions and age of at least one of the two most influential individuals. Stephen Boteach, a senior Proton scientist and coordinator of the collaboration, was approaching retirement and appeared less concerned with the long-term consequences of the alliance, in terms of potentially significant royalty payments, than he was with championing short-term results. He himself admitted to this:

Someone ten years down the road has got to worry about royalty payments. I am more interested in having something that is more expensive from a royalty standpoint but is more successful in the short term . . . In ten years I will be sixty-five and off and playing golf somewhere. (Boteach, Proton, May 1998)

Although it would be difficult to argue that the personalities, age, and personal ambitions of collaborating individuals were among the most important elements driving the programme, the data do seem to suggest some degree of influence on its evolution, potential, and effectiveness.

Contribution and performance

Despite efforts to substantially improve the likelihood of discovering a lead compound, the alliance produced few tangible results during its seven-year active existence. During the 1992–6 period, collaborating scientists published two joint scientific papers, and the organizations jointly filed two patent applications. Even if the project generated some interesting chemistry technologies, the natural products lead compound remained markedly absent. The alliance does appear to have been successful on other counts, however, as reflected in observations such as:

We see this as a successful collaboration and I am sure Proton do as well. It is successful to the extent that, first, the project team works seamlessly as a whole... and, second, undoubtedly interesting chemistries come out of the collaboration... It is in the lap of the gods as to whether, in that large reservoir of natural products, there happens to be one so effective against biological targets that it goes on to become a drug. (Annan, Bionatura, April 1998)

The bottom line is finding leads for them. But if you break it down to other objectives within a programme working towards that overall objective then, in terms of building a good working relationship and finding a good way to work with people, thus setting the foundation for finding a lead compound, it has been very successful. (Atkinson, Bionatura, May 1998)

This inherent serendipity was accepted also by Proton.

It is basically a fishing expedition. Our ultimate goal is to get a lead compound into some kind of development... So, in terms of the ultimate payoff, it has not been successful yet. But in terms of the way the collaboration has gone, allowing us to do the fishing, it has worked. You've gone out on a charter boat and they got you into the water and gave you the bait, and you went out there and didn't catch anything. (Allen, Proton, December 1998)

In the absence of a drug candidate, it thus appears that good interpersonal relationships have acted so as to promote continuity by helping to provide the right type of environment in which to identify new drug candidates. In addition to its interpersonal character, the twofold extension of the alliance was motivated primarily by the confidence of Proton in the quality of Bionatura's chemical libraries as well as the chemistry capabilities of its individual scientists, and Bionatura's enduring need for financial resources to continue its operations.

We can get broth samples from others and get a better deal from a financial standpoint, but they are not as astute from a biological standpoint as Bionatura, and don't have the history with us and don't have the ability to work together as well. And all of these things stand for something. (Boteach, Proton, May 1998)

You don't go into drug discovery expecting every screen to be a blockbuster. That is naive. You go into screening expecting that, as Pasteur said, 'Chance favours the prepared mind.' (Annan, Bionatura, April 1998)

A third extension of the ABC collaboration with Proton was announced by Bionatura Discovery in late 1998. Earlier that year, Hemingway, CEO of Bionatura, had initiated a strategic review of all its operations. Upon completion, at around the time of the signing of the extension agreement, Hemingway decided to actively seek partners for, to partially dispose of, or to completely dispose of, two of its subsidiary companies, including its ABC library.[1]

In April 1999, Bionatura Discovery Ltd, having never been a commercial success, was sold to EarthMed Discovery Inc., a Canadian biotech company that specializes in combinatorial biology. The assets transferred to the new owners included the ABC natural products library. As a result, EarthMed became a partner to the Proton collaboration. The two-tier programme became more complex, with the Bionatura Group providing access to the DEF library and EarthMed allowing for screening against the ABC library. Given that the social makeup of the newly acquired Bionatura Discovery was preserved (most scientists transferred with the discovery unit), the involvement of EarthMed appears to have had little significance on the working relationships between collaborating scientists. On an administrative level, however, the (now triadic) alliance has become vastly more complex. Though the Bionatura Group formally provided the DEF library and sat alongside EarthMed on the steering group, the operational management of its DEF facility had essentially been outsourced to EarthMed also. Consequently, from a day-to-day, operational perspective, Bionatura became increasingly less relevant.

Bionatura's disposal of MetaXen and its ABC discovery unit was driven primarily by a need to commercialize the Group and provide much needed cash inflows. As Bionatura failed to attract the two extra partner firms needed to complete the DEF consortium, the development costs of this specialist library had become excessive and drained any available cash reserves. In fact, shortly after the disposal, the Group decided to actively seek a buyer for its DEF library also – a move that would sever all ties to Pflegum Courtal. Informal negotiations took place between Pflegum Courtal and EarthMed for an extension to the ABC agreement,

[1] Chairman and Chief Executive's Statement, 1998 Annual Report, Bionatura Group plc.

but, at the time of writing this case, this appeared contingent on the ability of EarthMed to deliver 'proof of principle' of its unique combinatorial biosynthesis approach to drug discovery. To date, much of EarthMed's work remains confined to the theoretical domain. Given Pflegum Courtal's dissatisfaction with the added administrative complexity to managing two alliance partners, it is somewhat unlikely it will want to continue this relationship. Incidentally, Bob Fulghum, ejected by Bionatura, recently resurfaced in the industry as the founder of Brax, a Cambridge-based biotech startup.

Thematic discussion

As with the previous two case studies, this section makes a number of general observations on the strategic relationship between Bionatura and Proton (Pflegum Courtal).

Evolution

Akin to Plethora's collaborations with Rummidgen and Cambiogen, the alliance between Pflegum Courtal (Proton) and Bionatura evolved quite differently from that anticipated at its formation. The pharmaceutical twice deviated from agreed-upon research targets, added a focus on anti-fungals, and was given access to a new chemical library (DEF) midway through the duration of the relationship.

Longevity

Whether longevity is a useful indicator of success, as suggested by Lynch (1993), is doubtful in the context of the Bionatura experience. Seven years and two contract extensions have passed without generating significant drug candidates. Tallying up the years spent together in research would make the disappointment that much more difficult to digest. But, of course, this is contingent on one's definition of success.

Success

Apparently, an alliance can be deemed successful without having achieved its chief objectives – or even in the absence of any significant tangible accomplishments. During seven years of collaborating, the partner organizations have two joint scientific publications and two joint patents to their name. They have undoubtedly learned from the difficulty of doing natural products research and the rejecting of plausible scientific hypotheses.

Thus, in a Popperian sense one might argue for some degree of achievement. But in so far as the 'proof of the pudding is in the eating', the much sought-after lead compound remains as elusive as it did when the joint programme was first negotiated.

Learning

There appears to be ample evidence of tacit, and often joint, learning by both partners. The optimism of the early 1990s was overshadowed by the realism associated with the sheer difficulty of natural-products-based drug discovery. Dissatisfaction with the pay-per-screen arrangement prompted Pflegum Courtal to insist on a different arrangement, providing a higher probability of success, in its renegotiations with Bionatura. Disappointment with the output of the ABC library forced the partners to look for alternative means to optimizing lead compound discovery processes. The ensuing DEF library was heralded as a breakthrough and came to account for much of the joint efforts until it was realized by both partners that the technology had not only been costly, but was less successful than anticipated. Such developments appear to provide evidence of the tacit, joint learning processes that have characterized this alliance.

Change and reaction

As illustrated in Figures 5.2 and 5.3, changes in any one of the four institutionalized features of this alliance may occasionally have triggered retaliatory or compensatory changes in others. For instance, ongoing assessments of the outcomes of the joint programme after the initial four-year agreement caused Proton (Pflegum Courtal) to be dissatisfied with the low probability of successful discovery and the inability to make more extensive use of Bionatura's ABC library for multiple screens. This dissatisfaction forced the partner firms to renegotiate the operating rules of the collaboration, allowing for multiple screens to be performed on a fixed-fee basis, rather than on a pay-per-screen basis. Further, competitive pressures from synthetic and combinatorial chemistries forced Bionatura to pursue means by which it could remain an attractive alternative to these technologies. The joint development of DEF was a direct response to the call by Pflegum Courtal for greater efficiency, and vastly increased the chances of success in discovering a natural-products-based lead compound. That Proton played a vital role in the development of DEF is indicative of a collaborative research rather than a contract research (or 'fee-for-service') alliance.

However, changes in the social makeup of the alliance, through the departure of Bionatura's CEO Fulghum, and the replacement of the gatekeeper Tolkien, seem to have had little influence on its effectiveness and potential. Partial explanations are the dislike by certain senior Pflegum Courtal managers of Fulghum, and the conscious efforts by Bionatura to keep Tolkien involved in the alliance, albeit primarily at a social level. The latter did help provide a sense of continuity for those involved on either side.

As in the two previous case studies, one may find that individual actors relied on tacit social rules for their sensemaking and to legitimize their actions. For example, given its dissatisfaction with the low probability of success provided by an existing screening arrangement, which, in turn, was ratified within the context of successful alternative chemistry technologies, Proton considered it legitimate to coerce its partner to negotiate more favourable terms for the pharmaceutical. The asymmetrical power relationship between them, with Proton in control of the financial resources, appears to have helped provide it with the dominance it needed to pressure Bionatura into acceptance. Likewise, the ABC project, when evaluated against alternative methods of compound discovery, was seen as increasingly unattractive. Legitimized by the felt pressures of competing technologies, Proton suggested the development of a library of purified compounds (which became the DEF library). This development, in turn, created a two-tier structure within the alliance, based on separate contracts but centred around the same individuals. Finally, the case contains more common examples of such rules, including implicit 'gentlemen's agreements', a Popperian research logic, a real options investment logic, and the legitimizing potential of collaborating with established pharmaceuticals.

Symmetry

This relationship appears to be much less symmetrical than those discussed in the previous two chapters. Pflegum Courtal, given its financial muscle, was clearly able to 'drive a hard bargain' in extension negotiations, and remained dominant throughout the seven-year period. If anything, the absence of a good lead compound appears to have made Bionatura increasingly more dependent on its pharmaceutical partner.

Corporate culture

The attitudes of Proton and its parent company Pflegum Courtal to the alliance are quite different. Pflegum Courtal provided the financial resources for the joint research and its interests were clearly commercial, even predatory. Bionatura was merely seen to be a less expensive and less irreversible alternative to doing natural products chemistry in-house, and Pflegum Courtal appeared more interested in funding the current joint research than providing Bionatura with an opportunity to earn downstream royalties later on in the drug development process.

Proton, though still commercially driven, seems more intellectually curious and creative in seeking to optimize the probability of discovery and assisting in the development of new technologies. Being more academically oriented than would be typical of most pharmaceuticals, its scientists have been able to establish particularly good interpersonal rapport with their Bionatura counterparts.

Legitimacy

For Bionatura, the Proton collaboration appears to have served as a pathway towards legitimacy within the pharmaceutical sector. As with many biotech companies, its reputation as a potential collaborator is vitally important in securing future sources of revenues. It is therefore not surprising that biotech firms are usually more eager than their pharmaceutical partners to get announcements of newly agreed collaborations in the public domain as soon as is possible. By the same token, it is not uncommon for a small biotech firm to assess the commitment of its pharmaceutical partner to an alliance in terms of the time it takes the latter to release the information to the relevant press.

Alliance champions

The narrative draws out the importance of 'alliance champions', senior individuals who act as defenders and sponsors of the joint project within their respective organizations. Stephen Boteach assumed this role within Proton. His personal commitment to natural products chemistry can be traced back to his experiences whilst at rival pharmaceutical Merck, which successfully marketed a number of drugs derived from naturally occurring chemicals.

In this context, it is just as interesting to observe Boteach's apparent interest in achieving short-term results, and his corresponding lack of interest in the long-term consequences of surrendering royalty rights to Bionatura, given his age and personal ambitions. Being relatively close to retirement, the prospect of improving his handicap on the golf course appears to have outweighed any long-term interests in the financial consequences of the joint project. On the other hand, one might argue that commercial negotiations on the rights to intellectual property and down-stream royalties are governed primarily by the parent company, Pflegum Courtal, and hence would be of less interest to Boteach anyway.

Finally, the Bionatura and Pflegum Courtal experience appears to afford empirical support for two previously discussed theoretical perspectives on cooperative strategy. Bionatura's day-to-day operations are financed predominantly by its pharmaceutical partners, without whom it cannot survive. Pflegum Courtal, on the other hand, needs access to natural products chemistry and no longer has these capabilities in-house. This may, in fact, be a good illustration of the *resource-dependence* perspective (Pfeffer and Salancik, 1978).

It is the ultimate prospect of finding that product lead, and really having few other options in terms of this high quality resource to get natural products from. (Boteach, Proton, May 1998)

I think they [. . .] have seen the potential for future targets and do not want to lose their grip on natural products. (Musil, Bionatura, April 1998)

The unique natural chemistry capabilities of Bionatura constituted an imperfectly imitable and imperfectly mobile resource, and, besides providing a strategic justification for forming an alliance from Pflegum Courtal's perspectives, would also seem to provide empirical support for the *resource-based view* (Grant, 1991; Penrose, 1959; Rumelt, 1991; Wernerfelt, 1984).

We will return to these observations in the next chapter, by seeking to compare and contrast the experiences of Rummidgen and Cambiogen with Plethora, and of Bionatura with Pflegum Courtal.

6   Putting two and two together: revisiting theory and practice

This chapter seeks to provide a synthesis of the empirical chapters by means of a cross-case discussion. Chapters 1 and 2 may have generated expectations regarding the empirical work and, more broadly, the contributions of this book. It is thus appropriate that we start with identifying these expectations. These can, in turn, be used as criteria against which to evaluate the cases.

Revisiting the literature

It is important to realize from the outset that the case studies were intended as illustrations, and not as a representative sample (in the statistical sense) from which to draw universal conclusions. In fact, it is imperative that this be realized. While the three narratives perhaps expose limitations to our theories about alliance process, they are insufficient in themselves to produce a new theory. They may, however, be helpful in characterizing such a theory, or in suggesting what the theorizing process might entail. But this is material for the final three chapters.

Whereas Chapter 1 provided a review and brief critique of existing process models, the cases sought to illustrate these by example. In it, I proposed that our intellectual approach to alliances might be characterized by a-priori assumptions of constancy, homogeny, teleology, progress or rationality. I suggested that perhaps our understanding of them might profit from relaxing such expectations. Whilst recognizing that reductionism is part and parcel of explanation, we must be careful not to lose important details in so doing. Reducing alliances to their lowest common denominator risks depriving them of that which gives them their *raison d'être*: the relationships between specific individuals, the collective experience, the transfer of knowledge, the serendipitous discovery of a lead compound, the attainment of legitimacy, and so on. The extent to which the case studies differed may serve to endorse this observation. Strategic alliances, even those characterized by all the 'hard' sciences, remain after all distinctly social phenomena, albeit with a business purpose. Hence, the ensuing cross-case discussion must seek, as best as possible, to avoid any such assumptions.

Chapter 1 also provided a brief review of what appear to be some of the principal theories that help explain cooperative behaviour. Of these theories, six draw from economics and feature primarily in the strategy literature. The remaining four have their basis in sociology and are more prominent in the organization studies literature, although this distinction may be somewhat artificial. These theories were not originally developed to speak to alliances (particularly not their process dynamics) but have nevertheless been found useful in informing alliance research. Having outlined them briefly, the chapter concluded that, despite important merits, many appear overly deterministic and static, acontextual and undersocialized. These conclusions are broadly consistent with those of Child and Faulkner (1998), Das and Teng (2000), Faulkner and de Rond (2000), Gulati (1998) and Sydow and Windeler (1998). A more specific review examined alliance process theories. The most important and robust of these appear to be Ring and van de Ven (1994) and Doz (1996). Without diminishing the value of their contributions, which remain significant, the following discussion will seek to contrast these process frameworks with the empirical data.

Chapter 2 provided a brief introduction to the context of drug discovery. It emphasized the proliferation of alliances in biotechnology, pharmacology, and the life sciences, as well as the inevitable serendipity that continues to characterize it. Thus, the discussion will seek to highlight the influence of context on the evolution of these joint research programmes. Consistent with these expectations, this discussion will commence with a brief summary of the case studies, emphasizing the evolutionary dynamics of these alliances, the unintended consequences of action, and the relevance of context. It proceeds with a cross-case analysis structured along recurring themes in the alliance literature. This perhaps comprises the most substantial section of the chapter, leading us ultimately to restate and revisit a number of questions regarding alliance life.

Revisiting practice

Rummidgen and Plethora

The alliance between the pharmaceutical Plethora and biotech startup Rummidgen did not evolve free of controversy. During the nearly four-year research programme, the strategic justification for the alliance was changed twice. Once this was triggered by the unintended consequences of the marketing of a library of chemical structures by Rummidgen. Had Plethora's US-based negotiator of the alliance agreement not left the firm, the consequences might have been less dramatic, for much of the ensuing intellectual property rights (IPR) battle seems to have arisen from a fundamental misunderstanding of the intentions of the agreement. Further, given that this biochemistry-driven alliance was competing directly with one of Plethora's in-house chemistry units, and that the scientist in charge of this unit was asked to help coordinate the joint programme upon the departure of yet another Plethora manager (based at their UK office), the alliance fell on hard times.

Rummidgen, however, was not alone in suffering the unintended consequences of its actions. When Plethora made an offer of employment to one of its biotech partner's key scientists, trust relationships between collaborating individuals at both firms deteriorated and never quite recovered. Although Plethora alleged it had been acting in good faith, those at the biotech firm felt that a 'gentlemen's agreement' had been violated, and remained appalled at Plethora's defiant attitude. The case also illustrates how a 'fee-for-service' relationship, where trust might appear only moderately important (given its usually straightforward organization), can evolve into a collaborative relationship where objectives and research approaches are decided on jointly – and regress once again into a 'fee-for-service' arrangement, upon the erosion of trust relationships.

Despite having produced many novel chemical compounds, worthwhile strides in the development of combinatorial chemistry technologies, and learning opportunities for both partner firms, the alliance left those most intimately involved in it with mixed feelings about the relationship. The collaboration was not renewed after almost four relatively fertile years, and arguably well before having depleted its potential.

Cambiogen and Plethora

The ongoing alliance between Plethora and Cambiogen produces a quite different account. Although these two relationships overlapped in time, the underlying justification for the Cambiogen collaboration remained the same. This is especially interesting when considering that the biotech partner was subject to a merger *and* acquisition during the life of the alliance. A joint programme focused on fungal research came to include the chemistry capabilities of Perseptive Biosystems upon a merger, one year into the cooperative relationship, to form ChemAnalysis. A year later, ChemAnalysis was acquired by Cambiogen Pharmaceuticals, adding genetic and genomic capabilities to the alliance. Given rapid developments in genomics and genetics, this narrative illustrated the impact of a rapidly advancing scientific environment on an alliance. Ironically perhaps, despite it having failed to generate the sought-after lead compound, it is considered relatively successful by both Plethora and Cambiogen.

Bionatura and Pflegum Courtal

Different again is the account rendered by Bionatura and Pflegum Courtal, a relationship that survived eight years but without having entered a single drug candidate into the pipeline. Centred around a natural products chemical library called ABC, its strategic rationale was extended from a brief pre-alliance focus on retro-viruses in AIDS to a concentration on cardiovascular and CNS disease targets which came to include anti-fungals at the time of the first extension of the collaboration agreement, four years later.

Disappointed with the absence of a lead compound after the initial four-year period, and dissatisfied with the low probability of discovery provided by the current method of investigation, Proton (Pflegum Courtal's pharmaceutical research division) renegotiated the terms of the agreement so as to allow it to run an unspecified number of compounds against ABC screens, rather than to operate on a pay-per-screen basis. At the same time, Bionatura came under increasing pressure from Proton to compete with the higher probabilities of successful discovery using synthetic chemistry technologies. As a joint effort with its pharmaceutical partner, Bionatura developed DEF, a library of purified compounds. It sought to fund the costs of the DEF project by means of a consortium of pharmaceutical partners, but failed to attract sufficient interest. Short of cash, the Bionatura Group was ultimately forced to dispose of two divisions. Although the joint programme remained intact, it evolved into a distinctively two-tier relationship, with Bionatura providing access to its DEF library and EarthMed, the new owners of Bionatura's discovery division, to ABC.

This case illustrated the serendipity of natural products chemistry discovery, the felt pressure to compete with alternative (bio)technologies, and the asymmetrical nature of a relationship dominated by a resource-rich pharmaceutical partner. It also highlighted the potentially enduring character of such a collaboration, particularly when faced with complex technologies and a difficult disease target, despite it lacking measurable success.

Thematic discussion

Chapter 1 began by raising questions that, having originally surfaced in loosely structured conversations with practitioners,[1] seemed relevant and also paradoxical: given high failure rates, how do we explain a growing

---

[1] For a detailed discussion of data and methods, refer to the appendix.

recourse to alliances whilst also assuming rational strategic management? Why have we persisted in approaching alliances with expectations of finding homogeneity whilst being well aware that they often unfold in very diverse and changing circumstances? Why are some apparently successful alliances dismantled before having exhausted their potential? Why are others deemed successful whilst being apparently void of any tangible achievements? Why do some survive despite being problematic? Why do others seem to get by despite apparently poor managerial decisions? Is alliance failure necessarily the consequence of managerial failure? While the first two of these will be revisited in later chapters, we may, in what follows, see what can be said on the others. Several speak to matters already familiar in the literature. Consistent with the case studies, the discussion is organized around themes so as to preserve a consistency with the concluding discussions to each.

Predictability

Each of the three alliances appears to have evolved quite differently from the expectations held at its formation. Founding scientists at the Cambiogen and Plethora alliance, and those involved in the Bionatura and Pflegum Courtal collaboration, had expected lead compound discoveries to have materialized much earlier in the joint programmes. As it is, after four and eight years respectively, neither was able to take a lead compound into the clinic. Their strategic objective appears as unsatisfied as it was at their formation, though important routes of inquiry were eliminated in the process. Given the uncertainty of drug discovery, this observation is perhaps not entirely surprising. One may merely not be able to predict the evolution of a research-based alliance with any degree of accuracy. By implication, many of the earliest process models in the strategy literature – primarily Achrol, Scheer, and Stern (1990), d'Aunno and Zuckerman (1987), Forrest and Martin (1992), Kanter (1994), and Murray and Mahon (1993) – appear of comparatively little relevance in this context.

This conclusion is reinforced when considering the rapid technological and scientific developments that have characterized the field and, by implication, the alliances inside them. Each joint research programme has, at some time, had to respond to these changes. Bionatura reacted to the felt pressure to develop new natural products technologies to keep pace with synthetic chemistries with the introduction of DEF. Plethora's alliances with Rummidgen and Cambiogen were continuously at risk of being rendered irrelevant due to those technologies that dominated their scientific fields during their formation rapidly becoming outdated.

Likewise, a partner may change its mind on the underlying strategic rationale for the joint programme. Pflegum Courtal twice deviated from negotiated research targets, and added a focus on anti-fungals as a disease target midway through the collaboration. Plethora twice altered the strategic justification for its alliance with Rummidgen towards very different activities in the drug development process. The merger of Myco and Perseptive to form ChemAnalysis, and the subsequent acquisition of ChemAnalysis by Cambiogen, could hardly have been foreseen by either Plethora or Myco, these being the founding partners of the alliance. Although, with the benefit of hindsight, each event became a welcome addition to the cooperative relationship, they did influence its evolutionary course by contributing new chemistry, genomic and genetic technologies, intellectual curiosity, and much greater bargaining power on the part of the biotech partner.

Most substantially, the unintended consequences of Rummidgen's decision to market a CD containing a prostaglandin library developed jointly with Plethora, and Plethora's decision to recruit one of Rummidgen's leading scientists to help build up an in-house facility, impacted significantly on the evolution and evolutionary potential of the alliance. Again, neither event could have been predicted at the start. Rather, as the case studies suggest, the life of an alliance may contain surprises and crises that are difficult to anticipate at its formation.

Evolution

The evolutionary trajectory of each of the alliances appears most akin to a *punctuated equilibrium* perspective, where longer periods of relative stability are interrupted by short periods of change. For Plethora and Rummidgen, these punctuations included the twofold change in the mobilizing strategic rationale by the pharmaceutical, the intellectual property rights rift triggered by the biotech company's decision to commercialize certain chemical structures, and the recruitment by Plethora of one of Rummidgen's scientists. In the case of Plethora and Cambiogen, such punctuations included the merger and subsequent acquisition and, possibly more materially, the six-month delay in renewing the collaboration agreement, causing much uncertainty to those individuals involved in it. For Bionatura and Pflegum Courtal, finally, these punctuations included the dissatisfaction with the low probability of discovery provided by the natural products discovery processes, discontentment with the pay-per-screen agreement, and disappointment with the absence of a sufficiently good lead compound to take into development. Had it not been for the 'proof of principle' established by compound AM-DB7, an amicable and effective working relationship, and resolute efforts by Stephen Boteach (Proton) to champion the relationship, it is unlikely that the alliance would have been extended beyond the initial four-year agreement. Another punctuation followed the decision by Bionatura's new CEO to commercialize the group and dispose of its hitherto unprofitable discovery division. Consequently, the two-tier nature of the alliance became more pronounced, with Bionatura providing access to its DEF library and EarthMed, the new owners of the ABC library, to ABC for screening purposes. A dyadic relationship had become a triadic one. The idea that the evolutionary trajectory of alliances may resemble a punctuated equilibrium paradigm appears consistent with the findings of Gray and Yan (1997) in a different context, and with Gulati (1998).

Notwithstanding such punctuations, it may be that, occasionally, the seeds of change were already present in the apparently stable interludes. Consequently, a punctuation may really be an expression of those underlying forces that, having depleted a reservoir of tolerance, erupt and instigate a change in the relationship. For instance, although the second change in the strategic rationale for the Plethora and Rummidgen collaboration was sudden and with immediate effect, the underlying agencies that prompted this change may have been gaining momentum in the intervening period of apparent stability just prior to the IPR controversy. The contentious recruitment of Karl Amis by Plethora, the negative imprint of Mark Amis on the alliance, the changing balance of power, and deteriorating trust relationships all appear to have helped pave the road towards a further punctuation. Then again, certain other events, including the first change of strategy by Plethora, the acquisition by Cambiogen of ChemAnalysis Pharmaceuticals, and EarthMed's purchase of some of Bionatura's assets, appear unrelated to such underlying, cumulative forces.

Archetypal evolution

Similar also are observations of evolution within alliance archetype, that is a fundamental change in an alliance from one type of collaboration to another. The Plethora and Rummidgen collaboration commenced as a *contract* research (or 'fee-for-service') relationship but developed into a *collaborative* research alliance in which partners interacted on a give-and-take basis, allowed for experimentation, exchanged proprietary knowledge on combinatorial chemistry and disease targets, and jointly negotiated relevant targets and research approaches. Upon the breakdown of trust relationships (following the IPR controversy and violation of a 'gentlemen's agreement'), and with the close involvement of Plethora's

US-based parent company, Plethora radically and abruptly redirected the collaboration towards technology development and transfer to its in-house facility. The relationship regressed into a far more straightforward 'fee-for-service' agreement.

A second example is the Bionatura and Pflegum Courtal collaboration, that evolved from a *dyadic* into a *triadic* relationship, with the addition of EarthMed upon the latter's acquisition of the ABC-related assets. Somewhat to its dissatisfaction, Pflegum Courtal now needed to interact with two biotech partners to access the same technologies under the collaboration agreement.

Success and performance

For a collaboration to be successful it should, in a strict sense, have accomplished its primary objective(s). For all three this objective was, at least at some stage, the discovery of a lead compound that, being sufficiently optimizable, could be taken into development and clinical trials. Alas, for both the Plethora–Cambiogen and the Bionatura–Pflegum Courtal collaborations this compound remained absent. In a discipline dominated by a hypothetico-deductive research tradition, the elimination of routes of inquiry can be considered as progress, albeit not, strictly speaking, success. Nevertheless, the alliances were deemed successful by many of the actors involved in them, both at a senior management and operational (or 'at the bench') level. This 'success' is attributed partly to the scientific progress made by eliminating certain routes of inquiry, though this has produced no short-term commercial success, partly to the amicable and effective interpersonal working relationships that have evolved, partly to the successful transfer of combinatorial or genetic technologies, and in part to mutual learning processes comprising (bio)chemistry capabilities, approaches to 'doing' research, and, more generally, the day-to-day management and long-term governance of research-oriented alliances. Alternatively, some individuals may have vested interests in celebrating 'their' relationship, irrespective of any measurable yields. This multiplicity and, at times, confusion surrounding the definition and measurement of performance is consistent with the assumptions that underpin Cohen, March, and Olsen's (1972) 'garbage can' model.

Longevity

Longevity may not be a particularly useful measure of success. Whereas the Plethora and Rummidgen alliance lasted for almost four years, it was arguably the most successful of the three in terms of tangible accomplishments. Though this appears consistent with Hamel (1991) and Hamel, Doz, and Prahalad (1989), it is at variance with Lynch (1993), who concluded that longevity is a measure of success and facilitated by good architecture (or governance structures). Rather, the enduring character of some alliances, particularly in the absence of any measurable feats, may be explained partly by the persistent desire of one partner to retain a foothold in a non-proprietary technology. Given few alternative providers of a similar technology this may be 'as good as it gets'. Both the Plethora and Cambiogen alliance and Bionatura's partnership with Pflegum Courtal serve as good illustrations. Moreover, given that the decision to extend a collaboration is partly contingent on the defence of it by a 'champion', this defence itself may be explained in part by prior experiences. For instance, the justification by Stephen Boteach for extending the Bionatura collaboration appears rooted in his firm personal commitment to natural products chemistry. This commitment is, in turn, explained by his experiences with this same approach to drug discovery whilst at rival Merck, and Merck's subsequent successes in this area of research. In fact, Merck is one of very few pharmaceuticals to have successfully brought natural-products-based chemistry drugs to market.

Drivers of change

Even if alliances exist to serve distinct strategic purposes, the evolution and evolutionary potential of those discussed here appears to have been precipitated by a number of factors. Changes in the Plethora–Rummidgen collaboration appear to have been pre-empted by the unintended, but significant, consequences of actions taken by both partners. When Plethora's parent company scientists became worried about violations of intellectual property rights they, through their senior management, demanded that Rummidgen no longer be informed of specific disease targets. Given the earlier departure of the chief US negotiator, these scientists had failed to appreciate the spirit of the collaboration and interpreted Rummidgen's actions as opportunistic and in violation of the agreement. The ensuing change in the strategic rationale for the alliance seems to have been an immediate consequence of a controversy, only augmented by the row over Plethora's recruitment of Karl Amis.

Further, partway through the collaboration, Mark Amis was brought in as a senior Plethora member of the steering group. His non-cooperative behaviour seriously limited its evolutionary potential. Threatened by a biotech partner competing directly with his in-house chemistry department, and unappreciative of Plethora's need for such a partnering arrangement (referred to earlier as the 'not-invented-here' syndrome), he failed to champion the alliance within his organization and made a continuation of the relationship difficult to justify. In this respect, the Plethora–Cambiogen alliance provides an interesting contrast, where Cambiogen's efforts complemented, rather than directly competed with one of the pharmaceutical's in-house research departments. Mark Amis was involved in both alliances but, in this particular instance, it was clearly in his own interest that the alliance should succeed. In sum, it appears that the drivers of change, and those limiting its potential, may have included trust and perception, as well as the fears, ambitions, and varied loyalties of specific individuals.

This observation takes the conclusions of Turpin (1993) and Inkpen and Beamish (1997) that, in the absence of partner continuity, there is a risk of 'corporate amnesia' one step further. For the absence of partner continuity (or, more specifically, the replacement of a collaborative actor with a non-collaborative one) can *harm* the perceived success and future potential of the alliance. This happens not merely as a result of forgetting the original intentions of the partnership but, rather, by including an individual with private interests, thus crippling the relationship in a more determined and deliberate fashion. Such fluidity of participants, as observed here, is consistent with Cohen, March, and Olsen (1972), and can significantly influence decision-making processes.

Likewise, continuity in an alliance can be sustained through effective and amicable interpersonal relationships. Such has been the case with Plethora–Cambiogen and Bionatura–Pflegum Courtal. For instance, the unique ability of Robert Gray to liaise between Plethora and its biotech partner during six months of difficult and indecisive extension negotiations provided Cambiogen with a degree of transparency, and a resultant sense of security, which it otherwise might not have attained. Also, the longevity of the Bionatura–Pflegum Courtal collaboration, despite having failed to produce a promising lead compound, appears due partly (but not entirely) to the competence-based and character-based trust between collaborating individuals, and to the championing efforts of Stephen Boteach who, based on his previous experiences with Merck, remained a firm believer in natural products chemistry. Moreover, when the ABC library was acquired by EarthMed, in April 1999, the transition appeared relatively trouble-free, perhaps primarily because the social composition of the alliance, at the level of the individual actors, remained unaffected.

In sum, neither change nor continuity may be fully explained by just strategic or economic justifications,[2] though these may tender useful

---

[2] Among these explanations, I include transaction cost theory, market power theory, resource-based theory, game theory, and agency theory, as each appears informed primarily by either economics or strategy.

partial explanations. For instance, the competitive pressures from combinatorial and synthetic drug discovery processes forced Bionatura to develop more efficient technologies. Likewise, dissatisfaction with the low probability of success provided in the first four-year agreement pressured it to accept an alternative model whereby Pflegum Courtal was allowed an unspecified number of screens. Finally, the longevity of this alliance in particular can be explained partly by the felt need of the pharmaceutical to access unique natural products chemistry capabilities that it no longer possessed in-house.

Management

The management of these alliances appears to have been more akin to ongoing processes of mediation, adaptation, and navigation,[3] than that of careful planning and controlling. The Plethora–Rummidgen alliance, for instance, faced difficulties that regularly required the mediation of senior management. Several such events happened unexpectedly to at least one of the partners and, by implication, remained largely outside managerial control. In the case of the Plethora–Cambiogen alliance, both the merger of Myco with Perseptive and the subsequent acquisition by Cambiogen would have been difficult to anticipate (so as to allow for control), but required senior management at both partner firms to make adaptations so as to preserve continuity, appropriate the newly available chemistry, genetic, and genomic technologies, and maximize the chances of successful drug discovery.

As for Bionatura, upon developing its DEF library, it was unable to complete the consortium by attracting an additional two partners and did not succeed in persuading Pflegum Courtal to increase its financial stake in this project. Due partly to the financial difficulties of Bionatura, now faced with mounting development costs, its subsidiary ABC-based research division was disposed of. EarthMed, the new owner, became partner to the alliance by default.[4] As a result, Pflegum Courtal had to adapt to the added administrative complexity of the three-tier relationship. Further, the obvious lack of control over drug discovery, given its

---

[3] Implying only occasional changes – navigation entails the avoidance of conflict, where possible.

[4] Apparently, Bionatura had tried to sell both the ABC and DEF libraries with its disposal of its subsidiary ABC-based research division, but EarthMed was unwilling to take on the financial implications of purchasing the DEF library. The DEF contract with Pharmagen, one of Pflegum Courtal's competitors and partners in the consortium, provides for substantial remuneration payments (believed to be as much as US$1 million) should this library be sold to a third party before the contractually stipulated termination date.

serendipitous character, required Bionatura to accept vastly revised conditions proposed by the pharmaceutical when negotiating the agreement, and made it realize the benefits of higher up-front payments at the expense of downstream royalties. Again, these developments would appear more characteristic of adaptation than control. The notion of alliance management as a process of adaptation has already been recognized in the literature (e.g. Arino and de la Torre, 1998, Doz, 1996, and Ring and van de Ven, 1994), and the empirical evidence introduced here seems strongly supportive of it.

There remains a final observation on the management of these three alliances. Particularly in the Plethora–Rummidgen and Pflegum Courtal–Bionatura programmes, it seems that the collaboration depended in great measure on the nature and quality of interpersonal ties. One might suggest that it was perhaps too dependent on these interpersonal ties and at risk of blinding individuals to the necessity of viewing the alliance as embedded in a wider social and economic system. To what extent does this constitute a failure of management to provide clear and consistent managerial explanations of what is going on and why, rather than allowing the alliance to subsist on rumour, fear, and individual ambition?

Organizational learning

Although learning was never explicitly stated as an objective for the formation of any of these three alliances, each partner acknowledges that it has constituted a meaningful element in the process of collaborating. Plethora attempted to appropriate the combinatorial chemistry capabilities from Rummidgen and disseminate these skills to its newly set-up in-house facility. Likewise, it sought to appropriate the genetic and genomic technologies of Cambiogen. Rummidgen, in turn, came to recognize the legitimate need in the pharmaceutical sector for the large-scale manufacture of compounds, which today constitutes an important share of its revenues. With respect to learning about alliance management, based on its experiences with Plethora, Rummidgen invested in videoconferencing facilities and now insists on regular conferencing with all of its partners to nurture and maintain multi-point communications (i.e. involving more than just one individual from each partner company), in sharp contrast to the single-point communications that were typical of the Plethora programme. As for Bionatura and Pflegum Courtal, each grew to be more realistic about the prospect of natural products discovery, as evidenced in the pharmaceutical's efforts to increase the probability of success by negotiating more favourable terms, and the recognition by the biotech company that it needed to develop a new technology so as to remain competitive with alternative discovery processes. Also, having learned the benefits of good interpersonal relationships, Bionatura purposefully seeks to preserve these by inviting past members of the steering group to joint social activities.

In sum, it appears that the learning opportunities furnished by the alliance helped generate a perception of success, have served to promote continuity, and have exposed partnering firms to new approaches to doing research whilst allowing them to become better at negotiating, structuring, and managing alliances. This, individually, is consistent with Powell, Koput, and Smith Doerr's (1996) emphasis on learning as the development of partnering routines. In the case of Plethora and Rummidgen, learning about each other seems to have contributed to the erosion of trust relationships. By implication, assessments of performance and success were based not solely, or even primarily, on rational (e.g. economic or strategic) considerations. Rather, notions of success and performance appear the products of cognitive processes of individuals within alliances, who subsequently share these with others involved in the collaboration and within their organization.

Legitimacy

For biotech startups, establishing alliances with large pharmaceuticals such as Plethora and Pflegum Courtal remains an important route towards gaining legitimacy within the industry. It is therefore not surprising that Rummidgen, Bionatura, and Cambiogen have each been keen to emphasize these partnerships in their publications and quick to make public announcements regarding them. The acquisition by EarthMed of some of Bionatura's assets appears to have been motivated partly by its ongoing alliance with Pflegum Courtal, providing EarthMed with the opportunity to add a third and major pharmaceutical partner to its portfolio. Subsequent publications and public announcements by EarthMed suggest as much.

Equally important is the effect of an alliance on the reputation of a biotech partner. For instance, Rummidgen risked losing a potentially lucrative alliance with an IT services provider due to a negative reference by a senior Plethora manager. It is interesting to observe, first, the extent to which the opinion of a single individual was assumed to represent the view of an entire organization and, second, the fact that this individual did not have first-hand experience with the actual collaboration. Rather, his opinion appears to have been based on hearsay. Ironically, the reputation of partner firms may thus be relatively rapidly disseminated within partner organizations, even by those individuals not immediately involved in the collaboration.

Revisiting the questions

At the start of this chapter, I reiterated the questions that arise in relation to the ongoing phenomena of alliances. This section attempts to provide some tentative answers.

Firstly, why are some apparently successful alliances dismantled before having exhausted their potential? Plethora's alliance with Rummidgen provides an interesting contrast to its ongoing collaboration with Cambiogen. Plethora's agreement with the former was not renewed again despite the relationship not having exhausted its technical potential. Rummidgen scientists, for better or worse, thought the pharmaceutical incapable of replicating its specialized chemistry capabilities in-house. During a little less than four years, the collaboration generated a large number of chemical compounds to be evaluated by Plethora, and Rummidgen appears to have been largely able to deliver on targets set by its partner. In contrast, Plethora's relationship with Cambiogen was extended beyond this four-year period even in the absence of a lead compound – a chemical compound sufficiently active against anti-infectious disease to be taken into development. This contrast becomes more pronounced when considering Pflegum Courtal's alliance with Bionatura, which was extended three times but had little to show for it. So, why was the Rummidgen alliance, whilst successful, abandoned, arguably before having been sapped of its potential? Perhaps the mutual abandonment of the alliance by Plethora and Rummidgen can be explained by a number of factors: a fundamental lack of trust following the recruitment of Karl Amis and the IPR controversy; a refusal to champion the alliance by at least one key Plethora manager; a lack of support from the US-based pharmaceutical parent company upon the departure of an alliance negotiator and champion, and following the IPR controversy; a reciprocal fear of exploitation; a fear of creating in Rummidgen a competitor, particularly given the biotech company's remarkable success in negotiating more substantial alliances with large chemical companies, and its rapid growth; and the diminishing importance of Plethora in Rummidgen's portfolio of business relationships. Maybe Rummidgen had served its purpose and become redundant now its combinatorial chemistry capabilities had been transferred to Plethora's in-house laboratory, spear-headed by a former Rummidgen scientist? Or, more likely, the truth lies somewhere in the middle, comprising a complex combination of these various elements.

But why were the Cambiogen and Bionatura collaborations rationalized as comparatively successful but void of any tangible achievements? Why do such alliances survive despite being seemingly problematic? Again the answers may comprise a combination of elements: the amicable working relationship; mutual trust; the absence of any credible threat of Bionatura integrating forward, though this threat was felt as legitimate by Plethora about Cambiogen; scientific progress in the Popperian sense of having eliminated relevant routes of inquiry; the potential for testing yet other hypotheses or drawing on new technologies; strong championing efforts on either side; continual dependency relationships by the smaller partners for lack of resources; and a lack of alternative providers of similar technologies.

Finally, why do others seem to get by despite apparently poor managerial decisions? Must alliance failure necessarily be the consequence of managerial failure? In each of the case studies, intervention by senior managers remained important. Theirs was largely a 'fire-fighting' role, in being forced to mediate in interorganizational as well as interpersonal conflicts and to respond to contingencies. Certain events, including the merger and takeover, the poaching of a scientist, the entry of a third party, the lack of success, and the departure and admission of individuals, would have been difficult, if not impossible, to foresee. However, did the involvement of Mark Amis not constitute a managerial failure on the part of Plethora, in failing to anticipate his conflict of interests? Did Rummidgen fail to secure proper, written authorization by Plethora before marketing its prostaglandin library? Should this not have been a fairly straightforward administrative task? And could Plethora not have ensured a better handling of the Karl Amis affair? What should hopefully be evident is the nature of these various elements in being not exclusively economics or corporate strategy motivated, but being importantly social. To a significant degree, it is the individuals who wrote the plots of the alliance stories.

These observations are supportive of van de Ven and Ring (1994) and Doz (1996) in calling for managerial intervention when appropriate, and the importance of organizational learning (Powell, Koput, and Smith Doerr, 1996). Clearly, management cannot warrant the discovery of drug candidates, nor ensure that an alliance follows a pre-planned developmental trajectory, nor predict the full consequences of individual or organizational actions, nor eliminate ambiguities in interpreting organizational behaviour or changes in the environment, nor accurately anticipate the personal ambitions of individuals involved in the alliance and the consequences of their involvement in, or departure from, it. Even so, they also appear to call for relaxing assumptions of teleology as governing process, and management as the primary agent of change and performance.

More generally, our desire to systematize process, to be able to construct an elegant microcosm of alliance life, and to discover an underlying order may be the logical consequence of a subtler, deep-seated tradition. Precisely what this intellectual tradition entails is explained in Chapter 8.

7   Strategy, structure, and structuration: the general in the particular

If the three alliance narratives are any indication of the nature of alliance life generally, one might be excused for supposing that the pursuit of a single theory is an arduous task. To suggest – as a lowest common denominator – that alliances begin, mature, and end is not exactly rocket science. Neither is this helpful to practitioners – the nature of cooperation in various stages may well differ greatly from alliance to alliance; some may never quite reach maturity but skip straight from an introductory period into decline; others may be able to overwrite this evolutionary pattern through innovation, renegotiation or by virtue of unanticipated events. Besides, the strategic and managerial implications associated with each stage are anything but straightforward.

However, despite their potential individuality and unpredictability, there *is* order in alliances even if it is not the kind of order that easily allows for prediction. Using the narratives as an empirical platform, this chapter will seek to illustrate that this is so. Alliance life may genuinely be one of paradox: regardless of any inconsistency, irrationality, and unpredictability on the part of human agency, its conduct remains informed by deep-seated social norms. To take a simple and relatively familiar example, in their interactions individuals will tend to rely on social rules, such as politeness. This particular social norm may differ in application depending on context but appears fairly generic in content. Being courteous seems the *natural* thing to do. Yet, in being polite we, perhaps unintentionally, reinforce it as a socially binding imperative to inform any future interactions. It is not until we choose to violate such conventions (for example, by being persistently rude) that these social rules are subject to change. This notion of human conduct as being embedded in social constitutions is now relatively well recognized, particularly with the popularization of Anthony Giddens's contributions to social theory. In extending the pluralist argument, this chapter draws on Giddens's (1984) structuration theory. It accepts many of its assumptions, particularly the recursive nature of action and structure and the reproductive element in human conduct, but differs in that it sees alliance life as far more open ended. It agrees with Giddens on the enabling function of structure; that although individuals draw on deep-seated social structures they need not be constrained by them. Paradoxically, it accepts also that there exists a tendency in human conduct towards order (or in reproducing the status quo) but is more open to voluntarism and change. In processes of both reproduction and change, human actors rely equally on the same underlying social institutions. The theoretical implications of such a view are twofold. First, paradoxically, order and generality do not necessarily afford predictability. Second, and most relevantly, it allows one to simultaneously detect the general *and* the particular, the general *in* the particular, and the particular *in* the general.

The general in the particular

In recognizing the complexity, heterogeneity, and potential inconsistencies of human conduct, Giddens (1984) thought social life to be best understood as comprising an iteration of structure and action in which each interacts with, and informs, the other. Structure is recursively implicated in the process of social reproduction, and no longer just constrains action, as Durkheim hypothesized, but also enables it through roles of signification (or sensemaking), legitimization, and domination (or empowerment). In differentiating between structure and action, Giddens sought to bridge the traditional dichotomy between static and deterministic notions of structure on the one hand, and voluntarism on the other (Barley and Tolbert, 1997). The two are different but clearly related – structure is to action what language is to speech. As language enables conversation, so does conversation help the evolution of language by introducing new word configurations and new vocabulary or by retiring 'old-fashioned' words and expressions.

Giddens conceptualized the relationship between agency and structure not as one of two distinct phenomena, or a dualism, but as representing a duality (Giddens, 1997: 25). Structure is the precondition and consequence of agency, whereas the activities of human agents are inseparable from structure in being 'structured' by it. Emerging from this duality is an intellectual lens that explains the production and reproduction of social systems as a function of human interaction, but informed by underlying social structures. For the purposes of our argument, this duality suggests that strategic alliances can be usefully viewed as both the precondition and outcome of human conduct.

They are given life, and evolve, within distinct social contexts by equally diverse individuals. The latter rely on social structures – societal norms, conventions, rules, and resources, both tacit and explicit – for their everyday activities whilst they, in the majority of cases, cannot help but reproduce those very same structures. Each day is informed by the one before.

Similar phenomena exist in the process of drug discovery. Those engaged in biotech collaborations will tend to rely on tacit 'gentlemen's agreements' in their interactions – an example being that of not using each other's laboratories as a breeding ground for future recruits. In the process of so doing they, perhaps inadvertently, reproduce these social structures. It follows that structure provides a context for action to unfold whilst action itself feeds back into structure. Structure conveys institutional definition. It expresses the hardening of certain aspects of the alliance. Its overarching strategic justification, for example, is not likely to change on a weekly basis but to remain stable for some time; without some degree of permanence and stability, notions of purposefulness and effectiveness would be meaningless. Arguably, the same is true for the operating rules of an alliance, its governance structure, the type of research activities it is engaged in, the technologies that are put to use, and the individuals and organizations involved in it.

Although structure – viewed thus as the sedimented remains of prior interactions – may serve to inform practice, human actors do enjoy a fair degree of voluntarism. Though they may be conscious of certain institutional constraints, rules, and resources, they need not be constrained by them. 'It is men themselves,' wrote Friedrich Engels to Plekhanov, 'who make their history, but within a given environment which conditions them.'[1] Unlike being subject to gravitation, leaving us with no more choice about falling than a branch, actors *can* choose to challenge social practices. That is, human agency, whilst unable to disobey those laws it shares with other things, can, in fact, confront those rules peculiar to it (Lewis, 1943). We are not quite like the pitiable man in an amusing verse by Maurice Evan Hare (1905):

> There was a young man who said, 'Damn,
> It is borne upon me that I am
> A creature that moves
> In predestinate grooves –
> Not even a bus, but a tram.'

In granting human agency a greater degree of voluntarism, the pluralist perspective thus departs slightly from Giddens's theory of social constitution. It simply suggests that in processes of reproduction and change human actors still draw on the same underlying social institutions.

---

[1] As cited in Sartre (1963: 31).

Although there may still exist a natural tendency towards maintaining the status quo, change is quite possible.

Giddens's emphasis on studying social life through structural reasoning is considered anti-empiricist and anti-positivist. Rather than focusing primarily on immediate observations, as is typical of positivism, social explanation is conceived of as embedded in deep-seated structures underlying thought and behaviour. Further, Giddens's perspective on universal laws appears at odds with empiricist conceptions of reality. He claims:

[There are] no universal laws in the social sciences, and there will not be any – not, first and foremost, because methods of empirical testing and validation are somehow inadequate but because [. . .] the causal conditions involved in generalizations about human social conduct are inherently unstable in respect of the very knowledge (or beliefs) that actors have about the circumstances of their own action.[2] (Giddens, 1984: xxxii)

What Giddens appears to suggest is a social world of such complexity that simple causal relationships are difficult to come by. He thinks it too unstable for this to be plausible. In this he shares the concerns of Kuhn, Feyerabend, Dilthey, and others, on the traditional dominance of a naturalist- and functionalist-informed research programme, boldly labelled, by Giddens, the 'orthodox consensus' in the social sciences (Baert, 1998). Perhaps not surprisingly, Giddens's theory of the social world is expansive as it attempts the consolidation of several. As he himself acknowledges, his theory incorporates ideas from Heidegger's existentialism, Gadamer's hermeneutics, Schutz's phenomenology, Garfinkel's ethnomethodology, Foucault's and Derrida's post-structuralism, and Erikson's and Freud's studies of child development (Baert, 1998: 94). Consequently, structuration theory contains important elements of: (a) a 'double hermeneutic';[3] (b) a notion of human reflexivity and (c) tacit knowledge;[4] (d) an enabling dimension to social structure; and (e) the importance of trust and tact. First, given that individuals interpret their social environment and, accordingly, impregnate it with meaning, a

---

[2] It is a little curious, perhaps, that he himself seems to fall prey to his own criticism, as his (universal) claim that there are no universal laws would seem self-contradictory.

[3] A 'double hermeneutic' refers to the multi-layered nature of interpretation. For example, the empirical sections of this thesis essentially present my interpretations of the evolution and process dynamics of real-life alliances. These narratives are based in large part on interviews with those closely involved in them. Interviewees provided me with interpretations of situations as they perceived them. You, the reader, in turn, will provide some interpretation of my work; one which is based on my interpretation, which is based in part on the interpretation of those directly involved with alliances. Hence, yours is an interpretation of an interpretation of an interpretation, or a triple hermeneutic.

[4] Tacit refers to that which is implicitly held. For instance, silence may be interpreted as meaning implied agreement.

difficulty arises for social researchers. Not only do they need to interpret their subject matter, but this subject matter itself contains meaning. This phenomenon is generally known as a 'double hermeneutic'. Second, Giddens argues that individuals are reflexive beings that continually monitor their actions whilst reflecting on their consequences. This knowledge is subsequently incorporated in future behaviour rendering action purposive: though people might lack clear intentions in everyday life, they are nevertheless reflexive of their own behaviour and that of others. Third, they are the products of particular organizational culture contexts, having to 'toe the party line', and thus aware of local rules, local etiquette, and expectations. Hence, action is path and context dependent. Fourth, and this is where his account may differ from Durkheim, Giddens views social structures as *enabling* as well as constraining. Individuals rely on rules and resources (structures) for their day-to-day interactions and subsequently, though perhaps not intentionally, reproduce them. For instance, individuals in alliances rely on trust as a basis for their interaction. When a trust relationship is violated, this can have significant implications for future interactions. Structure is essentially a precondition for human activity. Finally, he suggests that trust and tact are crucial features of social interaction. On various occasions, Giddens refers to the way in which individuals routinely 'repair' the moral basis of their interactions, using tact and remedial practices or helping others save face (cf. Baert, 1998). Based on Freud's and, particularly, Erikson's theories on child development, Giddens views the development of trust, and the parallel evolution of self-consciousness, as the foundation of the capability for reflexive behaviour.[5] Indeed, not only is trust a prominent feature in Giddens's treatment of structuration theory, but it is also helpful in the analysis of everyday human interaction within interorganizational partnerships, particularly in a context as unpredictable, and including such high stakes, as biotech research.

Giddens's notion of *structure*, viewed as rules and resources, consists of institutionalized[6] features of a social system that have stabilized across time and space, and constitute memory traces that are intrinsic to, and enable, social practice. Drawing on a now familiar metaphor:

It is not *in spite of* language that we are able to think or intervene, but it is precisely *because of* the existence of language that we are able to do so. (Baert, 1998: 105)

---

[5] Giddens relies on Erikson to identify three stages in the development of trust: (a) basic trust versus mistrust; (b) autonomy versus shame and doubt; and (c) initiative versus guilt (Erikson (1963) and Giddens (1984: 51–60)).

[6] By the term 'institutionalized', I mean the establishment of particular practices or customs, or even a stable social composition of a society, group or alliance.

Structure, however, also includes those practices more typical of alliances such as, for instance, a division of labour, implicit gentlemen's agreements, pre-existing social ties (social capital), the social composition of alliances, commitments to specific technologies, alliance agreements, performance appraisal systems, and operating rules. People draw upon these structures to exercise agency and, given the assumption of bounded rationality, their actions will have some unintended consequences. Social systems are reproduced relations between people or collectivities that have stabilized into institutionalized social practices. And the very reproduction of these systems comprises the process Giddens refers to as *structuration*.

An analysis of strategic conduct

A structurationist reading of the case studies allows us to look more closely at the rules and resources that informed the behaviour of those involved. It seeks to draw out the tacit orders that signify power structures, mediate sensemaking processes, and legitimize specific courses of action. The process of arriving at meaningful explanations of what is going on, and why, is ongoing and underpinned by deep-seated social structures. Consistent with Giddens's definitions, we briefly examine the three processes – sensemaking, legitimization, and domination – in each alliance. Such processes can be seen to be mediated by largely unquestioned social structures. Metaphorically speaking, they provide the language – the vocabulary and grammatical rules – for the ensuing story lines. By relying on illustrations taken directly from the cases, this discussion will seek to uncover some of these structures.

Plethora and Rummidgen

Sensemaking   When Plethora proposed a first change in the focus of the collaboration from lead optimization to lead discovery, this development was not wholly unwelcome to Rummidgen. As Coe pointed out, within the field of biopharmaceutical research it was considered important to have skills in both areas. Thus, it made sense to go along with Plethora's proposal. Moreover, as some expected Rummidgen's future to lie in drug discovery, these expectations not only ratified but also *legitimized* the biotech firm's acquiescence. The simultaneous decision of Plethora to pursue a mixtures-based approach was interpreted rather differently. 'Mixtures' was seen to be a 'been there, done that, didn't work' technology and in stark contrast to the business philosophy of Rummidgen as a provider of 'novel' solutions.

Making mixtures was contrary to our business philosophy. Mixtures were cheap, nasty, and didn't work. The whole industry was moving away from mixtures and Plethora wanted to get back into this area. We had evolved past this stage and to be told to go back into it is like being told to go back to kindergarten. (Coe, Rummidgen, April 1998)

Rummidgen's compliance this time appears not to have been legitimized by an expectation of adding value to the firm, but typical of an asymmetrical power relationship dominated by a resource-rich pharmaceutical partner.

When Plethora reacted abruptly to Rummidgen's marketing of the prostaglandin library by refocusing the collaboration yet again, it may have surprised its biotech partner. What is of interest here is the sheer difference between the meanings ascribed to this event by the partnering firms. Rummidgen felt its actions *made sense* and had been *legitimized* by the 'spirit' of the alliance – an understanding between the arbitrating parties during the formation negotiations that the firm could leverage the collaboration to position itself more firmly in the pharmaceutical industry as an independent entity. However, with the departure of Plethora's chief US negotiator, other Malibu-based scientists interpreted this opportunistic move as a direct violation of the agreement. This one development resulted in two distinct interpretations, and legitimized Plethora's subsequent decision to refocus the alliance, it being much less trustful of its partner.

When, in May 1999, Plethora patented a co-development with Rummidgen, but as a single discovery, it fell prey to its own criticism of violating the alliance agreement. What is significant here is the reaction of the biotech firm's CEO, Derrek Lodge, to this development. Rather than filing a formal complaint with the patenting authorities, he chose to lodge 'brownie points' with Plethora, leaving it indebted to Rummidgen to provide an, as yet undefined, favour in return. Here perhaps surfaces the first of several tacit structures: the 'I scratch your back, you scratch mine' principle. An expectation of reciprocation of a favour is implied. This expectation of reciprocity – or of responding in kind – has been debated in various intellectual traditions, and is likely to be present in many of our everyday life activities. Clearly, it is not distinctive to business organizations. In fact, the political philosopher John Rawls thought it essential to the survival of the human species, as argued in his *A Theory of Justice*:

The basic idea is one of reciprocity, a tendency to answer in kind. Now this tendency is a deep psychological fact. Without it our nature would be very different and fruitful social cooperation fragile if not impossible . . . Beings with a different psychology either have never existed or must soon have disappeared in the course of evolution. (1999: 433)[7]

By implication, it may be treacherous to draw the line between those social structures that are characteristic of a single firm (e.g. Merck) or a specific industry (e.g. pharmaceutical) and those that are more widely held at the level of societies (e.g. the British) or cultures (e.g. Anglo-Saxon). The interrelationships between these are far from straightforward, and my treatment here has sought to avoid what may well be a theoretical minefield.

Finally, Plethora's surprise at the unanticipated success of Rummidgen as an independent and independently profitable biotech company appears indicative of a contemptuous attitude towards smaller partner firms. This observation appears evident also in Plethora's silence during the Karl Amis recruitment issue and, at the level of the individual, in Mark Amis's lack of respect for Coe. Rummidgen were the 'new kids on the block' and, surprisingly, these new kids were getting rich fast. Collaborating individuals at Plethora appear to have had some difficulty mentally adjusting to this increasing discrepancy in earning power, particularly as they felt they helped provide the means in the first place.

Legitimization   An interesting tacitly held rule surfaces in the aftermath of the conflict surrounding Plethora's hiring of Karl Amis. Rummidgen maintained that their partner had violated a (tacit) 'gentlemen's agreement', or norm, not to use each other's organization as a breeding ground for new recruits. In fact, such agreements appear quite common in the industry and are often taken for granted, being not usually incorporated in the written contract. Viewed thus by Rummidgen as a violation of the 'spirit' of the collaboration, Plethora rationalized the situation differently. Though apparently well aware of this tacit understanding, it felt it had no choice but to hire Karl Amis, as he would have left the biotech company anyway. Hence, it would be preferable under all circumstances to offer Amis a position, as the only foreseeable alternative was to see him leave for a competing firm. It thus appears that individuals within both organizations drew on the same underlying virtual order to structure their actions. However, Plethora, being aware of it, was not constrained by it. Instead, it chose to justify its actions by relying on a different set of rules – those dictated by competition. Moreover, during this period Plethora claimed it could not disclose the nature of the negotiations with Amis due to an industry-wide ethical code that serves to

---

[7] As quoted in Fukuyama (2002: 121).

protect the interests of the job-seeker. Rummidgen had little sympathy for Plethora's reliance on a formal, explicit code of conduct, suggesting that 'in the real world' this code is violated all the time. Its response is perhaps suggestive of another prevailing order, namely that of being truthful and transparent under all circumstances.

This episode appears to suggest that organizations, and the actors inside them, may claim to rely on orders other than tacit ones, depending on which appear to best serve their self-interest. This observation does not negate the existence of underlying social structures, but merely suggests that individuals and organizations need not be wholly bound by them. Plethora's opportunism, exhibited most clearly in the final leg of the alliance, is more easily digestible in view of Hornby's comment that 'the collaboration is a means to an end'. Whereas Rummidgen appears to have used Plethora as a means to gaining *legitimacy* in the wider pharmaceutical industry, Plethora recognized in Rummidgen an opportunity to transfer combinatorial chemistry technologies to an in-house facility. The perceived IPR violation, and subsequent distrust, provided Plethora with an added rationale, and the necessary legitimacy (or sanctioning ability), to set up this facility during the latter half of the alliance.

Reputation is a key strategic resource in the pharmaceutical industry, explaining not only Rummidgen's intentions of gaining industry-wide legitimacy through an alliance with a much-reputed pharmaceutical, but also the concerns that arose out of a negative reference provided by a Plethora agent. Of interest here is the perceived credibility extended to this individual as legitimately representing the organizational experience.

Two further observations may be relevant. First, Rummidgen worked hard at producing a first plate of deliverables to Plethora, so as to establish credibility with its partner and, in turn, allow Plethora agents to champion the alliance within their organization. Put differently, early success would enable Plethora scientists to legitimate the joint effort and drum up support for it. Further, for the alliance to have been extended beyond the three-year period would, from Rummidgen's standpoint, require Plethora to admit that it had treated its partner unfairly. This perception of unfairness, of course, implies the biotech company's reference to some underlying moral standard or norm. However, for Plethora to openly acknowledge its mistakes would require it not only to recognize that mistakes were made, but also allow potentially for a loss of face, or organizational pride. Given the importance of reputation, this appears unlikely ever to happen at the organizational level, though apologies were exchanged informally between Lodge (Rummidgen) and Green (Plethora) at the interpersonal level.

Domination   The narrative alludes to the generally asymmetrical, but evolving, power relationship between a financially well-endowed Plethora and startup Rummidgen. Several instances can serve as examples of Plethora's dominance, particularly earlier on, in the collaborative relationship, including its decision, and ability, twice to refocus the alliance, to suddenly but successfully impose ideas upon its partner, to dictate a mixtures-based research approach against the advice of Rummidgen, to get by without providing adequate feedback to its partner firm, as well as the offhand and seemingly insensitive manner in which it managed the Karl Amis issue. However, as Rummidgen became successful in its own right, it was able to negotiate an extension of the contract at a higher than expected cost to Plethora. In other words, it appeared to have gained some degree of legitimacy within the industry, granting it a much increased bargaining power.

At the level of the individual, although Hornby (Plethora) and Coe (Rummidgen) were assigned operational responsibility for the alliance, neither appears to have been given sufficient power to deliver on commitments. The various interpersonal conflicts that resulted from unkept promises required the mediation of senior managers Lodge (Rummidgen) and Green (Plethora). Thus, even though in theory each should have been equipped with adequate authoritative resources to manage the collaboration, in reality neither was.

Plethora and Cambiogen

Sensemaking   Due to complexity of anti-fungal research ('it's a damn difficult thing to do...') and the correspondingly low success rate in drug discovery, any measure of alliance success appears to have been largely perceptual. As the narrative indicates, the 'feel-good' factor surfaces as a significant contributor to the felt success of the joint programme. Moreover, actors appeared to tacitly draw on a Popperian research logic to rationalize accomplishments and legitimize the alliance. They proceeded to define achievements in terms of disconfirmed (and rejected) hypotheses – routes of inquiry that were tried but failed to produce a result ('The alliance may still have been successful... even if you have learned how not to do something.'). Consistent with this underlying logic, joint research progresses only incrementally, and even somewhat artificially, for the much-coveted broad-spectrum anti-fungal lead compound remained as elusive as it did in early 1995. Yet, the alliance appeared a success story within both partner organizations ('Out of those ten, we probably think of the Plethora relationship as our best collaborative relationship.'). In sum, in the absence of having achieved the stated objective, alliance success seems to have been rationalized, and the alliance legitimized, using incremental measures of success and relying on subjective frameworks, including mutual respect, the practice of 'due diligence', and amicable interpersonal interactions.

At an organizational level, it is a cost–benefit calculation that surfaces as a mental framework to have informed and legitimized Plethora's continued commitment. For the purposes of establishing its legitimacy more firmly in the pharmaceutical industry, an extension of the alliance would naturally be in Cambiogen's interest, even in the absence of tangible measures of success. For Plethora, however, the choice seems to have been more difficult, as further escalating its resource commitments would, by implication, serve to increase the probability of creating in Cambiogen a future competitor. That this decision came not without difficulty seems evident from the six-month delay in finalizing its commitment to the extension. Ultimately, the benefit of access to genetic and genomic technologies were thought to outweigh the risks of competition.

During these six months, the insecurity that was experienced, organizationally as well as individually (for those engaged in the joint research programme), was offset partially by Gray (Cambiogen), who, by leveraging his personal friendship with a former Plethora colleague, was able to keep individuals at Cambiogen informed of sentiments at Plethora.

Chris and I were able to have some very frank conversations. We don't need to hide behind the company line. We can just be honest with each other as to where things stood. (Gray, Cambiogen, May 1999)

What is of interest here is the extent to which sensemaking processes at Cambiogen were informed by informal human interactions rather than any formal corporate statements. Informal reassurances appear to have played a significant role in sustaining individuals at Cambiogen during the intense insecurity.

An underlying cultural prejudice surfaces from the interpersonal interaction between alliance agents, where it was deemed necessary to over-communicate and undersell results. Viewed in context, this appears to have signified a reaction to the optimism and self-confidence that is, for better or worse, sometimes thought to characterize American corporate life more generally ('If your partner says it's brilliant, it is probably OK.').

Legitimization   Akin to the Rummidgen collaboration, Cambiogen and Plethora appear to have been conscious of a tacit 'gentlemen's agreement' – an implicit understanding that any act of 'poaching' scientists would be highly inappropriate. That both parties were aware of this virtual order seems fairly evident from the interview data ('It is like

Common Law, it is not written down but you know what you should and shouldn't do ... it would not be kosher.'). Nevertheless, Cambiogen, though aware of it, chose not to be bound by it, and made job offers to two Plethora employees. Its implicit recognition of having violated a moral code of conduct seems evident from an explicit sensitivity towards Plethora in seeking to discuss this openly beforehand. Plethora itself now fell victim to a non-legitimate act ('There was a bit of "hmmm ... that's not very nice." It was interesting to see the film played from the other side.').

As regards the crucial role of the informal communications between Gray (Cambiogen) and a former Plethora colleague, it is significant that both individuals were held to legitimately and credibly represent their organizational viewpoints, despite their relatively junior positions. In fact, the importance of trust – both competence- and character-based trust – featured in various places throughout the alliance.

Domination   By virtue of its primary role as financier of the alliance, Plethora (particularly its US-based headquarters) continually emerged as ultimately the more dominant of the two partners ('Plethora calls the tune.'). On the other hand, concessions on experiments in which Cambiogen scientists had a specific intellectual interest would appear indicative of Cambiogen's increasing negotiating power. The successful unfolding of Cambiogen as a profitable biopharmaceutical, attested by an increasing portfolio of pharmaceutical partners, has almost certainly contributed to this. Interestingly, when conflicts did arise they were re-solved at a managerial level. This deliberate detachment of scientists from the business rationale for the alliance, for better or worse, may have con-stituted an attempt to isolate power struggles to the level of management ('... it's better to let scientists continue being friends and working to-gether.').

At the level of the individual, power struggles seem to have been largely absent. The attitude of Mark Amis to Cambiogen is markedly different from that to Rummidgen, though this may have been due primarily to the complementary nature of this collaboration. Whereas Rummidgen was seen to be in direct competition with his in-house chemistry facility, any lead compounds from the Cambiogen alliance would feed into his department for optimization. Hence, unlike the previous collaboration, any success with Cambiogen served Amis's self-interest.

Pflegum Courtal and Bionatura

Sensemaking   In view of the difficulty of natural-products-based drug discovery, and the absence of a drug candidate, measures of alliance success appear mostly subjective. As the narrative suggested, the 'feel-good' factor also emerges here as contributing significantly to its felt success. Apart from two joint publications and two jointly-held patents early on in the collaboration, any tangible accomplishments remained elusive. As with the previous case, actors are seen to draw again on a Popperian research logic to rationalize accomplishments and legitimize the alliance, defining achievements in terms of rejected hypotheses. Consistent with this underlying logic (one that is taken for granted in the industry), joint research progresses incrementally. In the absence of having achieved the stated objective, success appears to have been rationalized – and the alliance legitimized – using such incremental measures, whilst relying also on subjective statements of mutual respect, the practice of 'due diligence', and amicable interpersonal interactions. In fact, the felt importance of maintaining existing social ties appears obvious from Bionatura's deliberate efforts at inviting Tolkien to social gatherings, despite him having left the alliance.

Yet another reason supported Pflegum Courtal's ongoing rationalization of its investment in Bionatura. Given a particular R&D budget, its pharmaceutical research division, Proton, would periodically select a number of new 'real options' in which to invest while evaluating which existing options to exercise by extending collaboration contracts. Being far from unique in pursuing this type of strategy (it is similar to Plethora's 'PlethoraGen' programme), the investment would be expected to pay off if even just one of the resultant alliances produced a drug candidate. That the Bionatura collaboration was extended several times appears indicative partly of the biotech firm's biological astuteness, as well as Boteach's (Proton) personal ambitions in the field of natural products chemistry. Based on his many years with Merck, his attitude seems one of 'if they can do it, so can we'.

What may help explain the apparently good interpersonal ties that existed within the joint programme is a shared intellectual curiosity. Both Proton and Bionatura retained ties to local universities. Boteach and Annan were both affiliated with local academic programmes for which they provided lectures occasionally. However, Pflegum Courtal, the pharmaceutical parent, surfaced as far more commercially oriented. Consequently, whereas interpersonal interactions appeared sufficiently amicable and respectful, the commercial negotiations were not without difficulty. The narrative provides several illustrations of this, particularly those involving ex-CEO Fulghum. It also illustrates Pflegum Courtal's apparent opportunism with respect to their partner ('So you set some very high hurdles for them and, hopefully, they will never be able to reach them ... We want to keep them out.').

A final point of interest concerns the seemingly short-term concerns of Proton's Stephen Boteach. Being rather less concerned with long-term royalty issues (though this is probably of greater concern to Pflegum Courtal), his self-interest focused primarily on optimizing the chances for discovering a natural-products-based drug candidate before retirement.

Legitimization   Bionatura's interest in continuing its collaboration with Pflegum Courtal was based in part on its chronic need for cash inflows, but partly also on maintaining legitimacy and credibility within the pharmaceutical industry ('We would be gutted if Pflegum Courtal decided not to continue with us.'). This perception of legitimacy is imperative to negotiating future partnerships with established pharmaceuticals. Bionatura's failure to complete the DEF consortium by attracting two more partner organizations may suggest a failure of attaining credibility. Both Pharmagen and Proton were founding partners with Bionatura at the time of the DEF development and, therefore, may already have had a vested interest in an escalated commitment. Any subsequent failure to attract new partners may have signified, and signalled, a lack of legitimacy with competing pharmaceuticals.

Finally, as with the previous two case examples, Proton and Bionatura appear to have drawn on a tacit understanding not to use each other's organizations as a recruiting ground for scientists. As opposed to the previous two cases, neither organization violated this 'gentlemen's agreement'. When raised, the issue met with instant recognition by individuals at both partner firms. Nor do there appear to have been any instances where individuals have taken the initiative to 'jump ship' and approach the partner organization.

Domination   Perhaps unsurprisingly, Pflegum Courtal (Proton) continuously emerges as the dominant partner. For example, Bionatura's lack of negotiating power led to a situation in which it barely broke even financially on the first four-year period of the collaboration. In the mean time, however, Proton was allowed to change previously negotiated targets twice without compensating Bionatura. Further, Proton coerced Bionatura into increasing the probability of successful discovery, and its efficiency, with the development of DEF, and a new deal structure whereby the pharmaceutical was allowed an unlimited number of screens. Also, apparently, Proton exceeded the quantity of chemical samples allowed by the formal agreement on several occasions without penalty. Moreover, the pharmaceutical appears the main beneficiary of the relationship, at least in financial terms. It was unwilling to escalate its commitment to DEF beyond the minimum requirement of £2 million, despite attempts of Bionatura to persuade Proton otherwise, and insisted on an equity exchange rather than cash payment. Finally, individuals at Pflegum Courtal (rather than those at Proton), on various occasions, appear defiant towards their biotech partner. The caricatures of Bob Fulghum (Bionatura) by Evelyn Murdoch (Pflegum Courtal) are anything but flattering ('He was a real pain in the neck...We call him "the whiner"...I always thought he was a bit schizo really...One of our secretaries does a wonderful imitation of him, because he calls so frequently to whine about why this is not enough...oh, it was just pathetic!'). What seems to emerge is a 'prince and pauper' screenplay – the image of a struggling biotech startup trying to make ends meet with inadequate funding provided by a much larger and largely insensitive pharmaceutical partner.

Whereas in the previous two case studies both biotech partners successfully emerged as legitimate and profitable organizations in their own right, rendering them increased bargaining power, Bionatura largely failed to do so. After nearly eight years the alliance had still not produced the elusive drug candidate. Instead, Bionatura was forced to sell off parts of its business in order to stay afloat. And, unless the joint programme happens upon a promising lead compound soon, the alliance may well die a natural death.

Criticisms

Structuration theory has been criticized on at least two accounts. First, despite the concept of the duality of structure being strong in accounting for the reproduction of social structures, it appears less well equipped to explain their transformation. As explained above, this predicament is not insurmountable, for there appears to be nothing in Giddens's treatment of structuration theory that makes it inadequate as a theory of change also. The theory does not exclude the possibility of change. Rather, the process of inventing a new structure appears no different from the process of reproducing existing structures, for in both contexts actors draw on existing structures. Confronted with the *unintended* outcomes of their actions, people may reflect on what was previously taken for granted and develop discursive knowledge regarding previously unacknowledged social structures. When this knowledge is acquired collectively it can become the basis for a structural, rather than mere incremental, change (Baert, 1992). Surely, it is only to be expected that individuals draw practical consequences from their experiences and put this practical knowledge to work in their everyday pursuits (Bourdieu and Wacquant, 1992).

A second line of criticism concerns the difficulty of delineating between action and structure. Giddens's contention that institutions only exist in so far as they are instantiated in everyday activities risks conflating structure with action (Barley and Tolbert, 1997). For where does action end and structure begin? And how can one avoid reducing structure to action and speak of institutions as existing separately from activity? Barley and Tolbert (1997), speaking to this criticism, suggest that it is of value only in an epistemological, rather than ontological, sense. From an epistemological perspective, they suggest, it makes good sense to use separate indicators for structure and action. There exist practical reasons for distinguishing between the two. In their own words:

> Unless researchers use separate indicators of institutions (which span settings and time) and actions (which are localized to a specific setting), they can neither argue convincingly that the two map the same principles nor show how actions implicate structures broader than those of setting itself. [Also] researchers require an empirically viable means of linking the two realms ... The value of defining scripts in behavioural terms and treating them as pivots between an institution and action is that it allows one to explicate the basis for one's inferences about systems of action, while simultaneously providing a point of reference for gauging the acceptability of deductions from transituational indicators of an institution and its implications for the logic of an interactive order. (1997: 99)

In a nutshell, the distinction, albeit slightly artificial, is helpful. Action and structure are intricately interrelated and one cannot speak of one without implicitly referring also to the other (Bouchikhi, 1993). A theory of alliances must therefore propose a scheme for studying both of these aspects of alliances. It is its first and most important epistemological implication.

A second feature of a structurationist epistemology is a strong emphasis on process. It is only as one comes close enough to the everyday reality of alliances that one can try to understand *how* people's actions and interactions are empowered and constrained by their, largely structural, context, of which the alliance is a part, and how they, in turn, produce, reproduce or transform these alliances. A third epistemological implication concerns the goals of social theory more broadly. More precisely, it affects a subscription to Giddens's epistemological position that empirical work in social sciences should be concerned with *verstehen* (understanding) social phenomena as opposed to producing normative theories. This does not reject the legitimate need for theories on the performance and management of alliances that may help pilot deliberate intervention. Quite to the contrary. Effective intervention can *only* be guided by a genuine understanding of phenomena. An analogy with the medical field may help. Prior to the discovery of aspirin people tried curing migraine using homespun remedies, including trepanning (drilling a hole in the skull), driving nails into fetishes, rubbing peppermint leaves on one's forehead or placing a wet cloth on it. The longevity of some of these practices (e.g. trepanning continued in Europe well into the sixteenth century) appears indicative of some success, though perhaps only in particular circumstances (e.g. a hangover or stress-induced headache) or with certain individuals (e.g. those with psychosomatic disorders). In fact, it was not until medicine had developed a thorough understanding of human physiology and the various sources of pain that the development of an effective, and consistently effective, cure became a realistic possibility.

In sum, structurationist theory contributes a number of characteristics to the study of alliances. Action and structure, it usefully suggests, are mutually implicated. Action is legitimized (sanctioned), ratified (made sense of), and empowered (given sufficient resources to be able to be carried out) by existing social structures. Thus, legitimization, signification, and domination are necessary preconditions of action, and structural dimensions of social systems. Action helps shape social structures by reproducing or transforming them, as the case may be. The structure of alliances, containing in it the sediments of prior transactions, is thus both the mediator and outcome of action. Human actors are a central feature of this process of structuration as it is they who act, generally under the constraint of existing social structures, though they need not be bound by these. They continuously reflect on the consequences of their actions, which may bring about unexpected change, transforming social structures. In a real sense innovation is replication, but replication is itself an agent of change.

Despite a theoretical appearance, owing to its link with a strong intellectual tradition, the approach advocated in this chapter is intended to contain a fair dose of realism. Yet, it does not advocate simple recipes nor predict an orderly and consistent alliance life. Every alliance is likely to be a unique phenomenon and some appear able to flourish given a fair amount of ambiguity. Consequently, there may not necessarily be one best way of managing them. Yet despite the relative idiosyncrasy and unpredictability of those involved in alliances, there is also order in their conduct. But it is the sort of order that does not easily afford grounds for prediction. Nor does this view negate the role of management or the importance of learning processes. It merely argues that multiple forces are at work and must be confronted purposefully and forcefully by managers, who must also be willing to understand that there can be no a-priori guarantee to secure any planned outcomes.

8   The hedgehog and the fox: the particular in the general[1]

If the theory review of the first chapter seemed a little critical, its critique was intended primarily at atomistic approaches to alliance life. The case studies should have been sufficient indication of their limitations and, in the specific cases of Ring and van de Ven (1994) and Doz (1996), also their contributions. Without seeking to diminish such contributions, one wonders whether these do not risk seeing alliance success primarily as the product of voluntary and purposive managerial intervention. Population-level approaches, conversely, may risk being too deterministic – in leaving too little room for chance and choice – and too expecting of progress. Clearly, the case is not against those who explain alliance life but those who explain away its quintessence and individuality. Experience precedes form, and may ultimately be more important than it.

The previous chapter suggested that, despite their individuality, there is order in alliance life. Order exists where (and to the extent to which) actors draw on underlying social structures to inform their strategic conduct. The chapter provided several examples of structuration processes from the case studies. But it delivered only the first segment of a multilectic account (cf. Huff, 1981), in leaving the idiosyncratic yet to be formally accounted for. While structuration theory may have been helpful in explaining order, we lack a formal theory to answer and justify the peculiar. This chapter invites the reader to consider a particular tradition in intellectual history – objective value pluralism – as a compelling platform on which to construct such a theory. The ensuing perspective, informed by the works of Isaiah Berlin and the eighteenth-century Romantics, affords a socialized appreciation of alliances, comparatively free of expectations on their constancy, homogeny, teleology or progress. This chapter thus comprises the conclusion of what is probably best described as a pluralist perspective on alliances.

---

[1] Excerpts from this chapter first appeared in de Rond (2002).

The following excerpt seems appropriate as an introduction: 'In every description of a battle there is a necessary lie,' wrote Tolstoy, 'resulting from the need of describing in a few words the actions of thousands of men spread over several miles, and subject to most violent moral excitement under the influence of fear, shame and death' (1983: 1310). As an afterthought to his epic novel *War and Peace*, this reflection may not be entirely irrelevant to our project. What was true of the official historical accounts of the 1812 Napoleonic wars may be true also, albeit perhaps to a lesser degree, of alliance studies. In writing about them we seem to have sought traits that afford generalization, prediction, and prescription – in the absence of compelling evidence that these are ordinarily the properties of alliances. Yet they are thought to be critical qualities in a discipline as keen to speak to practitioners as ours. Indeed, is this attitude not as much metaphysical as it is physical?

One might contend, however, that the ability to generalize and predict are not, and should never be, the sole, or even chief, goals of alliance research. As a matter of fact, we have adopted theories that, whilst considered successful, do not allow for either. For instance, although Darwin's theory of natural selection may help explain diversity and evolution within and between species, it is less helpful in predicting what the next generation of species will look like. Yet, despite being primarily descriptive, Darwin's theory remains extraordinarily robust. Within our own discipline, it speaks to population ecologists (e.g. Hannan and Freeman, 1977) and those interested in process (e.g. Koza and Lewin, 1998; van de Ven and Poole, 1995). And the reverse is also true. Consider, for instance, the migration of geese just prior to the start of winter. Though one might be able to predict winters quite effectively, this does not imply an understanding of them. For, surely, if geese *cause* winters by their departure, one could sustain the summer by grounding every goose in sight.

Theory needs to speak to the practitioner, particularly when it concerns a discipline as applied as ours. Affording prediction and prescription, however, is but one way in which to speak to practice. Theories can be compelling and useful despite being primarily explanatory. Moreover, good description can foster better prescription, though one should be careful never to make prediction the sole criterion for good theory. To use another analogy from medicine, it was not until the medical profession understood the various causes of heartburn that it was able to replace homespun remedies with H2 antagonist or proton pump inhibitors, resulting in such blockbuster drugs as Zantac.

This tendency towards generalization and simplification in management is the subject of an amusing but wry verse (a parody on a familiar

Christmas song) by the economist and *Financial Times* columnist John Kay:[2]

> On the first day of Christmas, my true love sent to me *The One Minute Manager*, by Kenneth Blanchard and Spencer Johnson. I thought she might be trying to make a point. On the second day of Christmas, my true love sent me *The Two Minute Motivator*. A touch of desperation here, I thought. But from the third day of Christmas on, the task became easier. I was pleased to receive Michael Porter's three generic strategies – cost leadership, differentiation and focus. On the fourth day, she presented me with the Boston Consulting Group matrix. There are four types of business in the firm's portfolio – cows, stars, dogs and question marks. On the fifth day, back to Michael Porter again, for the five forces of buyers, competitors, suppliers, entrants and substitutes. On the sixth day, who better to turn to than Jack Welch, for the six sigmas. And on the seventh day she pointedly drew my attention to Stephen Covey's *Seven Habits of Highly Effective People*. And like highly effective people, she stopped at seven. (Kay, 2002)

MBA core courses, the popular business literature, and the toolkits of consultants are usually packed with such lists. Kay continues:

> I once spent a session with a company which was debating how they should apply the concepts which had just [been] presented by their expensive consultants. Was the company a hunter or a gatherer? Were its customers empty-nesters or surfers? They couldn't do it. *They couldn't do it because the consultants' categories simply didn't match the way these managers instinctively saw their business or their customers.* Categorisation is inevitably rough and ready. We describe both blood and a pillar box as red although we know perfectly well that blood and a pillar box are actually different colours. The similarity seems more important than the difference. (Kay, 2002)

This partiality to prediction and its corollary, prescription, may be but a manifestation of a more urgent and deep-seated tendency in alliance research. I will seek to explain what this tradition might be, to try to discover the beliefs that sustain it, and to consider its potentially harmful consequences for the academic integrity of our discipline. Against the setting of an extant theoretical heterogeneity, as well as calls, by some, for a dominant paradigm, this chapter proposes an alternative theoretical position to help progress and differentiate our scholarship. When one accepts, so goes the argument, that the world of work is fundamentally diverse, pluralistic, and complex (an observation few are likely to forcefully contest) this inevitably calls for us to relax the monist orientation that appears to have informed our contributions thus far. Rather, what our discipline needs now is not more theoretical heterogeneity, nor a dominant paradigm to govern print and praxis, but theories *of* heterogeneity,

---

[2] His columns are available from his website www.johnkay.com

that is, theories that accept plurality, diversity, and complexity as onto-logical facts about the social world.

The hedgehog and the fox

As suggested by Glynn, Barr, and Dacin in a special issue of the *Academy of Management Review* on pluralism, our efforts at theory development may have embraced simplicity at the expense of accuracy.

The focus in much of organizational theorizing is to homogenize what is essentially a pluralistic world. On balance, organizational theorists have tended to emphasize the unifying principles that lend cohesion, focus, legitimacy, and identity; the result has been to problematize (or often overlook) the variety embedded in plurality. (2000: 726)

Studies of strategic alliances, despite drawing on an eclectic cluster of disciplines, are not unique in bearing the imprints of a parsimonic and monist tradition. For one finds this tradition woven into the fabrics of fields as varied as physics and politics, anthropology and archaeology, ethics and economics, religion and history. One of the fiercest and most articulate critics of monism was Isaiah Berlin. A Jew born in Riga but educated in England, Berlin was profoundly moved by the violence of the 1917 Russian Revolution (which he witnessed), but was also deeply influenced by the British empiricist tradition – its civilized, lucid, but sceptical treatment of anything catholic and rational. A contemporary and friend of A. J. (Freddie) Ayer, author of the classic *Language, Truth and Logic* (1936) and father of logical positivism in Britain, and J. L. Austin, a post-war critic of Ayer's work and pioneer of ordinary language philosophy, Berlin abandoned the Oxford philosophical tradition in pursuit of questions not then considered 'answerable'. Questions of meta-physics, theology, morality or politics are neither answerable by a-priori truths of logic and mathematics, nor translatable into simple atomistic and empirically testable propositions, and were to be assigned to 'the great bonfire of metaphysical rubbish' (Hausheer, 2002: 7). Epitomized in Wittgenstein's starting line in his *Tractatus-Logico-Philosophicus*, 'The world is all that is the case' (1992: 1), this was the dominant philosophical view at Oxford in the late 1950s. As recorded by the then-student Richard Swinburne:

The scepticism of Hume [had] given rise to logical positivism: the view that the only real things are sense impressions and (possibly) material objects of a size visible to the naked eye, and that our knowledge is limited to past, present and future alterations of sense impressions and material objects. And not merely our knowledge is limited; talk about anything else is meaningless. (1993: 182)

Indeed, 'what we cannot speak about we must pass over in silence', resolves the young Wittgenstein (1992). This, Berlin felt, denied too much of what we know to be true of human existence. There exist questions that are both genuine and important but to which there appear no ready-made, universal methods for resolving them. And this may be true even within as 'trivial' a research domain as that of interorganizational collaborations. In it, various theories have been proposed to explain their process dynamics, evolution, and performance. In trying to answer the 'how' question, these theories inevitably invoked the 'how come' question – or 'why do alliances unfold as they do?' The 'how' appears to entail the 'why', but it is the 'why' that seems most difficult to answer. To this there may not be a single, uniform solution. And there is no a-priori reason to think that may be the case even for 'how' questions. Berlin's intense dissatisfaction with the intellectual tradition of his day, his firm belief in the incompatibility of legitimate human values, and his observation that human beings were not infinitely malleable, drove him to read the neglected works of eighteenth-century Romantics Giambattista Vico (1668–1744), Johann Georg Hamann (1730–88),[3] and Johann Gottfried von Herder (1744–1803). And it is here that Berlin made a stunning and life-changing discovery. As recorded by his former pupil Roger Hausheer:

> As it now appeared to Berlin, and as he often repeated throughout his long life, all schools and movements of Western thought from, say, Plato until around the middle or the last of the eighteenth century... no matter how greatly they differed amongst themselves, rested upon the unexamined belief that behind all the variety and chaos of common human experience and opinion there lies one single objective world of facts and values which are in principle discoverable once and for all. Moreover, that if we but hit upon the proper method of investigation and apply it correctly, then we will discover what these are. And finally that the result will be a logically unified body of truth on all the genuine questions of theory and practice, of the nature of reality and the nature of true conduct which, once it has been uncovered, will be immutably valid for all men at all times and places. This was Berlin's first major discovery. (2002: 12)

These largely unquestioned tenets, comprising the very backbone of our Western intellectual tradition, affirm that harmony, predictability, and organization are, in fact, the stuff of reality. Bringing them to light, using reason (and reason alone), will help us answer the basic questions of life: what and why things are, were, and are likely to be. All questions, including normative ones, are essentially answerable. Of course we may never know the answers in full. But, in principle, they are discoverable for they exist. Berlin explained it thus:

---

[3] See Berlin (1994) for an excellent description of J. G. Hamann's intellectual contributions.

Of course, we may never attain to these answers: human beings may be too confused by their emotions, or too stupid, or too unlucky, to be able to arrive at them; the answers may be too difficult, the means may be lacking, the techniques too complicated to discover; but however this may be, provided the questions are genuine, the answers must exist. If we do not know, our successors may know; or perhaps wise men in antiquity knew; and if they did not, perhaps Adam in Paradise knew; or if he did not, the angels must know; and if even they do not know, God must know – the answers must be there. (1999: 36)

This set of hypotheses (for that is what they are) is common to the Enlightenment, to twentieth-century positivism, to the monotheistic religions of this world, and even to extreme political movements witnessed in the twentieth century. For it was the Rousseau-like belief in the existence of a 'one right way to live' (we have only to discover it) that may have provided the corner stone for communism, Naziism, and fascism as efficient and utterly rational means of organizing society. As described by Berlin's biographer and Harvard professor Michael Ignatieff:

The Enlightenment *philosophes* . . . assumed that human values could be derived from facts about human nature. They believed that all men wanted the same things and that these things were not in conflict. The entire Western agenda of ameliorative reform derived from this optimistic rationalism. Berlin's dilemma was how to rescue what was positive in the Enlightenment project from what was tyrannous. (1998: 201)

Whereas the Enlightenment tradition implicitly suggested that conflicting values were a sign of intellectual frailty and correctable through rational reforms, Romanticists thought them unique to human existence. And it is with the Romanticists that Berlin sided on this issue: on the implausibility of a rational organization of society securely derived from objective, discoverable, and uniform human values and ideals. Immanuel Kant's proclamation that 'out of the crooked timber of humanity no straight thing was ever made' was to become one of Berlin's pet aphorisms.

This disagreement with the atomistic 'one best way' approach to social organization was characteristic of, but not unique to, Berlin. In Greek philosophy, one finds the Sophists in search of an alternative to the intolerable conclusions of the Presocratics, particularly the extreme monism of Parmenides. As summarized by the twentieth-century philosopher W. K. C. Guthrie, 'If the monistic hypothesis led to denying the reality of the apparent multiplicity of the world around us, then in the interests of the phenomena that hypothesis must be rejected' (2000: 5). This moving away from monism to pluralism became a distinctive feature of Sophist philosophy. Despite their marked individuality, Sophists were empiricists and practically minded, and united in their stance against the assumed unshakeability of human laws, customs, and religious beliefs, as if these

were rooted in an unchanging natural order. Human society, in its organization, was to be a mere microcosm of the order of nature, 'involving
the conception of the universe as a divinely constructed and close-knit
organism, which goes back to Plato and beyond' (Guthrie, 1998: 6). It
is here that eighteenth-century German Romanticism may have repeated
the violent intellectual retort of fifth-century Greek Sophism.

Berlin argued that if one were to espouse the rationalist belief, life would
be rendered a mere jigsaw puzzle – we lie among the idle fragments trying
to figure out a way of putting the puzzle together. But together it must
fit. Berlin's (1999a) narrative on Tolstoy's view of history, entitled *The
Hedgehog and the Fox*, serves as an exceptionally insightful illustration.[4]
'The fox knows many things, but the hedgehog knows one big thing,'
quotes Berlin from the Greek poet Archilochus (1999a: 3). The hedgehog
is the *monist*, the fox the *pluralist*. Hedgehogs will always seek to interpret
everything in the light of some single, all-embracing system. They are, as
Berlin puts it, always trying to connect, always trying to represent things
as in some sense fitting or not fitting into some single pattern in which they
passionately believe. They are consistently viewing things and measuring
their significance in terms of some unifying principle, as opposed to being
interested in things for their own sake. Incidentally, this seems to have
been Durkheim's thrust also. To quote Berlin:

There exists a great chasm between those, on one side, who relate everything to a
single central vision, one system, less or more coherent or articulate, in terms of
which they understand, think and feel – a single, universal, organizing principle in
terms of which alone all that they are and say has significance – and, on the other
side, those who pursue many ends, often unrelated and even contradictory, connected, if at all, only in some *de facto* way, for some psychological or physiological
cause, related by no moral or aesthetic principle. These last lead lives, perform
acts and entertain ideas that are centrifugal rather than centripetal; their thought
is scattered or diffused, moving on many levels, seizing upon the essence of a
vast variety of experiences and objects for what they are in themselves, without,
consciously or unconsciously, seeking to fit them into, or exclude them from, any
one unchanging, all-embracing, sometimes self-contradictory and incomplete,
at times fanatical, unitary inner vision. The first kind of intellectual and artistic
personality belongs to the hedgehogs, the second to the foxes. (1999a: 3)

What Tolstoy's genius saw was not *the one* coherent and orderly world, but
always, 'with an ever growing minuteness, in all its teeming individuality, with an obsessive, inescapable, incorruptible, all-penetrating lucidity
which maddens him, *the many*' (1999a: 71). Tolstoy was a fox yearning
to be a hedgehog. In the words of Ignatieff, 'this distinction [between

---

[4] Interestingly, Isaiah Berlin happened upon the 'hedgehog and fox' metaphor at a party
game, where he was told of a line from the Greek poet Archilochus by the then-student,
Lord Oxford.

hedgehogs and foxes] seemed to capture the fissure between Tolstoy's fox-like gift as a novelist for conveying the fine detail of human life and his hedgehog-like search for an overarching theory of human existence' (1998: 173).

The controversial philosopher Paul Feyerabend (1999), taking great pleasure in the physical and cultural diversity of this world, made a strikingly similar observation. Our efforts to make sense in varied and complex contexts by drawing on abstractions, metaphors, and stereotypes, he argued, appear to suggest that one can gradually unravel the (one) truth. What is more, by virtue of all local entities being lawfully, or causally, related, we expect to be able to manipulate or predict them. However, as now acknowledged by some mathematicians and physicists, particularly those working on complexity theories, even the simplest of dynamic systems are seen to create extraordinary difficulty in terms of predictability (Gleick, 1998: 7, 8). Noted as early as 1931 by Carl L. Becker in his Storrs Foundation lectures to Yale University:

It is one of the engaging ironies of modern thought that the scientific method, which it was once fondly hoped would banish mystery from the world, leaves it every day more inexplicable. Physics, which it was thought had dispensed with the need of metaphysics, has been transformed by its own proper researches into the most metaphysical of disciplines. The more attentively the physicist looks at the material stuff of the world the less there is to see. (1960: 24)

That prediction has hitherto been thought to be a plausible test of theory is, in part, the legacy of logical positivism – the belief, among other things, in symmetry of explanation and prediction, testability as a gauge of good theory, and a clear-cut distinction between facts and values. As recently put by the editors of a special issue of *Organization Science* on complexity theory:

Organizational scholars seldom come to grips with nonlinear phenomena. Instead, we tend to model phenomena as if they were linear in order to make them tractable, and we tend to model aggregate behaviour as if it is produced by individual entities which all exhibit *average* behaviour. (Anderson et al., 1999: 233; italics added)

Theories that allow for accuracy in prediction are deemed the most desirable, despite perhaps failing to explain exactly how these regularities and predictions come about (Baert, 1998).

The epistemological challenge

Alliance process theories, to the extent to which they seek uniformity, consistency, and rationality, are comparatively 'hedgehog' in orientation. Life cycle models, in their atomistic and rigid linearity, are severely limited in allowing for rapidly changing technological environments, the multiplicity and fluidity of strategy, the regeneration of a research project, and the element of surprise. The empirical world may not contain anything like a 'statistically average' alliance. Teleological approaches, though vastly more realistic than the reductionist theories they sought to improve upon, may still risk being too expectant of management as the centripetal force behind the evolution and success of alliances. Their rhetoric, at any rate, is managerial. Despite these criticisms, the proposed iteration by Ring and van de Ven (1994) may well be the most open ended. Evolutionary models are different again, in that they explain alliance process at the population level and risk being too deterministic and too expectant of progress. While it may be difficult for linear models to coexist with iterative ones, these iterative theories can coexist with population-level approaches. Their points of view differ, as do the underlying disciplines on which they draw (socio-psychology versus biology), and one can derive different lessons from each. They are helpful, whether considered independently or jointly, albeit not perfectly compatible. This observation is consistent with van de Ven and Poole (1995).

Even so, each approach remains characterized by expectations that are comparatively monist, in assuming, a priori, the existence of order and constancy, uniformity and rationality. In our life cycle, teleological, and evolutionary approaches we may have persisted, inadvertently or otherwise, in three persuasive but largely unexamined beliefs: (a) that to all genuine questions there is only one true answer; (b) that true answers are discoverable through the application of reason; and (c) that, when combined, these true answers cannot be in conflict with one another. True to our monist intellectual tradition, they must form a stable and universal body of theory (cf. Becker, 1960; Berlin, 1991, 1996, 1998, 2000a, 2000b). As in arithmetic, there is but one true solution to a given sum. A single and predictive theory of alliances, in other words, has always remained a distinct and desirable possibility. Even if we have not found it yet, the idea of a single, perfect theory exists – at least in principle.

If only men would learn how little the cleverest and most gifted among them can control, how little they can know of all the multitude of factors the orderly movement of which is the history of the world; above all, what presumptuous nonsense it is to claim to perceive an order merely on the strength of believing desperately that an order must exist, when all one actually perceives is meaningless chaos. (Berlin, 1999a: 48)

To some extent, of course, this trimming down of variety is part and parcel of the scholarly enterprise. It is an obligation also on the part of managers.

One of the central issues for strategic leadership in the modern corporation becomes the defraying of excessive complexity and ambiguity. The ability to deliver clear, simple, and evocative messages that balance future goals with present needs seems to be a crucial simplifying routine in times of tension and change. (Pettigrew, 2001: 43)

However, as is the case with ancient manuscripts, not all translations are equally good; some, in refusing to explain away inconsistencies, provide insight where others leave fragments of the puzzle shrouded in obscurity.

A provocative argument, put forward by Jeffrey Pfeffer (1993), responds to this theoretical heterogeneity (but not to its monist and reductionist character) by suggesting that we may benefit from efficiencies gained by converging on a dominant paradigm to guide research in the field. The argument is essentially epistemological. Citing the works of Cole (1983) and Kuhn (1970), Pfeffer mirrors organization studies to the physical sciences and, perhaps mistakenly, concludes that too much heterogeneity can be harmful to the field. He suggests that, instead, control over publication is best placed into the hands of an elite who subscribe to the same scholarly praxis.

Pfeffer's controversial viewpoint has been much debated. Particularly helpful criticisms, whilst remaining confined to the realms of epistemology, are provided by Cannella and Paetzold (1994) and van Maanen (1995). The former suggest that Pfeffer's argument is fundamentally flawed; that knowledge, whether in the arts or sciences, is essentially socially constructed. This is a good but not new argument. Constructivism has a long and illustrious history. John van Maanen's (1995) rejoinder to Pfeffer proposes that it is neither feasible to conjure up a paradigm of sufficient appeal to voluntarily unite the community of scholars, nor practicable to will or legislate into existence any such unity of praxis.

Neither the existing theoretical heterogeneity – providing insightful but incomplete theories – nor the dominant paradigm advocated by Pfeffer may supply a particularly well-suited epistemology for the empirical study of alliance life. Rather, if one is prepared to accept the ontological statement that the empirical social world is a diverse and complex place, at whichever level, one must follow through with the epistemological consequence that research may be best served by being grounded in theories that accept this complexity up front. Or theories *of* heterogeneity. Or the *fox*.

Towards theories *of* heterogeneity

When one accepts that the empirical world is fundamentally heterogeneous, ambiguous, and complex, this necessitates the relaxing of a central feature of our western intellectual tradition: the deep-seated belief that there is a single harmony of truths into which everything, if it is genuine, in the end must fit (Berlin, 2000a: 14). Theories *of* heterogeneity (or pluralist theories) make no such assumption. The social world is neither considered exceptionally orderly or predictable, nor do we expect this to be true of organizational phenomena despite the constraints imposed by their institutional frameworks. Disorder and ambiguity may be found at the industry, organizational, and individual level. Thus, the ontological assumptions that sustain such theories will typically view alliances as open ended, self-generating, and largely self-organizing, capable of rapid change but only sporadically as circumstances dictate, subject to coexisting but opposing forces that do not necessarily favour efficiency, less sensitive to the external environment than are 'open' systems, and able to remember and carry information. This approach is not entirely dissimilar to that advocated by Gharajedaghi and Ackoff (1984). From a systems theory perspective, they proposed a study of organizations as *social systems*, to contrast with more common mechanistic and organismic treatment. A social systems approach proposes to study organizations synthetically (or as whole systems), assuming that their different parts are dynamic and nonlinear, and their interaction complex, recursive or highly iterative (Mathews, White, and Long, 1999). These properties would seem to suggest two things. First, an interdependence between different organizational components would allude to the coexistence of cooperative and competitive relationships within organizations. Second, by implication, evolution would appear to be largely unpredictable.

Pluralism is defined here more precisely as *objective value* pluralism, or the belief in a plurality of values and ideals which men can and do seek (Rescher, 2000). These values are objective in that the pursuit of them is an intrinsic part of being human.

The fact that men are men and women are women and not dogs or cats or tables or chairs is an objective fact; and part of this objective fact is that there are certain values, and only those values, which men, while remaining men, can pursue. (Berlin, 1999a: 51)

Pluralism differs from relativism in an important respect: it expects us to find certain alternatives to be rationally superior to others. This judgement is entirely rational in that certain ideas may be seen to be more rationally appropriate than others given a particular context. It is not a matter of preference or taste (as in preferring tea over tonic) as in relativism, nor is it predicated on indifference (or 'anything goes'). In contrast with relativism, pluralism is not equally accepting of the various incompatible standpoints on offer, leaving one with no rational basis to choose one reality over another. Instead, it suggests that those existing in different circumstances may have their own good reasons for seeing an alternative as rationally appropriate.

That is why pluralism is not relativism – the multiple values are objective, part of the essence of humanity rather than arbitrary creations of men's subjective fancies. Nevertheless, of course, if I pursue one set of values I may detest another, and may think it is damaging to the only form of life that I am able to live or tolerate, for myself and others; in which case I may attack it ... But I still recognize it as a human pursuit. I find Nazi values detestable, but I can understand how, given enough misinformation, enough false belief about reality, one could come to believe that they are the only salvation. Of course they have to be fought, by war if need be, but I do not regard the Nazis, as some people do, as literally pathological or insane, only as wickedly wrong, totally misguided about the facts, for example in believing that some beings are subhuman, or that race is central, or that Nordic races alone are truly creative, and so forth. I see how, with enough false education, enough widespread illusion and error, men can, while remaining men, believe this and commit the most unspeakable crimes. (Berlin, 1999a: 52–3)

The Italian philosopher and novelist Umberto Eco provides an illuminating example of exactly what pluralism entails. Reflecting on the demise of Ptolemy's theory in the Copernican revolution, Eco says this:

The force of the Copernican revolution is not only due to the fact that it explains some astronomical phenomena better than the Ptolemaic tradition, but also to the fact that it – instead of presenting Ptolemy as a crazy liar – explains why and on which grounds he was *justified* in outlining his own interpretation. (1992: 150–1; italics added)

The legitimacy of arguments, in other words, depends greatly on the context in which they are created and exist. The distinction between relativism and pluralism seems subtle but is worth remembering, particularly given what appears to be the gradual erosion of relativism as an intellectually acceptable alternative to modernism. Pluralism is also superior to relativism for pragmatic reasons in that it demands of us the articulation of one justifiable standpoint rather than steering us into an intellectual quasi-cramp. Even so, pluralists join relativists in their call for democracy as the only acceptable solution to social complexity and diversity.

Being thus pluralistically oriented – in believing deeply in the coexistence of multiple legitimate but incompatible ideas – the approach outlined here allows for equally desirable ends to conflict, forcing management to orchestrate the conflicting claims of cooperation and competition, autonomy and control, trust and vigilance, integration and differentiation, innovation and replication, justice and mercy. To paraphrase G. K. Chesterton (1996), it allows one to see two or more images at once and yet see all the better for it. Paradoxically, however, performance cannot readily be predicted, and yet there is a sense of the predictable about it (cf. Marion, 1999).

In crafting a pluralistic approach to the study of alliance evolution, particularly one applied to drug discovery alliances as an empirical illustration, we remember the counsel of Tolstoy who, upon an exhaustive effort to detail the complex mental and moral lives of Russians comes to a remarkable conclusion. Faulting historians for giving the 1812 Napoleonic war aims that never existed, he says this in his epic *War and Peace*:

> To study the laws of history we must completely change the subject of our observation, must leave aside kings, ministers, and generals, and study *the common, infinitesimally small elements by which the masses are moved.* No one can say how far it is possible for man to advance in this way towards an understanding of the laws of history; but it is evident that only along that path does the possibility of discovering the laws of history lie. (1983: 881; italics added)

Tolstoy could not but notice the particular, the diverse, the coexistence of equally valid but incompatible ideals – a people made happy by quite different things. Or as put by the German Romantic J. G. von Herder, 'The happiness of man is in all places an individual good ... the offspring of practice, tradition, and custom' (1968: 71).

Closer to our own discipline, early examples of theories of heterogeneity have broken the surface. Complexity-based theories have been applied to explain the formation of, and change inside, social systems, including organizations (e.g. Axelrod and Cohen, 1999; Marion, 1999). Cohen, March, and Olsen's (1972) 'garbage can' approach may be viewed as a relatively early example in the organizations literature, given its assumptions. Structuration theory, credited to the sociologist Anthony Giddens (and essentially a 'complex' theory), has been applied to the study of alliance effectiveness (e.g. Sydow and Windeler, 1998) and their process dynamics and evolution (e.g. de Rond, 2000). Bouchikhi (1998) appropriated the ontology of complex systems theory to generate a constructivist perspective on organizations, built on the assumption that human behaviour is relatively undetermined, multidirectional, and contradictory. Boisot and Child (1999) drew on structuration theory and complex systems theory to propose a treatment of organizations as complex adaptive systems, and concluded similarly that most organizations will exist in a poised state somewhere between order and chaos. A parallel assumption sustains the work of Brown and Eisenhardt (1998). Calls for less parsimonious and more eclectic theoretical approaches to the study of organizations are not particularly novel (e.g. Huff, 1981), but calls for theories and empirical applications are. Interestingly, social scientists are looking, once again, at the natural sciences to provide explanatory frameworks.

Relevance and implications

The relevance of accepting diversity and complexity (an ontological position) and adopting a strategy of building theories of heterogeneity (an epistemological position) becomes clear when examining its corollary – that if our discipline is to be organized at all, and not left to chaos, hunches, and the play of chance, then it can be organized only in the light of monist principles and laws (cf. Berlin, 1998: 327). As the philosopher of science Nancy Cartwright forcefully argues:

If nothing further were at stake, I should not be particularly concerned about whether we believe in a ruly world or in an unruly one, for, not prizing the purity of our affirmations, I am not afraid that we might hold false beliefs. The problem is that our beliefs about the structure of the world go hand-in-hand with the methodologies we adopt to study it. The worry is not so much that we will adopt wrong images with which to represent the world, *but rather that we will choose wrong tools with which to change it.* (1999a: 12; italics added)

For instance, a view of organizations as being continuously subject to a set of coexisting, dialectical forces produces a different set of managerial implications than more traditional approaches. Whereas a traditional treatment may call for monitoring, managerial intervention, and control, a pluralist-based perspective would prefer to view management as a subtle activity, tolerant to ambiguity and some disorder, and involved in ongoing processes of balancing, adaptation, and navigation, implying only infrequent changes in itinerary. Whatever theories of heterogeneity may be constructed within, or adopted by, strategy scholars, they will probably share a number of characteristics. First, they will accept variety as an ontological fact about the empirical world. Heterogeneity, accordingly, becomes a point of departure, rather than a corollary, no longer necessitating theoretical concessions. Second, they seek to leave aside any a-priori expectations as to manageability, constancy, consistency, internal structure, life span, performance, and success. They focus on what is. Third, they will actively encourage variety in methodology, allowing one to employ a portfolio of research tools, without sacrificing transparency and rigour. Fourth, they will almost inevitably sacrifice efficiency in favour of realism; but perhaps our discipline might be better served by an emphasis on the latter. At the expense of using a well-worn cliché, Rome wasn't built in just one day. Fifth, their criteria for theory choice and development will be primarily explanatory, rather than being exclusively predictive. Sixth, they are quite likely to emerge as snapshots of the theorizing process, rather than as full-blown theories. To paraphrase Weick (1995), theories may take the form of approximations, reflecting not intellectual impotence nor indolence, but 'interim struggles' as scholars inch towards stronger theories of heterogeneity.

Seventh, it may well be that innovation in any social science – as appears the case with the natural sciences – is necessarily an anarchic enterprise. Whilst anarchism is not attractive politically, it may be excellent medicine for epistemology. Violations of existing epistemological and methodological approaches may well be critical to progress. As Feyerabend concludes in his historical review of science, 'the idea of a method that contains firm, unchanging and absolutely binding principles for conducting the business of science meets considerable difficulty when confronted with the results of historical research' (1993: 14). A very similar conclusion is reached by Durschmied (1999), though applied not to the history of science, but, interestingly, that of warfare.

Eighth, if we come to see the world of organizations as fundamentally pluralistic, as did Leo Tolstoy and Isaiah Berlin, we must be prepared to relax our zeal for prediction and control. Pluralism and prediction are not necessarily compatible. Pluralism believes not merely in the multiplicity, but in the *incommensurability* of the values of different cultures and societies; the coexistence of incompatible ideals – the fact that men are not made happy by the same things (Berlin, 2000b). In contrast to our Western intellectual tradition, it denies the necessity of regularity, compatibility, harmony, progress, and perfection. Hence, how can prediction follow naturally from better description? Description may produce understanding but not necessarily prediction. A better appreciation of the forces shaping organizational life, however, will still generate implications for management. Theory still has much to say to practice, albeit from a different set of premises.

Ninth, in building theories of heterogeneity – theories that accept pluralism as an ontological statement about the world of organizations – we are likely to find the works of such scholars as Isaiah Berlin and the German Romantics to be a useful resource. By denying the necessity of regularity, harmony, compatibility, and progress (the fruits of the Enlightenment), the Romantics sought to emphasize instead the inspiration, subjectivity, and primacy of the individual. Romanticism, though difficult to define precisely given its many strands, is innately contradictory: it comprises the primitive and untutored as well as the complex and cerebral; the novel and mysterious as well as the familiar and nostalgic; the pursuit of knowledge and yet also the rejection of it.

Tenth, and on a more speculative note, to the extent that our present research may have cloaked itself, at times, in pretensions of objectivity – generating legitimacy but risking detachment – future efforts may benefit from leveraging our imaginative faculties, enabling us to enter contexts that may not naturally be our own and allowing our output to bear the mark of our varied personalities. It is during the long periods of reflection that precede the writing – and that are an intrinsic constituent of theorizing and sensemaking – that this imaginative faculty is at its most active.

Thanks to the imagination, to its flattering touch, the cold skeleton of reason acquires living, rosy flesh; thanks to it the sciences flourish, the arts are embellished, woods speak, echoes sigh, rocks weep, marble breathes and all inanimate objects come to life. (Joseph de la Mettrie (1709–51), 1996: 15, 17)

In sum, if one accepts the ontological claim that the empirical world of alliances is potentially varied, disorderly, inconsistent, subject to contradictory forces, and socially complex, then theories of heterogeneity would appear the most logical epistemological consequence. In fact, it may not be until we adopt such theories that we can simultaneously see at work, describe, and explain the irregularity and relative unpredictability of human agency; the coexistence of order and chaos; the spontaneous appearance of order in an disorderly environment, but without yielding to predictability; its drawing on potentially incompatible value systems; it being both empowered and constrained by underlying social structures, and simultaneously focused on the pursuit of multiple but not always congruent agendas; organizations as mediated by the interplay of coexisting but diametrically opposed forces that surface at the level of the environment, the organization, and the individual, at the atomic and the everyday level – driving organizations into a poised state somewhere between synergy and entropy, stability and change. It is thus that we may help humanize one of the most important spheres of life. That, to be sure, must be a central aim of this book.

So here we have it. Berlin's objective value pluralism and Giddens's structuration theory may combine into a perspective that emphasizes the particular of alliances whilst seeing in them also the general. For the particular remains impregnated with the universal. Social facts cannot be abstracted from the potential idiosyncrasies and inconsistencies of human conduct. But neither can this conduct be removed, except artificially, from collective social structures that inform, legitimize, and sanction it. And yet the general is experienced only ever in the particular. Some things can only be known through particulars despite a vast literature imparting universals. Ironically, we, true to our monist tradition, have tended to invest our intellectual lives in pursuit of universals despite living most of our everyday lives by samples of one.[5]

Clearly, there is the particular and the general. There is the particular *in* the general but so too the general *in* the particular. Individuals express their individuality but do so in part by drawing on the sedimented remains of prior interactions. Whilst it is they that compose the plots of the stories, the stories themselves belong to the same genre. The 'whodunit' may give away the general idea but exposes not the perpetrator.

---

[5] And, ironically, so have some of our most successful corporate leaders. Jack Welch, Bill Gates, Warren Buffet, each lacking breadth of experience, serve as telling examples, having spent most of their working lives inside a single institution. The idea of 'samples of one' came from the insightful article by March, Sproull, and Tamuz (1991).

9   The legitimacy of messiness

'Would you tell me, please, which way I ought to go from here?' asked Alice in Wonderland.[1] Hers is a legitimate question (particularly when lost), and should perhaps be the starting point for this concluding chapter. What, if any, are the implications of a pluralist perspective for our understanding of biopharmaceutical alliances? How might it challenge the way we think about alliances generally? Despite it being principally descriptive, has it any use for practice? What should be clear is that there is not ever likely to be a single recipe for managing them. Nor is there necessarily a one-best-strategy for the pursuit and use of alliances – its value would have been destroyed in the act of its discovery.

Strategic alliances have continued to proliferate in the face of high failure rates. It would be too easy to conclude that managers are either irrational or incompetent. Whilst this may be true occasionally, a good part of the problem lies in our thinking about them. Beneficiaries of a monist intellectual tradition, we may have persisted in three rarely questioned beliefs: (a) that to all genuine questions there is only one true answer; (b) that true answers are discoverable by applying reason; and (c) that these true answers cannot be in conflict with one another but must fit into a coherent body of theory (Berlin, 1999a). A single and durable theory of alliances, in other words, has remained not only possible but also desirable – for the ideal exists in principle. Yet are not organizations likely to experience human divisiveness, ubiquity of interests, idiosyncrasies, personalities, histories, and loyalties despite the inevitable institutional constraints they place on their members? Business organizations remain distinctly social phenomena – personal, political, social, and moral life carries on inside them. Moreover, we that write about alliances may be faulted for these same characteristics. Why then have we persisted in the expectation of finding constancy, progress, teleology or an underlying

---

[1] Alice is the fictional heroine of Lewis Carroll's *Alice's Adventures in Wonderland* (1865). Lewis Carroll was the pseudonym of Charles Lutwidge Dodgson, a logician and mathematician at Christ Church, Oxford, who based his character on Alice Liddell, daughter of the then Dean of Christ Church, for whom he also wrote the book.

order? It is such expectations that this book has sought to relax. Pluralism, as the epistemological alternative to monism, may better allow one to observe all that can be seen – even if it is irrelevant to existing theory.

This book sought to achieve three related objectives: (a) to respond to a lack of empirical research and theory development on alliance dynamics and evolution in a governance- and performance-dominated alliance literature; (b) to help remedy a felt imbalance in this literature towards alliances as strategic, financial or economic phenomena, at the expense of their social, contextual, and historical characteristics; and (c) to relax any monist assumptions we may traditionally have taken to them. It took as its focal point those alliances dominated by sophisticated technologies, chemistry, biology, biochemistry, physics, biophysics, structural modelling, and crystallography – all natural sciences – and placed them within the context of the relevant alliance process literature. This strategy should have yielded two broad observations. First, teleological frameworks are a considerable improvement on life cycle explanations of alliance life. Even so, they may risk explaining their evolution principally as the product of managerial intervention and leaving too little room for serendipity, the possibility of irrationality, and inevitability. To this extent, the case narratives contained events neither easily nor normally accounted for by such approaches. Second, this juxtaposition of theory and empirical data forced us to think more deeply about the assumptions we bring to our theorizing about alliances. Our understanding of alliance life, I suggested, may be improved by examining their diversity and the role of human agency in authoring their various plots. Thus what our discipline may need is not more theoretical variety but theories *of* variety – or pluralist theories. The practice of merely adding together different theories, as one might do with metaphors, does not amount to a theory of variety. While they may provide useful, partial explanations, such theories remain built on the premise of homogeny. Theories *of* variety comprise a fundamentally different category, for their starting premise is heterogeneity.

Within a pluralist perspective, human agency takes centre stage. Coherent with structuration theory, the conduct of those involved in alliances is ratified, legitimized, and sanctioned by deep-seated social rules and resources that are themselves the consequence of prior interactions. Surely, it is only likely that individuals learn from their experiences and put this practical knowledge to use in their present-day activities (Bourdieu and Wacquant, 1992). A pluralist perspective, however, grants them a far greater degree of voluntarism than one might expect from reading Giddens (1984), for there appears to be nothing in structuration theory that prevents it from being also a theory of change. Individuals

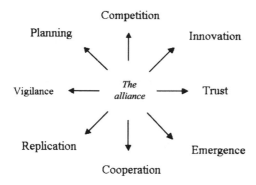

Figure 9.1: Dialectical tensions in alliances (adapted from Bouchikhi, 1998)

may be aware of the past but need not be constrained by it. In sum, despite the peculiarity of alliance life there is order – but order of a different sort. There is the general *and* the particular, the general as existing *in* the particular, the general as only ever experienced *through* the particular, and the particular *in* the general. And what at first might have seemed a marriage of incompatibles may, in fact, help generate a more realistic appreciation of alliance life.

Beyond the findings that were specific to the case studies, this book makes three potentially important points relevant to alliance research. First, alliances may well be less orderly, less consistent internally, less homogeneous, less predictable, and less manageable (in the traditional sense) than previously supposed. Hamel, Doz, and Prahalad (1989) already alluded to the lack of harmony in alliances. But disharmony is not disorder. Whereas the former suggests conflict or lack of sympathy, disorder provides a much broader interpretation including not just the potential for conflict but the ubiquitous nature of strategy and resultant possibility of conflict, the lack of alignment of processes inside alliances, their lack of predictability, and their peculiarity. Second, human agency can play a more significant role than suggested in the alliance literature. It is they who write the plots of the stories. The argument agrees with Ring and van de Ven (1994) and Doz (1996) on the critical role played by middle managers (as opposed to just senior managers). Third, alliances may well be subject to dialectical but coexisting dynamics pulling the alliance in contradictory directions at any one time. Such forces can potentially include those of competition and cooperation, planning and emergence, control and autonomy, replication and innovation, expansion and contraction, conflict and compromise, justice and mercy (see Figure 9.1). As a result, alliances may, most of the time, exist in a poised state between synergy and entropy – divided by the incompatible and yet the legitimate. But perhaps it is exactly this balance of contradictions that constitutes the buoyancy of healthy alliances.

In sum, alliances may well be messier than previously thought. Ironically, this messiness may also be perfectly legitimate. For instance, not only do competing forces coexist but it may be quite useful for this to be so. Competition might still have to weed out the inefficient, even in alliances. Trust affords efficiency, particularly in an environment where legal contracts can trail months behind the actual joint work, but can be dangerous in the absence of vigilance. Planning and control likewise afford efficiency but can be constraining in the absence of emergence and autonomy. Penicillin and Viagra might never have been discovered otherwise. Autonomy and spontaneity are indispensable to alliance success but must be curbed by old-fashioned planning and control. This dialectical interplay helps explain the felt messiness of alliances.[2] But it also suggests that this messiness can be virtuous and entirely justifiable.

Contributions to theory

Consistent with its stated aims, this book has, I hope, made three identifiable contributions to theory. First, it added to the relatively scarce alliance process literature by contributing three longitudinal studies of evolving alliances, and a fresh theoretical lens for their study. Second, this perspective is a socialized one, in that it allows human actors a key role in shaping the process dynamics of alliances, and specifically sought a contextualized and historical treatment of them. Third, in so doing it sought to avoid making a-priori assumptions as to constancy, universality, manageability, and performance. Alliances just are. Incidentally, this study contributes also by emphasizing the possibility of a dialectical perspective. In so doing it moves beyond most of the literature into van de Ven and Poole's (1995) fourth and final quadrant (see Figure 1.5). Also, by using a similar empirical example to Doz (1996) one may see a contribution

---

[2] Dialectics is intended to be more open ended than as defined in the classical Hegelian and Marxist sense. Hegel, like Marx, expected the confrontation of dialectical forces to generate a new temporary equilibrium (thesis and anti-thesis collide and produce synthesis). In the dialectical view proposed here, there is no expectation of a new (and perhaps better) creation out of conflict. Fundamentally opposing forces merely coexist and may, or may not, generate new equilibria that may, or may not, be an improvement on what was before. This usage of dialectics outside of the strict Hegelian domain is not uncommon. As Zeitz explained, there exist many different interpretations of dialectics; Schneider (1971) articulated seven different definitions whereas Hall (1967) listed eight.

in arriving at a set of conclusions that highlight quite different characteristics of alliances.

Finally, this book pursued a pluralist treatment of alliances to contrast with monist approaches. Chapters 7 and 8, in particular, were dedicated to the characterization of a new sort of theory, combining features of structuration theory (to speak to their order) and objective value pluralism (to speak to the particular in alliances). This is inevitably a difficult challenge – the history of social and organizational theory is conspicuously marked by repeated attempts to mediate action and structural elements of social life (Baert, 1998; Coleman, 1986; Poole and van de Ven, 1989).[3] And this book is conceivably no real improvement on the contributions of great social thinkers, though arguably this was not its aim. It did intend to reiterate the need for a pluralist approach to alliance life, one that could accommodate structure as well as action, whilst speaking to chance coincidences also. To that extent it used rich empirical data to characterize existing explanations of the process dynamics and evolution of alliances, and invite theories of choice and chance, theories that speak to variety as well as similarity, to the particular as well as the general. Perhaps it is this absurdity that may ultimately afford a relatively complete perspective on alliance life. The book may thus be seen as responding to Poole and van de Ven's (1989: 576) call for experiments with what may seem incompatible theoretical positions (i.e. determinism, voluntarism, and serendipity), so as to specify the relationships, if any, among them and arrive at new and creative integrations that enhance understanding. It thus took on their proposed strategy of identifying 'theoretical tensions or oppositions', and using them 'to stimulate the development of more encompassing theories' (1989: 563). Any resulting theories may not be perfectly internally consistent but could at least house paradox. Clearly, we need theories to explain the particular alongside the general, so as to see the particular *in* the general, and the general *in* the particular – theories that permit voluntarism, determinism, and serendipity to jointly explain causality. For the stuff of alliance life is likely to be part choice, part chance, and part inevitability.

This, incidentally, is a future project worthy of consideration. What precisely is the relationship between choice, chance, and inevitability? Do serendipity and inevitability really exist at opposite ends of the spectrum? This, at any rate, sounds correct intuitively. To this extent it may be

---

[3] The most surprising example of this may well be Jean-Paul Sartre's *The Problem of Method* (1963), in which Sartre argued for the compatibility of existentialism and Marxism (or the voluntaristic and the deterministic). Sartre maintained that existentialism would cease to exist as a separate philosophy once Marxism is properly understood – a viewpoint that created some controversy, even among his followers.

interesting to briefly revisit Pfizer's experience with Viagra. The drug is frequently supposed to have been discovered by chance. And this is where we left it in Chapter 2. However, Pfizer's lucrative patent on Viagra was revoked by the UK High Court of Justice in November 2000 for reasons of 'obviousness'.[4] Lilly ICOS, a joint venture between Ely Lilly and ICOS Corporation to target erectile dysfunction, sought to invalidate and revoke the patent protection enjoyed by Pfizer for the medical use of a number of chemicals, including sildenafil citrate, the active ingredient in Viagra. Lilly ICOS worried that the patent might stand in its way of producing a competing anti-impotence drug. One of the chief arguments invoked by Lilly ICOS, the petitioner, was the fact that the patent[5] was 'anticipated by a single piece of prior art' and 'obvious over a number of pieces of prior art'. Put simply, the drug's discovery was inevitable. Anticipation by a single piece of prior art referred to a paper published in 1993 in the *Journal of the American Geriatrics Society* (Korenman and Viosca, 1993). Obviousness was pleaded based on two other publications, including an article in the prestigious *New England Journal of Medicine* (Rajfer et al., 1992; Murray, 1993) and a PhD dissertation completed at the University of California. Internal company documents, submitted at the time of the hearing, revealed that these publications had been taken notice of by at least four prominent scientists in addition to those at Pfizer.[6] Each article had surfaced in the early 1990s, thus preceding the patent by several years. Although the case of anticipation ultimately failed, Lilly ICOS was successful in persuading the court to invalidate Pfizer's patent for reasons of obviousness.

The *Lilly ICOS* v. *Pfizer* ruling may serve as a useful example of the complexity of causality in pharmaceutical R&D. Serendipity played a role, but so did voluntarism and inevitability. The same appears to have been true of 3M's development of Post-It Notes, where the special glue used had been available within 3M for several years. Or the development of Canon's Bubblejet technology with Ichiro Endo's serendipitous observation of a researcher accidentally touching the tip of an ink-filled syringe with a soldering iron, thus redirecting Canon's efforts towards producing the thermal inkjet printer.[7] Or the near-simultaneous discovery by Hewlett-Packard's Mr Vaught of the potential of using heat to shoot dots

---

[4] Case no.: HC 1999 No 01110. A full transcript of the case can be found at http://news.findlaw.com/cnn/docs/viagra/viagrapatent.html

[5] The patent is formally known as 'Pyrazolopyrimidones for the treatment of impotence'.

[6] Those mentioned by name include Dr Murray at SmithKline Beecham (now GlaxoSmithKline), Dr Silver of Sterling Winthrop, Dr Gristwood of Almirall, and Dr Hyafil of GlaxoWellcome.

[7] As described in *The Economist*, 21 September 2002, in a 'Technology Quarterly' supplement, pp. 24–5.

of ink directly onto paper by watching a coffee percolator in action, thus laying the theoretical foundations for Hewlett-Packard's Deskjet technologies through a process known as 'phreatic reaction' that worked but was not fully understood until a year later.[8] Or even Honda's much-debated entry into the US motorcycle market (Pascale, 1996). Chance, choice, and inevitability repeatedly surface as cooperating in the formulation and implementation of ideas. Chance coincidences may remain unrecognized unless accompanied by a larger context of inevitability to render them meaningful. As with voluntarism, chance appears to draw on such inevitable forces but also contributes to their future form (Giddens, 1984). The relationship may be similarly recursive. Hence, the following questions seem legitimate: to what extent is inevitability, rather than being the converse of chance and choice, also a precondition for both, as well as being their consequence? Is it possible to speak of one without necessarily implicating any other, and be hopeful of having provided a comprehensive account of alliance life?

Contributions to practice

Although it was not originally my aim to write for practitioners, it might be useful to see whether a pluralist approach to alliances can speak to practice. What, if any, might be the implications for those involved in their day-to-day unfolding? Whilst being careful not to draw general conclusions from a very limited sample, here are some possible implications.

First, alliances may experience a fair amount of disorder and instability, but can be successful in spite of it. Their messiness is likely to be perfectly legitimate and can be virtuous. As the early twentieth-century philosopher Otto Neurath (1882–1945) wryly observed, 'We are like sailors who must rebuild their ship on the open sea, never able to dismantle it in dry-dock and to reconstruct it out of the best materials';[9] this may well capture the essence of managing research driven collaborations. Second, though there may be beauty in simplicity, it may be useful not to try to keep things too simple. Complex interorganizational governance structures, where several individuals interact with, and are accountable to, each other, may provide a safety net should one such relationship collapse. Third, whilst detailed plans can quickly be rendered obsolete, the activity of planning itself remains immensely valuable. It helps identify any assumptions on industries, markets, and partners – a process that can be immensely valuable in its own right. Fourth, it may be best not to restrict alliance success to the measurement of pre-defined objectives. 'Fortune,'

---

[8] Ibid.   [9] As cited in Higgin (1999: 178).

said Louis Pasteur, 'favours the prepared mind.' Penicillin and Viagra would have never been discovered if not for the vigilance of surprise. On the issue of fortune, Machiavelli (1469–1527) presaged Pasteur:

A Republic has a fuller life and enjoys good fortune for a longer time than a principality, since it is better able to adapt itself to diverse circumstances owing to the diversity found among its citizens than a prince can do. For a man who is accustomed to act in one particular way, never changes . . . Hence, when times change, and no longer suit his ways, he is inevitably ruined. (1971: 431)

Fifth, those in charge must continue to explain what is going on, why the alliance exists, and precisely what is expected of those involved in it. There are few things more frustrating and, sadly, more common it seems than for scientists to be told to pack up one project to start another without adequate rationalization. Sixth, try to understand the strategic interests of the partner firm in the alliance. What, if anything, may cause it to re-evaluate its priorities, rendering some alliances redundant? Seventh, try to anticipate the competing interests of those involved in the collaboration – particularly within one's own organization. Ultimately, to use a metaphor, it is they who decide where to journey to, how fast to drive, when to stop and for how long, how to circumvent traffic jams or road blocks, how to respond to the behaviour of fellow road users, when and how to service the vehicle, and when to abandon it. Their private interests matter. Eighth, alliances demand consultation and compromise, where management must seek to recognize the legitimate claims and rights of individuals and groups inside them, avoiding extremes of there being only cooperation and no internal competition, only trust and no vigilance, only replication and no innovation, only justice and no mercy, only planning and no room for spontaneity, only control and no room for autonomy. Orchestrating their competing claims may well be key to collaborative success. In case these suggestions should not prove terribly original, one finds refuge in C. I. Lewis's suggestion that there is no a-priori reason for supposing that reality, once discovered, will prove interesting.

Limitations

Predictably, this book suffers from an obvious limitation. The empirical sample in it is small and the ability to generalize from it limited. This is the usual problem of induction. However, generalization was never its aim. Rather, it was to remedy a felt imbalance in the literature towards monist approaches to invariably complex phenomena. What the cases did empirically, the theory sought to do theoretically, namely to illuminate the limitations of monist approaches to alliance life. Besides, as Virginia

Woolf allegedly suggested, we must not take it for granted that life exists more fully in what is commonly thought big than in what is called small – an acute observation.

A second limitation relates to the nature of the data as relying, partly, on retrospective recall of informants. A potential source of bias consists in informants being quite likely to reconstruct the past to make it consistent with subsequent performance results and trendy story lines. March and Sutton's explanation is insightful in this respect:

> Performance information itself colours subjective memories, perceptions, and weightings of possible causes of performance. Informants exist in a world in which organizational performance is important. That world is filled with widely believed conventional stories about the causes of good and poor performance, and those stories are evoked by knowledge of performance results. As a result, retrospective reports of independent variables may be less influenced by memory than by a reconstruction that connects standard story lines with contemporaneous awareness of performance results. (1997: 701)

Given the longitudinal nature of the study, and the periodical interviewing of key actors, this criticism may be most relevant to the reconstruction of the alliance from the time of formation up to the date of the first interviews. This longitudinal approach, albeit perhaps not perfect, may have thus served to diminish the impact of this retrospective bias (Fischoff and Beyth, 1975).

A third limitation concerns its constructivist qualities (Berger and Luckman, 1967; Mir and Watson, 2000). It is inevitably difficult to separate researcher from subject, except artificially, and my treatment of the literature and empirical data may well have been subject to particular interests. This relationship, however, may well be one of necessity. For better or worse, research remains theory dependent. As the Cambridge historian E. H. Carr explains:

> The relation between the historian and his facts is one of give-and-take. As any working historian knows, if he stops to reflect what he is doing as he thinks and writes, the historian is engaged on a continuous process of moulding his facts to his interpretation and his interpretation to his facts. It is impossible to assign primacy to one over the other . . . The historian and the facts of history are necessary to one another. The historian without his facts is rootless and futile; the facts without their historian are dead and meaningless. (1961: 34–5)

As we enter the final pages of this book we look, perhaps in vain, for 'the fireworks'. Some such fireworks will hopefully have surfaced throughout the book. But so as not to disappoint, I leave the reader with a remarkable insight found in the pages of a novel familiar to many in our academic community. It is this: however deep we probe, in our search we may, besides much else, at last find ourselves. This poignant reflection is the subject of a controversial paragraph in David Lodge's *Small World*. In it, Morris Zap, a literary figure from America, is addressing a conference:

Now, as some of you know, I come from a city notorious for its bars and nightclubs featuring topless and bottomless dancers. I am told – I have not personally patronised these places, but I am told on the authority of no less a person than your host at this conference, my old friend Philip Swallow, who has patronised them [here several members of the audience turned in their seats to stare and grin at Philip Swallow, who blushed to the roots of his silver-grey hair], that the girls take off all their clothes before they commence dancing in front of the customers. This is not striptease, it is all strip and no tease, it is the terpsichorean equivalent of the hermeneutic fallacy of a recuperable meaning, which claims that if we remove the clothing of its rhetoric from a literary text we discover the bare facts it is trying to communicate. The classical tradition of striptease, however, which goes back to Salome's dance of the seven veils and beyond, and which survives in a debased form in the dives of your Soho, offers a valid metaphor for the activity of reading. The dancer teases the audience, as the text teases its readers, with the promise of an ultimate revelation that is infinitely postponed. Veil after veil, garment after garment, is removed, but it is the delay in the stripping that makes it exciting, not the stripping itself; because no sooner has one secret been revealed than we lose interest in it and crave another . . . Just so in [research]. The attempt to peer into the very core of [an organisation], to possess once and for all its meaning, is vain – *it is only ourselves that we find there*. (1984: 26–7; italics added)

Lastly, perhaps my interest in the relative messiness, complexity, unpredictability, and unmanageability of alliances arose partly from my sample. Drug discovery and development, comprising biotechnology and pharmacology, is a process fraught with uncertainty and serendipity. Early pipeline projects are especially sensitive to these properties. Hence it may be that alliances in more stable environments (i.e. in terms of industry, market, and internal composition) experience them to a much lesser degree. At least it would be interesting to find out. An extension of this research could build on the pluralist epistemology advocated here but applied to a fundamentally different industry (e.g. automotive, non-profit) or cultural context (e.g. by including firms located in Asian or Latin American regions).

Completing the circle

So how do we explain a growing recourse to alliances while at the same time assuming rational corporate strategic management? And why have we persisted in approaching them with expectations of finding homogeneity whilst knowing that many unfold in highly variable, heterogeneous environments? These being what appear to be the two remaining paradoxes of alliance life, I hypothesized that they should first and foremost be resolved at the level of epistemology – or at the 'how do we know what we know?' level. I hope it is now clear why this is so. To commence with the latter paradox, a pluralist epistemology will not entertain expectations as to homogeneity but instead allow alliances to be studied as they appear to present themselves. As for the former, a better understanding of the dynamics of alliances may help us better manage them. To paraphrase Cartwright (1999: 12), it may not matter whether we hold false beliefs. The real problem is that our beliefs tend to go hand in hand with the methodologies we adopt to study them, and the prescriptions we derive from these. The worry is thus not so much that we will adopt wrong images with which to represent alliances, but rather that we will choose wrong tools with which to manage them.

But perhaps the paradoxes that introduced the book are not so paradoxical after all.[10] Perhaps suggesting that the continued proliferation of alliances and their persistently high failure rates are paradoxical is to have misunderstood their point. Firms create alliances to achieve objectives that cannot easily be satisfied in-house such as, for instance, the acquisition of new knowledge, access to an existing knowledge base that provides the foundation and stimulus for the search for more of the same, or even simply access to finance or legitimacy. Any comparison with in-house venturing, as suggested in the first chapter, is thus, for the most part, inappropriate. As for the second paradox, to the extent that our appreciation of alliance life has been shaped by expectations of homogeny, constancy, teleology or progress, we might relax these premises and see what happens. In the words of René Descartes, 'In the matters we propose to investigate, our inquiries should be directed, not to what others have thought, nor to what we ourselves conjecture, but to what we can clearly and distinctly see and with certainty deduce, for knowledge is not won in any other way.'[11]

---

[10] This is a conclusion Ayn Rand might have liked. In her disconcerting *Atlas Shrugged* (1957) – a 1,074-page work of fiction in which she outlined her 'objectivist' epistemology and which went on to become one of the most influential novels of the twentieth century – Rand claimed that contradictions as such do not exist. What may appear to be contradictions can be shown not to be by the application of reason. Any such error lies not in the paradox but the premises that sustain it. Was she right? Her book was recommended to me by one of my MBA students (which goes to illustrate one of the pleasures of the teaching profession) with the warning that it might keep me up at night. It did.

[11] As quoted in Higgin (1999: 89).

Appendix: On methodology and definitions

The choice of biotechnology-based alliances was driven by a number of criteria. First, collaborations in biotechnology are increasingly common phenomena and have proliferated at an unprecedented rate over the past decade. Its growth rate is still one of the most prolific of any industry sector (Hagedoorn, 1993). Second, biotechnology-based alliances can exist to serve various different purposes, even simultaneously, and thus allow researchers to study alliances of different strategic intents within a single industry setting. Third, given that biotechnology has been nominated America's 'most promising' industry (James, 1995), that significant efforts have been made by several European economies to grow and nurture a biotechnology-friendly environment, and that the industry characteristically features collaborative ventures of all kinds, it is imperative that these cooperative processes are well understood if countries like the USA, the UK, and Germany are to retain a leadership role. The alliances discussed here comprise partners from the USA and the UK. Fourth, given the volatile and high-risk nature of the biotechnology sector, it is reasonable to expect managers within it to be as insightful as those in most other industries, particularly as regards the management of complexity, ambiguity, and change.

Data sources

I selected three cases, each of which tells a quite different story, but being unaware of the extent of this diversity until well into the empirical research. The case study process was designed to meet three tests of qualitative research (King, Keohane, and Verba, 1994; Yin, 1994). First, the use of mixed methods and triangulation sought to provide construct validity. In addition to relying on a pilot study[1] and extensive semi-structured

---

[1] The pilot study findings are not reported here, but comprised a case study of an international interbank alliance (between the Royal Bank of Scotland and Banco Santander), documenting nine years of cooperation.

interviews (in two stages), use was made also of archival and published data, and the results of a social network questionnaire (based on Labianca, Brass, and Gray, 1998). Second, replicating the research from the pilot study and stage 1 interviews across three further cases helped provide a degree of external validity. Third, the effort to provide transparency of the actual process, including the interview protocol, coding sheet, social network questionnaires, names of interviewees, dates of interviews, and original interview transcripts sought to demonstrate the study's replicability and, by implication, should provide some measure of reliability. Obviously, these data could not all be included in the book, but were retained by me. The interviews were guided by a protocol, yet one which was sufficiently flexible to allow them to retain a semi-structured character. The interviews were digitally recorded (on a portable MD player) and immediately transcribed. These transcripts were emailed to interviewees so as to verify missing data or misunderstood comments, or to respond to additional questions. The majority of participants made use of this opportunity, though relatively few additional insights were gained. These transcripts were subsequently coded using a coding sheet developed after Miles and Huberman (1994).

My approach was clearly inductive, following Strauss and Corbin (1990), Eisenhardt (1989), Parkhe (1993a), and Miles and Huberman (1994). Stage 1 of the research involved twenty-two semi-structured interviews and included middle managers and senior executives from biotech firms and pharmaceuticals, as well as specialists from management consulting and government, and industry experts from the media. The three subsequent case studies (stage 2) drew extensively from further interviews, thirty-two in total, but relied also on the business press, in-house publications, various Internet-based data sources (primarily Reuters and Datastream), and, in two cases, the actual alliance contract. These semi-structured interviews lasted anywhere from forty-five minutes to three and a half hours, and were conducted on location at regular intervals over an eighteen-month period. Those most closely involved with the alliance (both at senior and operational management level) were interviewed more regularly. Overall, there were relatively few people with significant involvement in each alliance. The focus of each interview was the individual's own factual experience with the partnership, the extent of their involvement with it, their interactions with others at the partner firm, their opinion on its relative success, and their recollection of events they thought important to the development of the relationship. This approach allowed me to observe every alliance in real time for eighteen months, whilst post-hoc reconstructing the alliances to their creation.

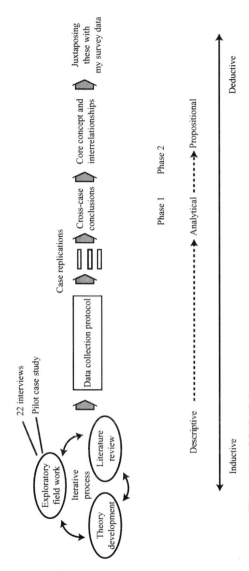

Figure A.1: Methodology

To better understand the nature and role of interpersonal ties, all interview participants were asked to complete a basic social network questionnaire based on Labianca, Brass, and Gray (1998) midway through the research. Only in one case was I not allowed to administer this questionnaire as it was considered intrusive. This survey sought to test for influence, trust, affection, as well as formality and frequency of communication, and allowed for triangulation with the opinions already expressed or implied in interviews. Pursuing an ego-centred approach (Wasserman and Faust, 1997), individuals were asked to nominate players with whom they had interpersonal ties. Upon their assessment of these ties, the individuals nominated were invited to participate also. This process continued through several rounds until the same names kept reappearing on the questionnaires, indicating that a dense and reasonably complete network had been captured. This instrument was useful also in highlighting important players that had not been interviewed. Due to the sensitive nature of the data, and on the request of those participating in the study, the names of companies and individuals have been changed. The case studies remain factually accurate.

Theory development

The theory development process was iterative and ad hoc. Having read through a fair bit of the alliance literature, I began, in late 1996, with an exploratory case study of the longstanding relationship between the Royal Bank of Scotland and Banco Santander. At the time I had no idea what meta-theories might be most useful in extending the literature. Nor did I think the banking industry to be particularly interesting. But one must start somewhere and, armed with a strong personal recommendation, access seemed easy. I conducted a series of interviews and wrote up the results in the form of a fifteen-page case study (unpublished). Lured by the hype, novelty, and controversy of biotechnology, I soon abandoned banking and embarked on a series of interviews with a variety of individuals – research directors of pharmaceutical and biotech firms, editors and journalists of journals targeted at the pharmacology and biotech industry, as well as industry-specific management consultants and funding agencies. The observations made then became the basis for the case study research.

The relevance of structuration theory became obvious only midway through the case interviews. Despite the diversity in alliance process there appeared to be a certain order – but not the sort of order I had encountered in the literature. Individuals involved in alliances, in their sensemaking and conduct, seemed to be drawing on deeper-seated social norms.

They considered certain things as acceptable whereas other behaviours clearly were not. Often neither type of conduct was fully accounted for in the formal contract. Everyone simply knew.[2] At the same time, the sheer variety encountered in just three research collaborations seemed insufficiently explained by the existing literature. There really didn't seem to be a theory of variety. Having committed to structuration theory, as an analytical framework for explaining order, it took a further twelve months to come across the writings of Isaiah Berlin. I was living in Oxford at the time and one of my great regrets is that of having discovered him too late, for Isaiah died in 1997. His intellectual legacy remained, however, and has had a profound impact on my thinking and research. By revisiting the concepts of pluralism, irrationality, and freedom (primarily through the works of neglected eighteenth-century Romantics), Berlin made some astonishing discoveries. This book is based on one such discovery. It remained for me to reconcile the claims of pluralism and structuration theory. I now believe that the theories are not necessarily conflicting, for there is nothing in structuration theory that prevents it from also being a theory of change. It best explains order (or the reproductive feature of social structure) but affords change. In drawing on these two disparate traditions we may be able to account for the particular and the general, to see the order in the particular and to find the particular in the orderly. In some ways the book does not reflect the actual research process, for in it the theory comes last. In reality, the theory came a little in the beginning, a little in the middle, and mostly at the end.

Given the importance of Giddens's (1984) ideas on structuration processes, it would seem only appropriate to consult him also on methodology. Giddens, however, says relatively little about empirical research in the context of a structurationist theory. His most elaborate statements appear contained within his 'A reply to my critics' (1989) and the final chapter of *The Constitution of Society* (1984). Following are five such statements, treated in this methodology section as 'criteria' for the conduct of social inquiry:

1 'All social research has a necessarily cultural, ethnographic or "anthropological" aspect to it.' (1984: 284)
2 'The study of day-to-day life is integral to analysis of the reproduction of institutionalised practices.' (1984: 282)
3 'Literary style is not irrelevant to the accuracy of social descriptions ... The social scientist is a communicator ... Thus the social sciences draw upon the same sources of description (mutual knowledge) as novelists or others who write fictional accounts of social life.' (1984: 284–5)

---

[2] Here it was probably helpful to have spent most of my life outside the life sciences.

4 'The study of context, or of the contextualities of interaction, is inherent in the investigation of social reproduction.' (1984: 282)
5 'As an operating principle of research, what structuration theory suggests is not that we should seek to categorise or classify the rules and resources involved in a given area of social conduct, but rather that we should *place the emphasis squarely upon the constitution and reconstitution of social practices.*' (1989: 298; italics added)

For Giddens, any case reconstructions should demonstrate an intimacy with the subject matter (see 1 and 2). Second, such descriptions should provide as accurate an account as possible by using verbatim quotations as vignettes to support or illustrate particular events, to preserve the integrity of these vignettes as to the original context in which they appeared, and to be cautious in word choice, given the reality-constructive power of narration (see 3). Third, it needs to be clear that strategic collaborations do not evolve in a vacuum but are subject to a changing context, including coevolving partner organizations, a coevolving competitive, technological, and scientific environment, and the unintended consequences of human activity (see 4). The conceptual framework outlined in Chapter 2 is consistent with each of these. Fourth, structuration theory should be employed as a 'sensitizing device' rather than a strict research regime for informing the empirical research (see 5). Indeed, the theory was never intended as a new method for the conduct of social research, but merely to provide a useful frame of reference for understanding the dynamics of social systems. Giddens's operating principle is translated into the case descriptions by focusing squarely on the *reproduction* of alliances, viewed as social artefacts, using the structurationist framework as its method. Essentially, this framework provides a transition from theory to method. It produces a generic language for describing alliances, at any point in time, as a particular combination of four institutionalized features: its social makeup, its strategic purpose, its content, and its operating rules. The evolution of alliances is theorized here as an ongoing process of reconfiguration of these four sedimented events whilst acknowledging also that these themselves are deeply embedded in underlying virtual structures. The case histories aim to reconstruct alliances using the structurationist framework by focusing on the interaction between, and alignment of, these four elements and a further three variables: performance assessments, coevolutionary developments within partner firms, and industry and competitive dynamics. Incidentally, the most cited 'structurationist' essay in organization studies is perhaps Barley's (1986) study of CT scanner adoption and social order in radiology departments. But obviously there is more than one way to operationalize the theory. Giddens is quite unspecific as to such empirical research.

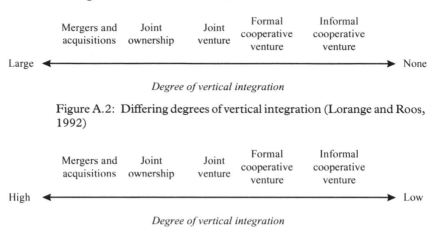

Figure A.2: Differing degrees of vertical integration (Lorange and Roos, 1992)

Figure A.3: Differing degrees of interdependence (Contractor and Lorange, 1988)

Definitions

As is well established by now, the literature on alliances has proliferated greatly since the mid-1980s. Indeed, the term 'alliances' is applied liberally to describe a diverse group of archetypes, including joint ventures, licensing agreements, outsourcing, collaborative research, joint product developments, consortia, even mergers and acquisitions. *The New Oxford Dictionary of English* proves unhelpful in narrowing the definition, suggesting merely that an alliance is 'a relationship based on an affinity in interests, nature, or qualities', tracing it back to its Middle English and, prior to that, French origins of *alier* (to ally). An influential publication by Lorange and Roos, in the early 1990s, improves on this, proposing that distinctions between various archetypes can be made when positing interorganizational relationships on a continuous scale between, on the one hand, free market transactions ('market') and, on the other, complete internalization ('hierarchy') (see Figure A.2).

Contractor and Lorange (1988) earlier proposed a similar scale, but based on degree of interdependency between the partners involved (see Figure A.3).

A more contemporary definition is provided by Harrigan (1986) and appears favoured by some (e.g. Faulkner, 1995; Gulati, 1995a). Paraphrasing Harrigan, I define alliances as:

Voluntary interorganizational relationships involving meaningful and durable exchange, sharing, or codevelopment of new knowledge, products, services or technologies.

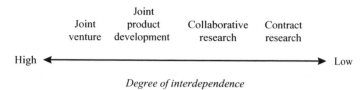

Figure A.4: Differentiating between alliance types in the biopharmaceutical sector

Such an inclusive treatment of the phenomenon will prove helpful in the empirical research, as alliances in biopharmaceutical research and/or development can surface in various forms. This was well understood by Zajac:

> Strategic alliances come in a wide variety of sizes and shapes, and the variety seems only limited by the creativity of the alliance originators. Those who have seen strategic alliance agreements know that they are sometimes so detailed and complex that they are measured by the inch rather than by the page...In other words, we have been so content to use the umbrella term of strategic alliances, yet this term in some ways diminishes our attention to the variety and complexity of alliance arrangements. (1998: 320–1)

Responding to his call for more attention to variety, I will distinguish between four types of dyadic relationships (my basic unit of analysis) in the empirical work, as follows (see, also, Figure A.4):

1 *Contract research*: a 'fee-for-service' type arrangement, not unlike the traditional buyer–supplier relationship, with relatively little mutual interdependency and integration.

2 *Collaborative research*: a joint effort to develop a particular science of technology involving the pooling or sharing of knowledge and resources and the sharing of results. The degree of interdependency and integration between partners is considerably higher than with contract research alliances.

3 *Joint product development*: a joint effort to develop a particular product with the biotech partner typically doing early stage research, and the pharmaceutical taking on the clinical development. As with collaborative research, the degree of interdependency and integration between partners is considerably higher than with contract research alliances.

4 *Joint venture*: the creation of a separate company for the purposes of conducting research or developing products, services or technologies, *in which each partner holds an equity interest*. The degree of interdependency between partners is relatively high as both have a real (equity) interest in seeing the joint venture succeed.

To improve the readability of the book, I vary my terminology, using 'alliance', 'interorganizational relationship', 'collaborative relationship', 'collaborative venture', 'collaboration', 'partnership', and 'cooperative relationship' to refer to essentially the same phenomenon: two or more organizations voluntarily engaging in meaningful and durable exchange, sharing or codevelopment of new knowledge, products, services or technologies.

Presaging criticisms about the constructivist, qualitative, and inductive nature of the research, I conclude with a commentary by the economist John Kay:

When I describe a business case study, someone will often say 'I was there and it wasn't like that'. But almost always these comments add a perspective on events without changing the basic analysis. There is no *true* story of how business develops. (*Financial Times*, 21 February 2001)

Of course, there are *stories*.

References

Achrol, R. S., Scheer, L. K., and Stern, L. W. 1990. Designing successful transorganizational marketing alliances. Marketing Science Institute: Cambridge, MA

Aldrich, H. 1979. *Organizations and Environments*. Prentice-Hall: Englewood Cliffs, NJ

  1999. *Organizations Evolving*. Sage: London

Aldrich, H. and Pfeffer, J. 1976. Environments of organizations. *Annual Review of Sociology* 2: 79–105

Aldrich, H. and Whetten, D. A. 1981. Organization-sets, action-sets, and networks: making the most of simplicity. In P. C. Nystrom and W. H. Starbuck (eds.), *Handbook of Organizational Design*: 385–408. Oxford University Press: New York

Amram, R. and Kulatilaka, N. 1999. *Real Options: Managing Strategic Investments in an Uncertain World*. Harvard Business School Press: Cambridge, MA

Anderson, E. 1990. Two firms, one frontier: on assessing joint venture performance. *Sloan Management Review* 31(2): 19–30

Anderson, E. and Gatignon, H. 1986. Models of foreign entry: a transaction cost analysis and propositions. *Journal of International Business Studies* 17(3): 1–26

Anderson, P., Meyer, A., Eisenhardt, K., Carley, K., and Pettigrew, A. 1999. Introduction to the Special Issue: applications of complexity theory to organization science. *Organization Science* 10(3): 233–6

Anderson, R. C. 1967. A sociometric approach to the analysis of interorganizational relationships. Institute for Community Development, Michigan State University: East Lansing, MI

Appleyard, B. 1999a. Where are we going? *The Sunday Times Magazine*: 39–41

  1999b. *Brave New Worlds: Genetics and the Human Experience*. HarperCollins: London

Arino, A. and de la Torre, J. 1998. Learning from failure: towards an evolutionary model of collaborative ventures. *Organization Science* 9(3): 306–25

Arnst, C. 2001. The birth of a cancer drug. *Business Week*, 9 July: 95–102

Auster, E. 1987. International corporate linkages: dynamic forms in changing environments. *Columbia Journal of World Business* 22(2): 3–7

Axelrod, R. 1984. *The Evolution of Cooperation*. HarperCollins: London

Axelrod, R. M. and Cohen, M. D. 1999. *Harnessing Complexity: Organizational Implications of a Scientific Frontier*. Free Press: New York

193

Ayer, A. J. 2001 [1936]. *Language, Truth and Logic*. Penguin: London

Badaracco, J. L. 1991. *The Knowledge Link: How Firms Compete through Strategic Alliances*. Harvard Business School Press: Boston, MA

Baert, P. 1992. *Time, Self and Social Being*. Ashgate: London
    1998. *Social Theory in the Twentieth Century*. Polity Press: Cambridge

Bailey, J. and Ford, C. 1996. Management as science versus management as practice in postgraduate business education. *Business Strategy Review* 7(4): 7–12

Bain, J. S. 1951. Relation of profit to industry concentration: American manufacturing, 1936–1940. *Quarterly Journal of Economics* 65: 293–324.

Barley, S. R. 1986. Technology as an occasion for structuring: evidence from observations of CT scanners and the social order of radiology departments. *Administrative Science Quarterly* 31: 78–108

Barley, S. R., Freeman, J., and Hybels, R. C. 1992. Strategic alliances in commercial biotechnology. In N. Nohria and R. G. Eccles (eds.), *Networks and Organizations: Structure, Form, and Action*: 311–47. Harvard Business School Press: Boston, MA

Barley, S. R. and Tolbert, P. S. 1997. Institutionalization and structuration: studying the links between action and institution. *Organization Studies* 18(1): 93–117

Barney, J. 1991. Firm resources and sustainable competitive advantage. *Journal of Management* 17: 99–120

Baum, J. A. C. and Calabrese, T. 2000. Don't go it alone: alliance network composition and startups' performance in Canadian biotechnology. *Strategic Management Journal* 21(3): 267–95

Beamish, P. W. 1985. The characteristics of joint ventures in developed and developing countries. *Columbia Journal of World Business* 20(3): 13–19
    1988. *Multinational Joint Ventures in Developing Countries*. Routledge: London

Beamish, P. W. and Delios, A. 1997. Incidence and propensity of alliance formation. In P. W. Beamish and J. P. Killing (eds.), *Cooperative Strategies: Asian Perspectives*, Vol. 3: 91–114. New Lexington Press: San Francisco, CA

Becker, C. L. 1960 (1932). *The Heavenly City of the Eighteenth-Century Philosophers*. Yale University Press: New Haven, CT

Benson, J. K. 1975. The interorganizational network as a political economy. *Administrative Science Quarterly* 20: 229–49

Berger, P. and Luckman, T. 1967. *The Social Construction of Reality*. Doubleday: New York

Berkeley, G. 1713 (1988). *Three Dialogues Between Hylas and Philonous*. Prometheus Books: New York

Berle, A. A. and Means, G. C. 1932. *The Modern Corporation and Private Property*. Harcourt, Brace and World: New York

Berlin, I. 1991. *The Crooked Timber of Humanity*. HarperCollins: London
    1994. *The Magus of the North: J. G. Hamann and the Origins of Modern Irrationalism*. Fontana Press: London
    1996. *The Sense of Reality: Studies in Ideas and Their History*. Pimlico: London
    1998. *The Proper Study of Mankind: An Anthology of Essays*. Pimlico: London
    1999a [1953]. *The Hedgehog and the Fox: An Essay on Tolstoy's View of History*. Orion Books: London

1999b. *The First and the Last*. Granta Books: London

2000a. *The Power of Ideas*. Chatto and Windus: London

2000b. *The Roots of Romanticism*. Pimlico: London

2000c (1992). *Conversations with Isaiah Berlin*. Interviews conducted by R. Jahanbegloo. Phoenix Press: London

2002. *Liberty*. Oxford University Press: Oxford

Bhaskar, R. 1989. *Reclaiming Reality: A Critical Introduction to Contemporary Philosophy*. Verso: London

Biworld, 1997. www.bioworld.com

Bleeke, J. and Ernst, D. 1991. The way to win in cross-border alliances. *Harvard Business Review* **Nov/Dec**: 129–35

1995. Is your strategic alliance really a sale? *Harvard Business Review* **Jan/Feb**: 97–105

Boisot, M. and Child, J. 1999. Organizations as adaptive systems in complex environments: the case of China. *Organization Science* 10(3): 237–52

Bouchikhi, H. 1993. A constructivist framework for understanding entrepreneurship performance. *Organization Studies* 14(4): 549–70

1998. Living with and building on complexity: a constructivist perspective on organizations. *Organization* 5(2): 217–32

Bourdieu, P. and Wacquant, L. J. D. (eds.) 1992. *An Invitation to Reflexive Sociology*. Polity Press: Cambridge

Brandenburger, A. and Nalebuff, B. 1996. *Co-opetition*. Doubleday: New York

Brecht, B. 1948. *The Good Woman of Setzuan* (E. Bentley, trans.). University of Minnesota Press: Minneapolis, MN

Brockhoff, K. 1992. R&D cooperation between firms: a perceived transaction cost perspective. *Management Science* 38(4): 514–24

Brown, S. L. and Eisenhardt, K. M. 1998. *Competing on the Edge. Strategy as Structured Chaos*. Harvard Business School Press: Boston, MA

Brunsson, N. 1985. *The Irrational Organization*. John Wiley: New York

Burt, R. S. 1992. The social structure of competition. In N. Nohria and R. G. Eccles (eds.), *Networks and Organizations: Structure, Form, and Action*: 57–91. Harvard Business School Press: Boston, MA

Bush, M. A. The role of the L-arginine nitric oxide cyclic GMP pathway in relaxation of corpus cavernosum smooth muscle, unpublished PhD dissertation, University of California

Cannella, A. A. Jr. and Paetzold, R. L. 1994. Pfeffer's barriers to the advance of organizational science: a rejoinder. *Academy of Management Review* 19(2): 331–41

Carr, E. H. 1961. *What is History?* Vintage Books: New York

Carroll, L. 1865. *Alice's Adventures in Wonderland*. Macmillan and Co.: London

Cartwright, N. 1999. *The Dappled World: A Study of the Boundaries of Science*. Cambridge University Press: Cambridge

Chesterton, G. K. 1996 [1908]. *Orthodoxy*. Hodder and Stoughton: London

Chi, T. 1994. Trading in strategic resources: necessary conditions, transaction cost problems, and choice of exchange structure. *Strategic Management Journal* 15: 271–90

Child, J. 1972. Organizational structure, environment and performance: the role of strategic choice. *Sociology* 6: 1–22

1997. Strategic choice in the analysis of action, structures, organizations and environment: retrospect and prospect. *Organization Studies* **18**: 43–76

Child, J. and Faulkner, D. O. 1998. *Strategies of Cooperation: Managing Alliances, Networks, and Joint Ventures.* Oxford University Press: Oxford

Child, J. and Rodrigues, S. 1996. The role of social identity in the international transfer of knowledge through joint ventures. In S. Clegg and G. Palmer (eds.), *Producing Management Knowledge*: 46–68. Sage: London

Ciborra, C. 1991. Alliances as learning experiments: cooperation, competition and change in hightech industries. In L. K. Mytelka (ed.), *Strategic Partnerships: States, Firms and International Competition*: 51–77. Pinter: London

Coase, R. H. 1937. The nature of the firm. *Economica N. S.* **4**: 386–405

Cohen, W. and Levinthal, D. A. 1990. Absorptive capability: a new perspective on learning and innovation. *Administrative Sciences Quarterly* **35**(1): 128–52

Cohen, M. D., March, J. G., and Olsen, J. P. 1972. A garbage can model of organizational choice. *Administrative Science Quarterly* **17**: 1–25

Cole, S. 1983. The hierarchy of the sciences? *American Journal of Sociology* **89**: 111–39

Coleman, J. S. 1986. Social theory, social research, and a theory of action. *American Journal of Sociology* **16**: 1309–35

Contractor, F. J. and Lorange, P. 1988. Why should firms cooperate? The strategy and economic basis for cooperative ventures. In F. J. Contractor and P. Lorange (eds.), *Cooperative Strategies in International Business*. Lexington Books: New York

Cook, K. 1977. Exchange and power in networks of interorganizational relations. *The Sociological Quarterly* **18**: 62–82

Cookson, C. 1999. [Untitled] *The Financial Times*, 7 September: 24, London

Copeland, T. E. and Keenan, P. T. 1998. Making real options real. *McKinsey Quarterly* (3): 128–41

Crighton, M. 1988. *Travels*. Ballantine Books: New York

Cyert, R. M. and March, J. G. 1963. *A Behavioral Theory of the Firm*. Prentice-Hall: Englewood Cliffs, NJ

Czarniawska, B. 1997. *Narrating the Organization: Dramas of Institutional Identity*. University of Chicago Press: Chicago

Das, T. K. and Teng, B. 2000. Instabilities of strategic alliances: an internal tensions perspective. *Organization Science* **11**(1): 77–101

d'Aunno, T. A. and Zuckerman, H. S. 1987. A life cycle model of organizational federations: the case of hospitals. *Academy of Management Review* **12**(3): 534–45

Deeds, D. L. and Hill, C. W. L. 1998. An examination of opportunistic action within research alliances: evidence from the biotechnology industry. *Journal of Business Venturing* **14**: 141–63

de la Mettrie, J. 1996. *Machine Man and other Writings* (A. Thompson, trans.). Cambridge University Press: Cambridge

de Rond, M. 2000. Alliances as social artefacts: a structurationist imagination: a study of the process dynamics and evolution of biopharmaceutical research collaborations. Unpublished DPhil thesis. Saïd Business School, University of Oxford: Oxford

2002. Reviewer 198, the hedgehog and the fox: Next Generation theories in strategy. *Journal of Management Inquiry* **11**(1): 36–46

Dierickx, I. and Cool, K. 1989. Asset stock accumulation and sustainability of competitive advantage. *Management Science* **35**: 1504–11

Dixit, A. K. and Nalebuff, B. J. 1991. *Thinking Strategically: The Competitive Edge in Business, Politics, and Everyday Life*. W. W. Norton: London

Dodge, H. R., Fullerton, S., and Robbins, J. E. 1994. Stage of the organizational life cycle and competition as mediators of problem perception for small businesses. *Strategic Management Journal* **15**(2): 121–34

Dodgson, M. 1993. Learning, trust, and technological collaboration. *Human Relations* **46**: 77–95

Donaldson, L. 1995. *American Anti-Management Theories of Organization: A Critique of Paradigm Proliferation*. Cambridge University Press: Cambridge

Dostoevsky, F. 1991 [1880]. *The Brothers Karamazov* (R. Pevear, trans.). Vintage Books: New York

Doz, Y. L. 1996. The evolution of cooperation in strategic alliances: initial conditions or learning processes? *Strategic Management Journal* **17** (SMS Special Issue): 55–83

Doz, Y. L. and Hamel, G. 1998. *Alliance Advantage: The Art of Creating Value Through Partnering*. Harvard Business School Press: Boston, MA

Durkheim, E. 1982. *The Rules of Sociological Method*. Macmillan: London

Durschmied, E. 1999. *The Hinge Factor: How Chance and Stupidity Have Changed History*. Hodder and Stoughton: London

Dyer, J. H. and Singh, H. 1998. The relational view: cooperative strategy and sources of interorganizational competitive advantage. *Academy of Management Review* **23**(4): 660–79

Dyer, J. H., Kale, P., and Singh, H. 2001. How to make strategic alliances work. *Sloan Management Review* **42**(4): 37–43

Eco, U. 1992. Reply. In S. Collini (ed.), *Interpretation and Overinterpretation*: 139–51. Cambridge University Press: Cambridge

Eisenhardt, K. M. 1989. Building theories from case study research. *Academy of Management Review* **14**(4): 532–50

Elton, G. R. 1967 (2002). *The Practice of History* (2nd edn.). Blackwell Publishers: Oxford

Erikson, 1963. *Childhood and Society*. Norton: New York

Evan, W. 1966. The organization-set: toward a theory of interorganizational relations. In J. D. Thompson (ed.), *Approaches to Organizational Design*: 173–91. University Press: Pittsburgh

Evans, R. J. 1997. *In Defence of History*. Granta Books: London

Fama, E. F. and Jensen, M. C. 1983. Separation of ownership and control. *Journal of Law and Economics* **26**: 301–25

Faulkner, D. O. 1995. *International Strategic Alliances: Co-operating to Compete*. McGraw-Hill: Maidenhead

Faulkner, D. O. and de Rond, M. 2000. Perspectives on cooperative strategy. In D. O. Faulkner and M. de Rond (eds.), *Cooperative Strategy: Economic, Business, and Organizational Issues*. Oxford University Press: Oxford

Feyerabend, P. 1993. *Against Method* (3rd edn.). Verso: London

1999. *Conquest of Abundance: A Tale of Abstraction versus the Richness of Being.* University of Chicago Press: Chicago

Feynman, R. P. 1998. *The Meaning Of It All.* Penguin: London

Fischoff, B. and Beyth, R. 1975. 'I knew it would happen' – remembered probabilities of once future things. *Organizational Behaviour and Human Performance* 13: 1–16

Forrest, J. E. and Martin, M. J. C. 1992. Strategic alliances between large and small research intensive organizations: experiences in the biotechnology industry. *R&D Management* 22(1): 41–54

Francis, A., Turk, J., and Willman, P. 1983. *Power, Efficiency and Institutions: A Critical Appraisal of the Markets and Hierarchies' Paradigm.* Heinemann: London

Fukuyama, F. 2002. *Our Posthuman Future: Consequences of the Biotechnology Revolution.* Profile Books: London

Galaskiewicz, J. and Wasserman, S. 1989. Mimetic and normative processes within an organizational field: an empirical test. *Administrative Science Quarterly* 34: 454–80

Garrette, B. and Dussauge, P. 1990. Towards an empirically-based taxonomy of strategic alliances between rival firms. 10th Annual Conference of the Strategic Management Society: Stockholm

Gates, S. 1989. Semiconductor firm strategies and technological cooperation: a perceived transaction cost approach. *Journal of Engineering and Technology Management* 6: 117–44

Gharajedaghi, J. and Ackoff, R. L. 1984. Mechanisms, organisms and social systems. *Strategic Management Journal* 5: 289–300

Giddens, A. 1989. A reply to my critics. In D. Held and J. Thompson (eds.), *Social Theory of Modern Organizations: Anthony Giddens and his Critics*: 249–301. Cambridge University Press: Cambridge

1997 [1984]. *The Constitution of Society.* Polity Press: Cambridge

Gleick, J. 1998 [1987]. *Chaos: The Amazing Science of the Unpredictable.* Vintage: London

Glynn, M. A., Barr, P. S., and Dacin, M. T. 2000. Pluralism and the problem of variety. *Academy of Management Review* 25(4): 726–34

Goldberg, C. 1999. Universities challenge Silicon Valley as high-tech incubators. *International Herald Tribune*, 12 October 1, 21: Paris

Gomes-Casseres, B. 1987. Joint venture instability: is it a problem? *Columbia Journal of World Business* 22(9): 97–102

1989. Ownership structure of foreign subsidiaries: theory and evidence. *Journal of Economic Behavior and Organization* 11: 1–25

Gordon, R. A. and Howell, J. E. (1959). *Higher Education for Business.* Columbia University Press: New York

Gove, A. 1998. Better living through chemistry. *The Red Herring* **May**: 52, 54

Grace, E. S. 1997. *Biotechnology Unzipped: Promises and Realities.* Joseph Hendry Press: Washington DC

Grant, R. M. 1991. The resource-based theory of competitive advantage: implications for strategy formulation. *California Management Review* **33**: 114–35

Gray, B. and Yan, A. 1997. Formation and evolution of international joint ventures: examples from US–Chinese partnerships. In P. Beamish and J. P. Killing (eds.), *Cooperative Strategies: Asian Pacific Perspectives*: 57–88. New Lexington Press: San Francisco, CA

Gray, P. 1999. Cursed by eugenics. *TIME Magazine*, 11 January: 84–5

Green, D. 1997. Survey – Biotechnology 97, *Financial Times* Supplement

Guetzkow, H. 1966. Relations among organizations. In R. Bowers (ed.), *Studies on Behavior in Organizations*: 13–41. University of Georgia Press: Athens, GA

Gulati, R. 1993. The dynamics of alliance formation. Unpublished PhD dissertation. Harvard University: Cambridge, MA

    1995a. Social structure and alliance formation patterns: a longitudinal analysis. *Administrative Science Quarterly* **40**: 619–52

    1995b. Does familiarity breed trust? The implications of repeated ties for contractual choice in alliances. *Academy of Management Journal* **38**(1): 85–112

    1998. Alliances and networks. *Strategic Management Journal* **19**(4): 293–317

Gulati, R. and Gargiulo, M. 1998. The dynamic evolution of interorganizational networks. Presentation at the 1998 Academy of Management Conference: San Diego

Gulati, R., Nohria, N., and Zaheer, A. 2000. Strategic networks, *Strategic Management Journal* **21**: 203–15

Guthrie, W. K. C. 1998 [1969]. *The Sophists*. Cambridge University Press: Cambridge

    2000 [1962]. *The Earlier Presocratics and the Pythagoreans*. Cambridge University Press: Cambridge

Hagedoorn, J. 1993. Understanding the rationale of strategic technology partnering. *Strategic Management Journal* **14**: 371–85

    1995. Strategic technology partnering during the 1980s: trends, networks, and corporate partners in non-core technologies. *Research Policy* **24**: 207–31

Hagedoorn, J. and Schakenraad, J. 1993. Strategic technology partnering and international corporate strategies. In K. S. Hughes (ed.), *European Competitiveness*: 60–86. Cambridge University Press: Cambridge

    1994. The effect of strategic technology alliances on company performance. *Strategic Management Journal* **15**: 291–309

Hakansson, H. 1990. Technological collaboration in industrial networks. *Engineering Management Journal* **8**: 371–9

Hall, R. 1967. Dialectics. *Encyclopedia of Philosophy, Vol. II*: 385–9. Macmillan: New York

Hamann, J. G. 1947–57. *Sämtliche Werke* (6 vols.) J. Nadler (ed.). Vienna

Hamel, G. 1991. Competition for competence and interpartner learning within international strategic alliances. *Strategic Management Journal* **12**: 83–103

Hamel, G., Doz, Y. L., and Prahalad, C. K. 1989. Collaborate with your competitors – and win. *Harvard Business Review* **67**(1): 133–9

Hamel, G. and Prahalad, C. K. 1996. Competing in the new economy: managing out of bounds. *Strategic Management Journal* **17**(3): 237–42

Hannan, M. and Freeman, J. H. 1977. The population ecology of organizations. *American Journal of Sociology* **83**: 929–84

Harbison, J. R. and Pekar, P. Jr. 1998. *Smart Alliances: A Practical Guide to Repeatable Success*. Jossey-Bass: San Francisco, CA

Hare, M. E. 1905. [Untitled]. In R. L. Green (ed.), *A Century of Humorous Verse (1850–1950)*: 285. Everyman's Library: London

Harrigan, K. R. 1985. *Strategies for Joint Venture Success*. Lexington Books: Lexington, MA

1986. *Managing for Joint Venture Success*. Lexington Books: Lexington, MA

Harrison, J. S., Hitt, M. A., Hoskisson, R. E., and Ireland, R. D. (in press). Resource complementarity in business combinations: extending the logic to organizational alliances. *Journal of Management*

Hatlestad, L. 1998. Biotech: the next great entrepreneurial wave. *The Red Herring* **May**: 47, 49

Hausheer, R. 2002, Keynote address. Presented at the Organization Theory in the 21st Century: from theoretical diversity to theories of diversity workshop, Brussels, 6–8 February

Hayward, S. 1998. Towards a political economy of biotechnology development: a sectoral analysis of Europe. *New Political Economy* **3**(1): 79–101

Hergert, M. and Morris, D. 1987. Trends in international collaborative agreements. *Columbia Journal of World Business* **22**(2): 15–22

1988. Trends in international collaborative agreements. In F. Contractor and P. Lorange (eds.), *Cooperative Strategies in International Business*: 99–110. Lexington Books: Lexington, MA

Heide, J. B. 1994. Interorganizational governance in marketing channels. *Journal of Marketing* **58**(1): 71–85

Henderson, R. and Cockburn, I. 1994. Measuring competence? Exploring firm effects in pharmaceutical research. *Strategic Management Journal* **15** (Winter Special Issue): 63–84

Hennert, J. F. 1988. A transaction cost theory of equity joint ventures. *Strategic Management Journal* **9**: 361–74

1991. The transaction cost theory of joint ventures. *Management Science* **37**: 483–97

Hennert, J. F., Kim, D. J., and Zeng, M. 1998. The impact of joint venture status on the longevity of Japanese stakes in US manufacturing affiliates. *Organization Science* **9**: 382–95

Herder, J. G. 1968 [1800]. *Reflections on the Philosophy of the History of Mankind* (T. O. Churchill, trans.) (Abridged and with an introduction by Frank E. Manuel (ed.)). University of Chicago Press: Chicago

Higgin, G. 1999. *Porcupines: A Philosophical Anthology*. Penguin: London

Huff, A. S. 1981. Multilectic methods of inquiry. *Human Systems Management* **2**: 83–94

Hume, D. 1740 (1995). *An Inquiry Concerning Human Understanding*. Prentice-Hall: Englewood Cliffs, NJ

Hund, J. 1982. Are social facts real? *British Journal of Sociology* **33**(2): 270–8

Ignatieff, M. 1998. *A Life: Isaiah Berlin*. Henry Holt and Company: New York

Inkpen, A. C. 1995. *The Management of International Joint Ventures: An Organizational Learning Perspective*. Routledge: London

1996. Creating knowledge through collaboration. *California Management Review* **39**(1): 123–40

1998. Learning and knowledge acquisition through international strategic alliances. *Academy of Management Executive* **12**(4): 69–80

2000. A note on the dynamics of learning alliances: Competition, cooperation, and relative scope. *Strategic Management Journal* **21**: 775–9

Inkpen, A. C. and Beamish, P. W. 1997. Knowledge, bargaining power, and the instability of international joint ventures. *Academy of Management Review* **22**(1): 177–202

Inkpen, A. C. and Crossan, M. M. 1995. Believing is seeing: joint ventures and organizational learning. *Journal of Management Studies* **32**: 595–618

Ireland, R. D., Hitt, M. A., and Vaidyanath, D. 2002. Strategic alliances as a pathway to competitive success. *Journal of Management* **28**(3): 413–46

James, G. E. 1995. Strategic alliances as 'virtual integration': a longitudinal exploration of biotech industry-level learning. *Academy of Management Journal* (*Best Papers Proceedings 1995*): 469–75

Jensen, M. C. and Meckling, C. 1976. Theory of the firm: managerial behavior, agency cost and ownership structure. *Journal of Financial Economics* **3**: 305–60

Jones, C., Hesterly, W. S., and Borgatti, S. P. 1997. A general theory of network governance: exchange conditions and social mechanisms. *Academy of Management Review* **22**(4): 911–45

Kant, I. 1781 (1991). *Critique of Pure Reason*. London: Everyman's Library

Kanter, R. M. 1989. *When Giants Learn to Dance*. Simon and Schuster: London

1994. Collaborative advantage: the art of alliances. *Harvard Business Review* **Jul/Aug**: 96–108

Kay, J. 2002. Categories and lists help us to make better sense of a complex world. But they must be chosen carefully. *Financial Times*, 2 January

Kent, D. H. 1991. Joint ventures vs. non-joint ventures: an empirical investigation. *Strategic Management Journal* **12**: 387–93

Kern, T. and Willcocks, L. P. 2000. Cooperative relationship strategy in global information technology outsourcing: the case of Xerox Corporation. In D. O. Faulkner and M. de Rond (eds.), *Cooperative Strategy: Economic, Business, and Organizational Issues*: 211–42. Oxford University Press: Oxford

Killing, J. P. 1982. How to make a global joint venture work. *Harvard Business Review* **May/June**: 120–7

King, G., Keohane, R. O., and Verba, S. 1994. *Designing Social Inquiry: Scientific Inference in Qualitative Research*. Princeton University Press: Princeton, NJ

Kogut, B. 1988a. A study of the life cycle of joint ventures. In F. Contractor and P. Lorange (eds.), *Cooperative Strategies in International Business*, Vol. 6: 169–85. Lexington Books: Lexington, MA

1988b. Joint ventures: theoretical and empirical perspectives. *Strategic Management Journal* **9**(4): 319–32

1991. Joint ventures and the option to expand and acquire. *Management Science* **37**: 19–33

Kogut, B. and Kulatilaka, N. 2001. Capabilities as real options. *Organization Science* **12**(6): 744–59

Korenman, S. G. and Viosca, A. D. 1993. Treatment of vasculogenic sexual dysfunction with pentoxifylline. *Journal of the American Geriatrics Society* **41**: 363–6

Kosko, B. 1993. *Fuzzy Thinking*. HarperCollins: London

Koza, M. P. and Lewin, A. Y. 1998. The co-evolution of strategic alliances. *Organization Science* **9**(3): 255–64

Kuhn, T. S. 1970 [1962]. *The Structure of Scientific Revolutions* (2nd edn.). University of Chicago Press: Chicago

LaBianca, G., Brass, D. J., and Gray, B. 1998. Social networks and perceptions of intergroup conflict: the role of negative relationships and third parties. *Academy of Management Journal* **41**(1): 55–67

Langreth, R. and Moore, S. D. 1999. Gene therapy, touted as breakthrough, bogs down in details. *Wall Street Journal – Eastern Edition*, 27 October 1999: 1

Lear, J. 1988. *Aristotle: The Desire to Understand*. Cambridge University Press: Cambridge

Leavitt, H. J. 1965. Applied organizational change in industry: structural, technological and humanistic approaches. In J. G. March (ed.), *Handbook of Organizations*: 1144–70. Rand McNally and Co.: Chicago

Leblebici, H., Salancik, G., Copay, A., and King, T. 1991. Institutional change and the transformation of interorganizational fields: an organizational history of the US radio broadcasting industry. *Administrative Science Quarterly* **36**(3): 333–63

Leonard-Barton, D. 1995. *Wellsprings of Knowledge: Building and Sustaining the Sources of Innovation*. Harvard Business School Press: Boston, MA

Levie, J. and Hay, M. 1998. Progress or just proliferation? A historical review of stages models of early corporate growth. Unpublished paper: London Business School

Levine, S. and White, P. E. 1961. Exchange as a conceptual framework for the study of interorganizational relationships. *Administrative Science Quarterly* **5**: 583–601

Levitt, B. and Nass, C. 1989. The lid on the garbage can: institutional constraints on decision making in the technical core of college-text publishers. *Administrative Science Quarterly* **34**: 190–207

Lewis, C. S. 1943. *Mere Christianity*. Macmillan Publishing Company: New York

Li, J. 1995. Foreign entry and survival: effects of strategic choices on performance in international markets. *Strategic Management Journal* **16**: 333–51

Lodge, D. 1984. *Small World*. Penguin Books: New York

Loizos, C. 1998. Chemical attraction. *The Red Herring* **May**: 70, 72

Lorange, P. and Roos, J. 1992. *Strategic Alliances: Formation, Implementation and Evolution*. Blackwell Publishers: Oxford

Lynch, R. P. 1993. *Business Alliances Guide: The Hidden Competitive Weapon*. John Wiley and Sons: New York

Macaulay, S. 1963. Non-contractual relations in business: a preliminary study. *American Sociological Review* **28**(1): 55–67

Machiavelli, N. 1971 [1531]. *Discourses on Livy* (L. J. Walker, trans.). Penguin: London

Macneil, I. R. 1974. The many futures of contracts. *Southern California Law Review* **47**(3): 691–716

1980. *The New Social Contract: An Inquiry into Modern Contractual Relations*. Yale University Press: New Haven, CT

March, J. G. 1981. Footnotes to organizational change. *Administrative Science Quarterly* **26**(2): 563–77

1991. Exploration and exploitation in organizational learning. *Organization Science* **2**: 71–87

March, J. G., Sproull, L. S., and Tamuz, M. 1991. Learning from samples of one or fewer. *Organization Science* **2**(1): 1–13

March, J. G. and Sutton, R. L. 1997. Organizational performance as a dependent variable. *Organization Science* **8**(6): 698–706

Marion, R. 1999. *The Edge of Organization: Chaos and Complexity Theories of Formal Social Systems*. Sage Publications: London

Martin, M. 1999. Pfizer moves in on deal between drugmakers. *International Herald Tribune*. 5 November: 1, 14: Paris

Mason, E. S. 1939. Price and production policies of large scale enterprises. *American Economic Review* **39**: 61–74

Mathews, K. M., White, M. C., and Long, R. C. 1999. Why study the complexity sciences in the social sciences? *Human Relations* **52**(4): 439–62

McCloskey, D. 1990. *If You're So Smart: The Narrative of Economic Expertise*. The University of Chicago Press: Chicago

1998. *The Rhetoric Of Economics* (2nd edn.). University of Wisconsin Press: Madison, WI

McKelvey, W. 1997. Quasi-natural organization science. *Organization Science* **8**(4): 352–80

Miles, M. B. and Huberman, A. M. 1994. *Qualitative Data Analysis*. Sage Publications: London

Mir, R. and Watson, A. 2000. Strategic management and the philosophy of science: the case for a constructivist methodology. *Strategic Management Journal* **21**: 941–53

Mitchell, G. R. and Hamilton, W. F. 1988. Managing R&D as a strategic option. *Research Technology* **31**: 15–22

Mowery, D. C. 1988. *International Collaborative Ventures in US Manufacturing*. Ballinger: Cambridge, MA

Mullis, K. 2000. *Dancing Naked in the Mind Field*. Pantheon Books: New York

Murray, E. A. Jr. and Mahon, J. F. 1993. Strategic alliances: gateway to the new Europe? *Long Range Planning* **26**(4): 102–11

Murray, K. J. 1993. Phosphodiesterase V inhibitors. *Drug News and Perspectives* **6**(3): 150–6

Musil, R. 1995 [1978]. *The Man Without Qualities* (S. Wilkins and B. Pike, trans.). London: Picador

Nasar, S. 2001. *A Beautiful Mind*. Faber and Faber Ltd: London

Nash, J. F. Jr. 1950a. Equilibrium points in n-person games. *Proceedings of the National Academy of Sciences, USA* **36**: 48–9

1950b. The bargaining problem. *Econometrica* **18**: 155–62

Nohria, N. 1992. Is a network perspective a useful way of studying organizations? In N. Nohria and R. G. Eccles (eds.), *Networks and Organizations: Structure, Form, and Action*: 1–22. Harvard Business School Press: Boston, MA

Osborn, R. N. and Hagedoorn, J. 1997. The institutionalization and evolutionary dynamics of interorganizational alliances and networks. *Academy of Management Journal* **40**(2): 261–78

Oviatt, B. M. and McDougall, P. P. 1994. Towards a theory of international ventures. *Journal of International Business Studies* **69**: 45–64

Park, S. J. and Russo, M. V. 1996. When competition eclipses cooperation: an event history analysis of joint venture failure. *Management Science* **42**: 875–90

Park, S. H. and Ungson, G. R. 1997. The effect of national culture, organizational complementarity and economic motivation on joint venture dissolution. *Academy of Management Journal* **40**(2): 279–308

Parkhe, A. 1993a. Messy research, methodological predispositions, and theory development in international joint ventures. *Academy of Management Review* **18**(2): 227–68

1993b. Strategic alliance structuring: a game theoretic and transaction cost examination of interfirm cooperation. *Academy of Management Journal* **36**(4): 794–829

Pascale, R. T. 1996. The 'Honda effect' revisited. *California Management Review* **38**(4): 78–91

Pekar, P. Jr. and Allio, R. 1994. Making alliances work: guidelines for success. *Long Range Planning* **27**(4): 54–65

Penrose, E. 1959. *The Theory of the Growth of the Firm.* Blackwell Publishing: Oxford

Pennings, J. M., Barkema, H., and Douma, S. 1994. Organization learning and diversification. *Academy of Management Journal* **37**: 608–40

Perrow, C. 1986. *Complex Organizations: A Critical Essay* (3rd edn.). McGraw-Hill: New York

Peteraf, M. 1993. The cornerstones of competitive advantage: a resource-based view. *Strategic Management Journal* **14**: 179–91

Pettigrew, A. M. 1987. Context and action in the transformation of the firm. *Journal of Management Studies* **24**(6): 649–70

2001. Crosstalk: Hambrick and Pettigrew on Leadership. *Academy of Management Executive*: 36–45

Pfeffer, J. 1982. *Organizations and Organization Theory.* Pitman: London

1993. Barriers to the advance of organizational science: paradigm development as a dependent variable. *Academy of Management Review* **18**(4): 599–620

Pfeffer, J. and Fong, C. T. 2002. The end of business schools? Less success than meets the eye. *Academy of Management Learning and Education* **1**(1): 78–95

Pfeffer, J. and Salancik, G. 1978. *The External Control of Organizations.* Harper and Row: New York

Pierson, F. C., et al. 1959. *The Education of American Businessmen: A Study of University-College Programs in Business Administration.* McGraw-Hill: New York.

Pilling, D. 2001. Big pharma sees the beauty of thinking small. *Financial Times (Inside Track)*, 2 April: London

Pisano, G. P. 1990. The R&D boundaries of the firm: an empirical analysis. *Administrative Science Quarterly* **35**: 153–76

Polanyi, M. 1966. *The Tacit Dimension.* Anchor Books: New York

Poole, M. S. and van de Ven, A. 1989. Using paradox to build management and organization theories. *Academy of Management Review* **14**(4): 562–78

Porter, L. W. 2000. Observations on business education. *Selections* **16**(2), 29–30.

Porter, L. W. and McKibbin, L. E. 1988. *Management Education and Development: Drift or Thrust into the 21st Century?* McGraw-Hill: New York

Porter, M. E. 1980. *Competitive Strategy.* The Free Press: New York

1985. *Competitive Advantage.* The Free Press: New York

1987. From competitive advantage to corporate strategy. *Harvard Business Review* **65**(3): 43–60

Powell, W. W. and Brantley, P. 1992. Competitive cooperation in biotechnology: learning through networks? In N. Nohria and R. G. Eccles (eds.), *Networks and Organizations: Structure, Form, and Action*: 366–94. Harvard Business School Press: Boston, MA

Powell, W. W., Koput, K. W., and Smith-Doerr, L. 1996. Interorganizational collaboration and the locus of innovation: networks of learning in biotechnology. *Administrative Science Quarterly* **41**: 116–45

Rajfer, J., Aronson, W. J., Bush, P. A., Dorey, F. J., and Ignarro, L. J. 1992. Nitric oxide as a mediator of relaxation of the corpus cavernosum in respect to nonadrenergic, noncholinergic neurotransmission. *New England Journal of Medicine* **362**(2): 90

Ramanathan, K. A. and Thomas, S. H. 1997. Explaining joint ventures: alternative theoretical perspectives. In P. W. Beamish and J. P. Killing (eds.), *Cooperative Strategies: North American Perspectives*, Vol. 1: 51–85. New Lexington Press: San Francisco, CA

Rand, A. 1985 [1957]. *Atlas Shrugged.* Penguin Books: New York

Rawls, J. 1999. *A Theory of Justice* (Revised edn.). Harvard/Belknap: Cambridge, MA

Rescher, N. 2000 [1993]. *Pluralism: Against the Demand for Consensus.* Clarendon Press: Oxford

Reuer, J. J., Zollo, M., and Singh, H. 2002. Post-formation dynamics in strategic alliances. *Strategic Management Journal* **23**(2): 135–52

Ricardo, D. 1891. *Principles of Political Economy and Taxation.* G. Bell: London

Ring, P. S. and van de Ven, A. H. 1994. Developmental processes of cooperative interorganisational relationships. *Academy of Management Review* **19**(1): 90–118

Rothaermel, F. T. 2001. Complementary assets, strategic alliances, and the incumbent's advantage: an empirical study of industry and firm effects in the biopharmaceutical industry. *Research Policy* **30**: 1235–51

Rumelt, R. P. 1984. Towards a strategic theory of the firm. In B. Lamb (ed.), *Competitive Strategic Management*: 556–70. Prentice-Hall: Englewood Cliffs, NJ

1991. How much does industry matter? *Strategic Management Journal* **12**(3): 167–85

Russell, B. 1957. *Why I Am Not A Christian.* Allen and Unwin: London

1980. *The Problems of Philosophy.* Oxford University Press: Oxford

Salk, J. and Shenkar, O. 2001. Social identities in an international joint venture: an exploratory case study. *Organization Science* **12**(2): 161–78

Sapienza, A. M. and Stork, D. 2001. *Leading Biotechnology Alliances: Right from the Start.* John Wiley and Sons: New York

Sartre, J.-P. 1963. *The Problem of Method.* John Dickens and Co. Ltd: Northampton

Schifrin, M. 2001. Partner or perish. *Forbes* **167**(12): 26–8

Schneider, L. 1971. Dialectics in sociology. *American Sociological Review* **36**: 667–78

Schumacher, E. F. 1995. *A Guide for the Perplexed*. Vintage: London

Seth, A. and Thomas, H. 1994. Theories of the firm: implications for strategy research. *Journal of Management Studies* **31**(2): 165–91

Shenkar, O. and Li, J. 1999. Knowledge search in international cooperative ventures. *Organization Science* **10**(2): 134–43

Shenkar, O. and Yan, A. 2002. Failure as a consequence of partner politics: learning from the life and death of an international cooperative venture. *Human Relations* **55**(5): 565–601

Shortell, S. M. and Zajac, E. J. 1988. Internal corporate joint ventures: development processes and performance outcomes. *Strategic Management Journal* **9**: 527–42

Simonin, B. L. 1999. Ambiguity and the process of knowledge transfer in strategic alliances. *Strategic Management Journal* **20**: 595–623

Smircich, L. and Stubbart, C. 1985. Strategic management in an enacted world. *Academy of Management Review* **10**(4): 724–36

Spekman, R. E., Isabella, L. A., MacAvoy, T., and Forbes, T. 1998. Alliance management: a view from the past and a look to the future. *Journal of Management Studies* **35**(6): 747–71

Spender, J.-C. and Grant, R. M. 1996. Knowledge and the firm: overview. *Strategic Management Journal*, Winter Special Issue **17**: 5–9

Starbuck, W. H. 1993. Keeping a butterfly and an elephant in a house of cards: the elements of exceptional success. *Journal of Management Studies* **30**(6): 885–921

Strauss, A. and Corbin, J. 1990. *Basics of Qualitative Research: Grounded Theory Procedures and Techniques*. Sage Publications: London

Swinburne, R. 1993. The vocation of a natural theologian. In K. J. Clark (ed.), *Philosophers Who Believe: The Spiritual Journeys of 11 Leading Thinkers*: 179–202. Intervarsity Press: Downers Grove, IL.

Sydow, J. and Windeler, A. 1998. Organizing and evaluating interfirm networks: a structurationist perspective on network processes and effectiveness. *Organization Science* **9**(3): 265–84

Taggart, J. 1993. *The World Pharmaceutical Industry*. Routledge: London

Tarnas, R. 1991. *Passion of the Western Mind: Understanding the Ideas that have Shaped Our World View*. Ballantine Books: New York

Tolstoy, L. 1983 [1869]. *War and Peace* (L. and A. Maude, trans.). Oxford Classics: Oxford

Turk, H. 1973. Comparative urban structure from an interorganizational perspective. *Administrative Science Quarterly* **18**: 37–55

Turpin, D. 1993. Strategic alliances with Japanese firms: myths, and realities. *Long Range Planning* **26**(5): 11–16

Unsworth, T. 1998. Cellmates. *The Sunday Times Magazine*, 14 June: 16–21: London

van Brunt, J. 1999. Innovation drives alliances. *Signals* (online magazine)
    2001. Grand ambitions. *Signals* (online magazine)

van de Ven, A. H. 1997. The buzzing, blooming, confusing world of organization and management theory: a view from Lake Wobegon University. Distinguished Scholar Lecture to the Organization and Management Theory Division of the Academy of Management, 11 August: Boston

van de Ven, A. H. and Poole, M. S. 1995. Explaining development and change in organizations. *Academy of Management Review* 20: 510–40

van Maanen, J. 1975. Police socialization. *Administrative Science Quarterly* 20: 207–28

1979. The fact of fiction in organizational ethnography. *Administrative Science Quarterly* 24: 539–50

1995. Fear and loathing in organization studies. *Organization Science* 6(6): 687–92

Vico, G. 1999 [1725]. *New Science* (D. Marsh, trans.). Penguin: London

von Hippel, E. 1988. *Sources of Innovation*. Oxford University Press: New York

von Neumann, J. 1928. Zur Theorie der Gesellschaftsspiele. *Math. Ann.* 100: 295–320

von Neumann, J. and Morgenstern, O. 1944. *Theory of Games and Economic Behavior*. Princeton University Press: Princeton

Walker, G., Kogut, B., and Shan, W.-J. 1997. Social capital, structural holes and the formation of an industry network. *Organization Science* 8: 109–25

Wasserman, S. and Faust, K. 1997. *Social Network Analysis: Methods and Applications*. Cambridge University Press: Cambridge

Weick, K. 1988. Enacted sensemaking in crisis situations. *Journal of Management Studies* 25(4): 305–18

1993. The collapse of sensemaking in organizations: the Mann Gulch disaster. *Administrative Science Quarterly* 38(4): 625–50

1995. What theory is not, theorizing is. *Administrative Science Quarterly* 40: 385–90

Wernerfelt, B. 1984. A resource-based view of the firm. *Strategic Management Journal* 5: 171–80

Werth, B. 1994. *The Billion Dollar Molecule: One Company's Quest for the Perfect Drug*. Touchstone: New York

Williamson, O. E. 1975. *Markets and Hierarchies: Analysis and Antitrust Implications*. The Free Press: New York

1985. *The Economic Institutions of Capitalism: Firms, Markets and Relational Contracting*. The Free Press: New York

Wittgenstein, L. 1992 [1921]. *Tractatus-Logico-Philosophicus* (D. F. Pears and B. F. McGuinness, trans.). Routledge: London

Wood, D. J. and Gray, B. 1991. Toward a comprehensive theory of collaboration. *Journal of Applied Behavioral Science* 27: 139–62

Yan, A. and Gray, B. 2001. Reconceptualizing the determinants and measurement of joint venture performance. *Advances in Global High-Technology Management* 5(B): 87–113

Yamawaki, H. 1997. Exit of Japanese multinationals in US and European manufacturing industries. In P. J. Buckley and J. L. Mucchielli (eds.), *Multinational Firms and International Relocation*: 220–37. Edward Elgar: Cheltenham, UK

Yeoh, P. L. and Roth, K. 1999. An empirical analysis of sustained advantage in the US pharmaceutical industry: impact of firm resources and capabilities. *Strategic Management Journal* **20**(7): 637–54

Yin, R. K. 1994. *Case Study Research: Design and Methods* (2nd edn.). Sage Publications: London

Young-Ybarra, C. and Wiersema, M. 1999. Strategic flexibility in information technology alliances: the influence of transaction cost economics and social exchange theory. *Organization Science* **10**(4): 439–59.

Zagare, F. C. 1984. *Game Theory*. Sage: London

Zajac, E. J. 1998. Commentary on 'Alliances and networks' by R. Gulati. *Strategic Management Journal* **19**(4): 319–21

1995. Airline alliances: flying in formation. *The Economist*, 22–29 July: 59–60

2002. Mercky prospects. *The Economist*, 13–20 July: 51

Zajac, E. J. and Olsen, C. P. 1993. From transaction cost to transactional value analysis: implications for the study of interorganizational strategies. *Journal of Management Studies* **30**(1): 131–45

Zald, M. N. 2002. Spinning disciplines: critical management studies in the context of the transformation of management education. *Organization* **9**(3): 365–86

Zeitz, G. 1980. Interorganizational dialectics. *Administrative Science Quarterly* **25**: 72–88

Index